Praise for the first edition of *Don't Blame Mother*:

"Sensitive and compassionate."
>—Harriet Lerner, author of *The Dance of Intimacy*
>and *The Dance of Anger*

"A compelling book. . . . Readers won't regard mothers in quite the same way again."
>—Carol Tavris, *Psychology Today*

"At long last! This is the book that redeems the mothers we have betrayed and the mothers we are."
>—*Lilith Magazine*

"*Don't Blame Mother* is intelligent, well-written, and vigorous."
>—*Journal of Women in Therapy*

"I would recommend this book to every man who has a mother he has ever slighted or contemptuously dismissed. Paula Caplan's book made me do an emotional double-take to face the . . . fact that I truly loved my mother, and for good reason."
>—Jeffrey Moussaieff Masson,
>author of *The Assault on Truth*

"I read *Don't Blame Mother* soon after my daughter fell into the pit of a life-threatening eating disorder and it really helped me keep my balance and not do too much self-blaming."
>—Sharon M. Abbey, co-editor of
>*Redefining Motherhood*

"Essential reading for every woman who has ever felt the love and pain of difficult interactions with her mother. Written with equal sensitivity and respect toward both mothers and daughters, this refreshingly hopeful book presents a major innovative contribution to our understanding of women's relationships within the family in the context of today's society."
>—Rachel Josefowitz Siegel
>co-editor of *Celebrat*

D0149114

Also by the Author:

Books

Children's Learning and Attention Problems
   (Co-authored with Marcel Kinsbourne)

Between Women: Lowering the Barriers

The Myth of Women's Masochism

Don't Blame Mother:
   Mending the Mother–Daughter Relationship

Lifting a Ton of Feathers:
   A Woman's Guide to Surviving
   in the Academic World

You're Smarter than They Make You Feel:
   How the Experts Intimidate Us
   and What We Can Do about It

Thinking Critically about Research on Sex and Gender
   (Co-authored with Jeremy B. Caplan)

They Say You're Crazy:
   How the World's Most Powerful Psychiatrists
   Decide Who's Normal

Gender Differences in Human Cognition
   (Co-authored with Mary Crawford, Janet Shibley Hyde, and
   John T. E. Richardson)

Plays

Call Me Crazy

Tikkun Olam: Repairing the World

Love's Hollow

The Test

Shades

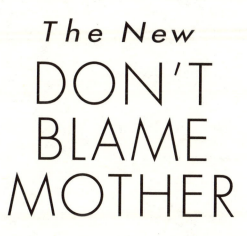

The New
DON'T
BLAME
MOTHER

Mending the Mother–Daughter Relationship

Paula J. Caplan, Ph.D.

Routledge
New York   London

Published in 2000 by
Routledge
29 West 35th Street
New York, NY 10001

Published in Great Britain by
Routledge
11 New Fetter Lane
London EC4P 4EE

10 9 8 7 6 5 4 3 2 1

Library of Congress Cataloging-in-Publication Data

Caplan, Paula J.
    The new don't blame mother : mending the mother-daughter
relationship / Paula J. Caplan.
      p. cm.
    Rev. ed. of: Don't blame mother. 1st ed. 1989.
    Includes bibliographical references and index.
    ISBN 0-415-92630-0 (pbk. : alk. paper)
    1. Mothers and daughters. 2. Women—Psychology. 3. Motherhood—
Psychological aspects. 4. Intergenerational relations. I. Caplan, Paula J.
Don't blame mother. II. Title.

HQ755.85.C355 2000
306.874'3—dc21

                                     99-054697

For my parents,
Theda Ann Karchmer Caplan *and* Jerome Arnold Caplan,

and my children,
Jeremy Benjamin Caplan *and* Emily Julia Caplan,

with all my love

Contents

Preface to
The New Don't Blame Mother

When you write a book to point out the mistreatment of an entire, enormous group of people, you hope that the book will quickly become irrelevant, that people will recognize the injustice of that mistreatment and put a stop to it. That is what I hoped for when I wrote *Don't Blame Mother*. Not for a moment did I believe my book alone would do the trick, but I believed that the burgeoning awareness of the unfair treatment of many groups of women would lead to a critical mass of work and revelation. I was optimistic enough to believe that, as Anne Frank wrote, most people are really good at heart, and that wholesale blaming and condemnation of mothers continued only because most people were not aware that they participated in it or that it was so unfair and did so much harm.

All these years later, as the new millennium dawns, far more books and articles, opinion pieces and systematic research reports, have been published on the subjects of mothers, and mothers and daughters—but, sadly, mother-blame remains pervasive and powerful.

Feminists have struggled to stem the tide of mother-blame even though they have simultaneously had to fend off the criticism that by doing so they were showing themselves to be radical feminists. How poignant this is, because feminism is aimed to ensure freedom and respect for people regardless of gender or parental status, and indeed it would be a radical change ("radical" coming from the Latin word meaning "root") if mothers were not automatically scapegoated.

When I began work on *The New Don't Blame Mother*, I found from a computer search of "mothers and daughters" that 737 books and articles on the subject had been published since the original edition of my book went to press nearly twelve years ago. Another computer search revealed that only about half that number had been published in the previous twelve years. "Mothers" as a topic had moved closer to the forefront of people's awareness, it seemed. And, as I shall describe later, a great deal of superb work has indeed been done. However, little of that work has been about the mother-daughter *relationship* and how to mend it when there is a rift (rather than, for instance, about such correlational questions as "Are alcoholic mothers likely to have alcoholic daughters?") and another computer search showed that even less has been specifically about mother-blaming, its scope, the harm it does, and ways to stop it. But happily, there is a growing richness of research on various groups of mothers, especially those marginalized by the dominant culture and subjected to even more condemnation and blame than middle-class, Anglo, able-bodied, heterosexual, married mothers.

In the following chapters I have incorporated a great deal of that new work, as well as thoughts and experiences I have had and changes that have taken place in the world since I completed the first edition. I have retained all stories from the first edition that illustrate something that still happens today, as well as references to earlier research when no recent research has superseded it.

In this preface, first I relate some of my experiences directly related to *Don't Blame Mother*—including letters from readers following its publication. Next, I address some of the recent, profound social changes that have affected the institution of mother-blame. Finally, I want to tell you enough about some of the new writing to give you a flavor of the deepening and broadening of the work on mothers and the mother-daughter relationship, so that you can see where to look for further reading. (See Bibliography)

New Developments since the First Edition

Early Conference Revelations

During the series of speaking engagements beginning in 1989 when I talked about *Don't Blame Mother*, I began to understand in a new way why mother-blaming is so powerful and so resistant to change, and I address that in chapter 3 of this edition. I believe this understanding is important; the more insight we have into the nature and use of mother-blame, the better will be our chance to reduce it.

In 1988, after my book went to press, Phyllis Chesler, Rachel Josefowitz Siegel, Janet Surrey, and I presented a panel on mother-blame at "Woman-Defined Motherhood: A Conference for Therapists," held at Goddard College. As far as we knew, this was the first major conference on mothers, and our panel the first public presentation on mother-blame, and we were amazed and deeply touched by the feelings it called forth. When I first wrote my book, I hoped it might get a few people thinking, but I had no idea how much women needed to discuss these issues.

One of the conference organizers, Jane Price Knowles, wrote that the panel on mother-blame "came as a stunning revelation . . . that shocked us into the recognition that it is almost impossible to think without mother-blaming. . . . I believe even the panelists themselves were surprised at how disturbing, painful, and ultimately powerful this panel proved to be. One woman said later, 'I felt overwhelmed by the sense of having been present at one of life's truly historic moments.'" Knowles also quoted two other women's responses to the panel and the conference. Melissa Meth described "learning how to forgive myself for not wanting to be a mother under the current definition of motherhood. I now understand it is okay to love myself and my mother instead of hating us both for being ourselves"; and Etta Bender Breit said, "Tears have washed my eyes throughout the weekend, as thoughts of myself as mother and of my mother replace what the experts have taught, wrongly."

What had the panelists said to inspire such feelings? Phyllis Chesler spoke about how young women wipe out of consciousness the knowledge of what their mothers—both biological mothers and "mothers" of feminism and scholarship—have done to pave their way, and about how devastating this is for literal or figurative mothers. Janet Surrey said therapists are trained to produce allegedly objective but in fact deeply blaming descriptions of mothers; she bravely listed adjectives she had used to describe patients' mothers in her own case reports: "engulfing," "controlling," "intrusive," "enmeshed," "seductive," "overprotective," "narcissistic," "unavailable," "ineffective," and "depriving." Applying her "self-in-relation" theory to mother-daughter relationships, she urged therapists to spend part of their time focusing on the joy and mutual growth that often arise from mother-daughter relationships.

Rachel Josefowitz Siegel said that old women are mistreated because every negative assumption about mothers is projected onto them while at the same time people expect them to be constantly giving. Siegel said, "When an old woman walks into the room, she reminds us of who we might become. She could be our mother, she could be our grandmother—she is not me, not us. *Old woman* is *mother* and *mother* is *old; old woman* is other. *Old woman* is a role, an image, a stereotype—she is not a person. . . . *Old woman* is not me; *old woman* is not what I want to be." Siegel also raised the question of why it is insulting to say, "You sound like a mother" but not to say, "You sound like a daughter."

I had proposed the panel, but I was completely unprepared for the richness of what these women said, the audience members' responses, and the depth and complexity of my own feelings. It seemed that mother-blame was much more powerful and multifaceted than I had even dreamed when I first wrote my book.

Soon after that conference, I spoke in northern Ontario about mothers and daughters and learned from some Native Canadian women there how, as children sent away from home to residential schools, they believed that their mothers *wanted* to send them away. Only after many years did they learn that their mothers had been threatened with imprisonment if they refused to send their children off, and the mothers had not spoken about this, for fear of worrying their children—heartbreaking evidence of the harm that politics and racism at the federal level have done to mothers and daughters. I wonder how many more such stories remain to be told.

Mothers and Daughters and Phil Donahue

The first interview for my book tour was television's *Donahue* show. A producer asked me to suggest other people who might appear on the panel, and one of the people I suggested was my mother. "She's bright, honest, and very funny," I said, "and she's a psychologist, too." The producer seemed uninterested. Perhaps everyone wants their mother to be on the show. I urged the producer to ensure that the show would not deteriorate into yet another mother-bashing session. I suggested that the most important and interesting thing we might do would be to talk to mothers and daughters who had overcome some of the problems between them. I also told her my parents were going to be in New York the day of the show for my father's college reunion at Columbia University, and I asked if they could sit in the audience. I was told that they would have to sit backstage in the Green Room.

Just before I was to leave for New York, the producer called and said, "Tell me again about your mother." I did, and she asked for Mom's telephone number. I replied that she had left home and was in another city visiting my brother on the way to New York, so I gave her his number. Later the producer called and said, "You were right. She's amazing! And she's agreed to be on the show." Mother said the producer had interviewed her and then asked if she would appear on the show. Mom, tongue in cheek, said, "When I packed my suitcase I didn't know I was going to be on *Donahue,* so I didn't bring anything appropriate to wear. If you'll take me to Bergdorf's and buy me a dress, I'll be on." The producer, wrongly assuming Mom was serious, said, "Oh, I'm afraid we're not allowed to do that. Is there anything else I can do for you?" Mom replied that she would appear if my father could sit in the audience, and the producer readily agreed.

The day of the show, the producer pulled me out of the makeup room in a panic. "It's your mother!" she said. I asked what was wrong, and she said, "I just tried to talk to her, and she didn't respond at all." I went to the Green Room and told Mom what the producer had said. "Oh!" she replied, "I have my hearing aids turned off. I didn't want to run the batteries down before the show started."

Just before the show began, both a producer and Donahue himself came into the Green Room and urged us to remember that time would fly once the cameras were on and that we might need to speak right up, get Donahue's attention, and grab the chance to say what we considered most important.

When we walked into the studio, a mother with her two teenage daughters was on the panel, as were a mother and her thirty-something daughter, who had recently returned to live with her mother while starting her own business. I had appeared on *Donahue* before and greatly admired Phil's keen intelligence, his wit, and his perceptiveness about social and political issues. That day, though, for what seemed like hours, he let the two teenagers and their mother spat about trivia, without bringing his or his audience's usual insightful commentary or analysis to bear. When he got to the adult daughter and her mother, they said that the two of them were living on their own; the daughter cooked, and the mother did the laundry. Members of the audience groaned, rolled their eyes, and said the mother still treated her daughter like a child by doing her laundry and a "role reversal" had taken place because the daughter was cooking for the mother. I pointed out that if we knew that two people—just people in the abstract—were living together, and one did the cooking and one the laundry, we would say, "Isn't that nice? They share the work." But when one of those people is a mother, we jump to pathologizing everything that happens.

Donahue then turned to my mother, who, in her first-ever media appearance, said that she wished other mothers would "get 'hep' the way I did years ago when I realized I'm not going to take the blame. I'm going to take the credit." Donahue asked about our relationship. She brightly replied that it was good, but sometimes I annoyed her, as when we argued about how loud she should turn up her hearing aids. The audience fell in love with her because of her courage in talking so easily about her hearing problem.

The show continued, filled with mother-blame, and about three-quarters of the way through, Mom called out, "Phil!" in the tone of voice she used with me when I was misbehaving. Donahue was at the back of the audience and did not hear. She called out two more times, getting louder, and he turned and said, "Yes, Mrs. Caplan." Mom looked straight into the camera and paused. I knew the producer was worrying about wasted air-time and assuming Mom had gotten confused or scared into silence. But I suspected her pause was for dramatic effect. She said forcefully, "This is an awareness hour. What should we be aware of? Everybody thought that with the feminist movement, mothers don't get blamed any more. That's not true. The research that Paula has done shows mothers are still getting blamed too much, and we've got to STOP IT!" In a few words, she had focused and encapsulated the point of the whole show. The audience cheered.

In the following months, as I waited in Green Rooms all over the country, the following scene often occurred. Another guest on the show would ask why I was going to appear. I would mention *Don't Blame Mother: Mending the Mother-Daughter Relationship*, and they would pause, then say, "Oh! I saw you on *Donahue.* You were good. Your *mother* was *terrific!*" Mom finds that difficult to believe, but it is true.

My Daughter and I Speak Together

In 1992 I invited my daughter Emily, then sixteen, to present a workshop with me on mothers and daughters. I had planned to talk about the material in my book at the first international conference on Judaism, feminism, and psychology in Seattle and thought it would be good to have a young daughter's perspective. Although Emily had always been supportive of my writing, she had not read *Don't Blame Mother.* We talked about her reading the book and giving her opinion about it. She was worried, because if she didn't like something in it, she wouldn't want to say that publicly. I told her that open discussion and debate were healthy and mattered a great deal to me. We agreed that she would not tell me ahead of time what she planned to say. In Seattle, I summarized the ideas in the book, and then Emily spoke. With delightful candor she said she thought that the book was not particularly useful to girls her age, who were understandably working hard to cope with all the teenage things they were going through. She told wonderful stories to illustrate her points, and the audience gave her a standing ovation. I thought every word she said was true, although I continue to believe in the importance of making children and teenagers aware of the existence and power of mother-blame, just as we point out the sexism in traditional fairy tales. They may not be ready to do much about it until they are older, but the knowledge will stand them in good stead as they grow.

Mother-Blame Takes the Stage

In the mid-1990s I returned to my early interest in theater as both an actor and a playwright. My first play, *Call Me Crazy,* dealt with the questions Is anybody considered normal? Who gets to decide? And what happens to people who are labeled abnormal? My friend Pat Hegnauer suggested that Sigmund Freud's mother might appear in the play. I loved that idea; in all the decades that Freud has received attention for his theories, in many of which he blames, demeans, and dismisses mothers, we've never heard what his mother thought. So Amalia Freud appears in *Call Me Crazy,* finally speaking her mind about how her son's views of women in general and mothers in particular made her—the mother of five daughters—feel. The audience hears her anguish as she struggles to decide whether she raised Sigmund right or overindulged him—after all, he was brilliant, she says, but maybe he had too much.

Letters from Readers

One of the most interesting consequences of writing a book is hearing people's reactions to your work. Both in letters from readers and in their remarks at book signings and lectures about mothers and daughters, the two most prominent themes were daughters' and mothers' longing to mend their relationships and joy when they did so, and the pain caused by mother-blame, especially from therapists.

In a particularly beautifully written example of the letters in the first category, a fifty-year-old woman wrote, "My relationship with my Mother has been revolutionized." They followed some of my suggestions about going over the mother's life history. Previously, wrote the daughter, "I had simply labeled her a bitter, angry immature woman"; but now, "for the first time, I was able to regard my mother as a person, an individual, a woman with feelings, problems, hopes, and expectations. I actually found qualities to admire, something which I never thought possible." Both she and her mother felt "elated" after doing that work. She said that, as her mother has grown older and developed health problems, her "guilt has grown because she and I have always had such a difficult time getting along. I knew that when she died I would feel unbearably sad that we had not been closer. Because of the strides we have made in this last year I will forever be grateful that she and I have grown closer and gained a better understanding of one another. Neither of us are easy people, and we both recognize this, but now, at least, we have a better basis from which to work and, even more important, a markedly improved attitude."

Another woman wrote that she had "begun to think that no one in a professional capacity would say a good word for mothers. [My husband] always blames me for [problems with the children] and gives me no emotional support whatsoever. I guess this contributes to my sorrow when I feel that my daughter is treating me the same way her father does."

Readers' comments about therapists' mother-blame were filled with a sense of pain and helplessness. One woman wrote, "Therapists do mother-bash. . . . I will send your book to my daughter and tell her to pass it on to her therapist. She tells me that he tells her to 'resign' from our relationship." Another writer, the mother of a psychologist-in-training, said, "This past decade [with my daughter, who is now forty] has been a continuous path of pain watching her absorb every myth you describe in your book. She is studying for her Master's degree in Psychology and continues to mother-blame with regularity, not only with her therapist once a week but also with her co-dependency group." Susan Davis, the book review editor of *New Directions for Women* magazine, who published a review of *Don't Blame Mother*, sent me the review with a note: "Because the reviewer I picked was a clinician, she didn't see the valuable message your book contains."

Not all clinicians blame mothers for everything. Therapists have become increasingly aware of the pressure put on us from the beginning of our training (in most, but not all, programs) to do knee-jerk mother-blaming. But mother-blame is still rampant, as will become clear in the following chapters.

Recent Changes: New and Intensified Dilemmas

Blame the Mothers or Blame the Brain?

The massive publicity surrounding the recent spate of horrendous mass murders committed by young people has had disturbing consequences. Although many experts report that national violence has in fact been on the decline, school shootings such as the one at Columbine High School have provoked desperate questions: What causes such horrors? How can they be stopped? *Who* can stop them? Unfortunately, the answers from both experts and laypeople fall into two categories. One is that the parents must be to blame. This means that mothers are more likely to be implicated; they are disproportionately the ones who are still expected to love children enough that they will not feel insecure and desperately angry, and to teach them safe ways to deal with their anger. This is the latest in the long history of blaming mothers for every social evil.

The other answer is that homicidal kids must be mentally

ill. Never mind that the term *mental illness* is used by therapists to explain behavior ranging from stuttering to reading disability, to feeling irritable and craving chocolate just before your period starts, to "still" feeling sad two weeks after a loved one has died. Even if no one has ever come up with a good definition of mental illness, to some people it seems easy to conclude that Columbine and the like were caused by "bad brains" or brain diseases. Although it would be comforting, and would take some pressure off mothers, if we could assume that frightening behavior is caused by brain disease, the truth is that people diagnosed as seriously mentally ill are *not* more likely to commit violent acts than other people.

If we limit our choices to blaming parents (mothers) or blaming the brain, we fail to recognize the significant contributions to violence made, for instance, by the availability of guns and the pandemic sense of alienation and loneliness. If we want to reduce the frequency and virulence of mother-blame, we need to be vigilant about its invocation as an explanation for every social evil.

More Social Changes

My children, who were in their teens when I wrote the first edition, are now in their mid-twenties. During the years in between, the frequency with which people their age do unconventional things to their hair and pierce and tattoo their bodies has dramatically increased. As a friend my age said about his daughter's pierced tongue, "I guess it's our turn not to understand." There have also been enormous changes in both the openness with which sexuality is discussed and the freedom with which is it practiced. Paradoxically, this has happened even as the fear of acquired immune deficiency syndrome (AIDS) has increased. When I was a teenager, beginning in the early 1960s, no girl I knew wanted her mother even to know that she did anything more than "let" a boy kiss her. Now mothers regularly struggle with such questions from their fourteen-year-olds as "Why *can't* my boyfriend spend the night here? You bought me condoms, so you know what we're doing. Wouldn't you rather have us do it here than in the park at night or the backseat of a car?" On a more encouraging note, where my generation used to worry what a boy would think of us if we did—or did not—let him kiss us or touch our breasts, with the focus on the boy, I more frequently (though not frequently enough) hear such comments from teenage girls as, "I didn't let him do that because I didn't feel ready," with the focus on the girl's own feelings. Since, as we shall see in later chapters, most of the work of dealing with these issues continues to fall to mothers, they can provoke ever more mother-daughter conflict and, therefore, more mother-blame.

Mothers have in recent years joined the paid workforce more frequently and more prominently, and the dilemmas posed by this double workload have made it necessary for me to add to my list of major myths that lead to mother-blame and cause or intensify mother-daughter problems. In chapter 5 you will find Myth Ten: Both stay-at-home mothers and mothers with paid jobs are "bad" mothers.

Other recent developments that further intensify and complicate expectations and assumptions about motherhood include:

- The burgeoning industry in reproductive technologies, which on the positive side has allowed some women to bear children when they otherwise could not have done so, but on the negative side has put enormous pressures on women to endure endless physical invasions, pains, and financial expense in order to bear a child that is "biologically theirs." Also on the negative side is that the women who are most likely to be able to use these technologies are "white," heterosexually married, and financially privileged.

- The increase in cross-national and cross-"racial" adoptions.

- The increase in the proportion of single mothers, as well as the move toward calling never-married ones "single mothers" rather than "unwed mothers," which was used when more of them were likely to be African-American or otherwise "nonwhite." This increase brings with it such major dilemmas as how to handle one's sex life and the children's questions about it while being a mother.

The Latest Theory and Research

As I mentioned, my computer search turned up 737 books and articles about mothers and daughters that have been published since the first edition of *Don't Blame Mother* went to press. Clearly, there is an explosion of interest in the subject. I'll start with the good news. Many of the pioneers of work on the experiences of mothers and mother-daughter relationships—Carol Gilligan, Judith Jordan, Alexandra Kaplan, Jean Baker Miller, Rachel Josefowitz Siegel, Irene Stiver, and Janet Surrey—have continued to produce glorious work in these fields. A great deal of that work is included in the bibliography of this book.

Canada is a hotbed of new work. Sharon Abbey, Andrea O'Reilly, and their colleagues organized the first international conference on mothers and daughters in 1997, and this was followed by conferences on mothers and sons, mothers and education, mothers in the African diaspora, and lesbian mothers. A number of excellent books based on presentations from these conferences have been published or are now being prepared. In 1998 Abbey and O'Reilly founded the Toronto-based Association for Research on Mothering (ARM), and in 1999 they began to publish the *Journal of the Association for Research on Mothering*. (For information write to 726 Atkinson, York University, 4700 Keele St., Toronto, Ontario M3J 1P3, or send e-mail to arm@yorku.ca.)

Also in Canada, the journal *Canadian Woman Studies/Les Cahiers de la femme* published a wonderful special issue in 1998 called "Looking Back, Looking Forward: Mothers, Daughters, and Feminism."

Other examples of the enormous variety of new work are:

- Mariana Cook and Jamaica Kincaid's *Generations of Women in Their Own Words,* a splendid book of photographs of daughters, mothers, grandmothers, and great-grandmothers, as well as their remarks about their relationships with each other.
- Phyllis Chesler's honest, compassionate *Letters to a Young Feminist*, in which she tells the next generation lessons she has learned and shows where we and they still need to go.
- Maureen Reddy's perceptive *Crossing the Color Line: Race, Parenting, and Culture.*
- *Sunbelt Working Mothers: Reconciling Family and Factory,* by Louise Lamphere and her colleagues.
- Shari Thurer's historical survey of motherhood myths, *The Myths of Motherhood: How Culture Reinvents the Good Mother.*

- Alix Kates Shulman's *A Good Enough Daughter,* a richly de-
  tailed description of, among other things, Shulman's efforts
  to find the realities of her mother's life among the myths.

Marginalized Mothers

A great deal of writing has appeared in the past decade that deals
with groups of mothers previously little studied because they are
marginalized, considered not "good enough" mothers because they
do not fit the dominant ideology, according to which the ideal
mother is heterosexual, at least middle-class, "white," able-bodied,
neither too old nor too young, born in the country where she
resides, and not imprisoned, as well as having children to whom
she gave birth and being married to the children's "white" father.
An invaluable resource is the new book *Mothering against the Odds:
Diverse Voices of Contemporary Mothers,* edited by Cynthia Garcia
Coll, Janet Surrey, and Kathy Weingarten, which includes chapters on a huge variety of marginalized mothers.

In the following chapters, as in the first edition, although much
of the research I mention and many of the stories I tell relate to
marginalized mothers and daughters, the primary focus is on the
similar ways that mothers are treated and mistreated. In this preface, I shall give some summaries of part of the recent work on
these marginalized women. Computer searches from 1988 to 1999
turned up many books and articles (see Bibliography) on adoptive
mothers, African-American or "Black" mothers, Asian mothers,
biracial children's mothers, Hispanic mothers, immigrant mothers, Jewish mothers, lesbian mothers, mothers of children with
disabilities, mothers with disabilities, mothers in prison, Native
American mothers, old mothers, poor mothers, single mothers,
and welfare mothers. To find anything at all on some of these
groups was reassuring, and in some categories I found a substantial body of work, such as the 54 listings for "Black" mothers and
the 317 for single mothers.

Several themes ran through the work on most or all of these
groups of mothers. One was how the members of each carry the
added burdens of fending off wrong, hurtful, and pathologizing
assumptions that are often made about them. For instance, any
mother not classified as "white" struggles with racist assumptions

about what "Black" or Hispanic or Asian mothers are really like, especially ways they are assumed to be inadequate—in the case of African-American mothers, "too powerful," and in the case of Asian mothers, "too passive." Women with disabilities or illnesses are often told they shouldn't even try to become mothers—though a wonderful antidote to this is the how-to book by Judi Rogers and Molleen Matsumura for mothers-to-be with disabilities. Lesbian mothers and mothers who are single for any reason are often at best considered unable to cope without a father figure in the house and at worst to be raising their children in unhealthy, even immoral environments. Adopted children are often assumed to be destined for trouble, since their birth mothers are considered deficient or damaged and their adoptive mothers deeply troubled by their inability to conceive their "own" children. Mothers of children with disabilities or illnesses—who are found in increasing numbers as physicians find ways to keep extremely premature, very disabled, and seriously ill children alive longer and longer—struggle in the education and medical systems against a vast array of prejudices about the disabled and the ill. Poor, homeless, and teenage mothers are assumed to be lazy and inadequate mothers.

For these and many other reasons, mothers from these groups are in greater danger of losing custody of their children. They are widely believed to be unable to raise happy, well-adjusted children. Thus, an important recent development has been research showing that, for instance, the children of lesbians and of homeless women are no more likely than other children to have impaired or disturbed attachments to their mothers or to have emotional and behavioral problems.

Authors of the new work document in moving detail the practical difficulties with which these mothers struggle. Mothers with disabilities, for instance, are often unable to take their children to physically inaccessible educational or cultural events—and even publicly funded special transportation must usually be ordered well in advance, making it difficult, for example, to take suddenly ill children to the doctor.

The most encouraging trend in the work on marginalized mothers is the increasing frequency with which the women tell their own stories either directly or through interviews with the authors. A few examples are Patricia Bell-Scott's *Double Stitch: Black Women Write about Mothers and Daughters*; Elaine Bell Kaplan's *Not Our Kind of Girl: Unraveling the Myths of Black Teenage Motherhood*; bell hooks's *Bone Black: Memories of Girlhood*, a jewel-bright, nuanced description of the wide variety of feelings she had about her mother as she grew up in the South; Kelly Williams's *Single Mamahood: Advice and Wisdom for the African-American Single Mother*; the forthcoming book of first-person accounts of Jewish mothers, edited by Rachel Josefowitz Siegel, Ellen Cole, and Susan Steinberg-Oren; Hamilton McCubbin and Elizabeth Thompson's *Resiliency in Native American and Immigrant Families*; Anne Adelman's work on women survivors of the Nazi Holocaust and their relationships with their daughters; and Joonok Huh's description of her relationships with her Korean mother and her daughter, now that she lives in North America.

Another encouraging trend is research focused on revealing strengths of mothers and children in these groups. This includes the findings that African-American mothers with HIV focus on their children's needs and act as educators of the wider community about HIV's dangers; that mothers with disabilities are happy to be mothers; that mothers diagnosed as mentally retarded who neglect their children have been able to learn and maintain child-care skills that eliminate the neglect; that many mothers of children with disabilities love keeping their children out of institutions and at home, where they "derive companionship, household assistance, and a sense of stability and continuity from their continued caregiving"; and that single-mother family members have more social interaction at dinner than members of married families. A particularly vibrant and growing body of literature is addressed to the strengths of African-American mothers. Beverly Greene describes how those who bore and reared children were highly valued in precolonial Africa and says that this respect for mothers has persisted in the United States, in spite of the horrendous ways African-Americans have been treated. She also discusses the ways that African-Amerian mothers have learned to teach their daughters the realities of racism and sexism and how to cope with them without being overwhelmed, while protecting them as much as possible and trying to instill sufficient self-confidence to fortify them in making their way in this world. Robert Strom and his colleagues found in their research that poor, African-American mothers derive great enjoyment from being mothers, and Patricia Hill Collins and Melvin Wilson describe the support that mothers receive from the African-American tradition of "othermothers," of many women within the family and the wider community sharing the tasks of child-raising.

New Work That's Cause for Alarm

In recent writing some deeply disturbing trends have appeared. In two enormous bodies of research, one on father-daughter incest and one on females with eating disorders, most work was based on the notion that mothers were primarily to blame. I address the work on incest at some length in chapter 3. With regard to eating disorders, in the vast majority of clinical studies and case reports mothers are the only possible causes of the disorders that were studied. This was regardless of patients' "race," even though for African Americans there were clear suggestions that both the daughters' and the mothers' attitudes about eating and weight were healthier than those for "whites." In some studies, the title of the article includes the word *parents,* although the study is only about mothers. It is obvious that if one only explores one of a huge number of possible causes, one will never understand the problem, and it makes me wonder what the reviewers and editors of these so-called scholarly journals are thinking when they publish articles with such sloppy logic.

How encouraging it is to discover work by authors who call these practices into question. Judith Rabinor criticizes therapists for "explaining" to eating-disordered girls and women how their mothers caused their disorders and then choosing interventions aimed at "fixing" the mothers. This mother-blaming can seriously damage the mother-daughter relationship, reducing the mother's ability to support her daughter. Rabinor finds this particularly unconscionable because, when therapists actually listen to mothers, they frequently hear that the mothers' husbands and fathers shamed them about their weight, often in front of their daughters. Isn't it understandable that a mother who has been mocked because of her weight will try desperately to protect her daughter from the same fate? Clearly, the problem does not originate in the mother. Further, since the media's obsession with undernourished females is well documented, it is surely irresponsible to disregard the enormous pressures placed on both mother *and* daughter to be exceedingly thin. Rabinor suggests that women's appearance "is often the most obvious or the only socially condoned form of power openly afforded her," and so it might be better to help the eating-disordered woman and her mother explore healthy ways to experience power.

I thought of Rabinor's work while watching a recent broadcast about singer Carnie Wilson's major stomach surgery, which was intended to allow her to lose a great deal of weight. The mother of this splendidly talented, accomplished woman said she hoped the surgery would allow her daughter to become "skinny" and "wonderful." It's understandable to feel furious at this mother for her value system; if only she had instead said that her daughter already *is* wonderful, and that she wished her daughter hadn't had to grow up in a society that condemns people it considers overweight. But it is also tragic for both mother and daughter that the mother has been so damaged by those values.

Similar patterns of only asking, How is mother at fault? rather than What various factors might be at fault? appear in articles about kids on drugs, about "borderline personality disorder" (the label often given to the emotional consequences of incest, which is usually perpetrated by a man), about nonsexual abuse and neglect of children, and about other problems. Elizabeth Hutchison points out a particularly troubling aspect of the blaming pattern. Welfare and other government agencies are more likely to investigate and blame mothers for abuse and neglect than to find out what kinds of services (money, food stamps, Medicaid, adequate housing, day care) might help them provide better for their children and treat them with greater patience.

Sometimes, my heart leaps, when somebody with some power finally seems to have gotten the point. That happened when I saw the April 5, 1998 special issue of the *New York Times Magazine's* title, "Mothers Can't Win." But as I read every word of that issue, I realized that, despite its promising title, it included only minuscule consideration of *why* mothers can't win and of what concrete steps could be taken to change this.

As you read *The New Don't Blame Mother* I hope that you will be inspired to take those concrete steps—not just for the sake of yourself or your relationship with your mother but for mothers everywhere.

Acknowledgments

I want to thank Phyllis Chesler, Rachel Josefowitz Siegel, and Janet Surrey for their early and ongoing, warm and enthusiastic support of the work on this book; my Routledge editor, Ilene Kalish, for believing in the importance of this subject and for her intelligent, perceptive suggestions and strong support; Janet Byer Barker for her wonderful hospitality and great company; the members of the Pembroke Center for Research and Teaching on Women for providing me a welcoming academic home; the Brown University Rockefeller and Science Library staff—including but not limited to Beth Coogan, Yvonne Federowica, Hans-Dieter Gomes, Jeanette Gomes, Frank Kellerman, Debra Nelson, Andrew Pereira, and Cynthia Soares—for their immense and irreplaceable practical help on a mammoth scale; my father, Jerome Arnold Caplan, Jacqueline Cook, Fran Goldscheider, Rachel Rosenfeld, and Walter Marshall and Bill Lohan of the United States Bureau of Labor Statistics for help with specific information; and, as always, my dear parents, Theda Ann (Tac) Karchmer Caplan and Jerome Arnold Caplan, and my dear children, Jeremy Benjamin Caplan and Emily Julia Caplan.

Acknowledgments for the First Edition

A book like this cannot be written in isolation. I was blessed to be able to write it from within a rich web of relationships.

I want to thank my agent, Connie Clausen, and her assistant, Guy Kettelhack, for setting me on the road to writing this book, and my editor, Janet Goldstein, for her brilliant, thoughtful, and painstaking work in helping me learn how to write this kind of book. Thanks also to Guy for keeping my spirits up when the going got rough.

My gratitude goes to many other people who have helped in various ways—to the memories of my maternal grandmother, Esther Shana Milner Karchmer, and my paternal grandmother,

Gertrude Dorothy Gorbach Caplan, for their love, their stories, and their inspiration; to my children—Jeremy and Emily, and my parents—Tac and Jerry, for their love, support, patience, and involvement in many ways in the writing and editing process; to Catherine Gildiner, Rachel Josefowitz Siegel, and Betty Jane Turner for carefully reading and sensitively commenting on the entire final draft; to Susan Gilbert Carrell, Jennifer Chambers, Margaret Grant, Donna Sharon, and Wendy Whitfield for reading and commenting on sections of the book; to Phyllis Chesler, Maureen Gans, Amy Hanen, Maria Matias, Kathryn Morgan, Frances Newman, Heather-jane Robertson, and Janet Surrey for providing warmth, suggestions, and/or helpful information; to my secretary, Julie Fung, for her kindness and her help with the typing and administrative work; to Chris Devon, Frieda Forman, Peggy Bristow, and the library staff at the Ontario Institute for Studies in Education, for help with the references; to Carola Barczak and Daria Love for teaching me how to keep up my stamina; to Janet Stickney for allowing me to use the title of her wonderful Don't Blame Mother conference as the title of this book; and to the students in my courses on mothers and my other women's studies courses, as well as the many other friends, patients, and former strangers who allowed me to interview them or who wrote to tell me their stories for this work. I also want to thank my family and friends for their patience in the face of my limited availability while I was involved in this project.

Since I failed to know my mother, I was denied the gift of knowing the other women who would cross my path.

—Pat Conroy, *The Prince of Tides*

1

Getting Started

How are we to be the mothers we want our daughters to have, if we are still sorting out who our own mothers are and what they mean to us?

—*Letty Cottin Pogrebin*

[In the story of mothers and daughters] the plot is not entirely of our own making. We may be free to unravel the tale, but we have not been free to create the social relations upon which it is based.

—*Marcia Westkott*

You're reading a book called *The New Don't Blame Mother,* so chances are, no matter how sad, upset, or angry you are at your mother, you'd rather improve your relationship with her than simply stay upset. This book is an offering to you, to let you know what has helped other mothers and daughters resolve their difficulties.

If you're busy blaming your mother or wishing you could "divorce" her, you are caught in a psychological prison. You can't get free, and you can't really grow up. There are practical problems. For example, you dread family parties: Your mother might not like what you're wearing. Or she might love what you're wearing and say to everyone, "Doesn't my daughter look gorgeous?!"—and you'd be mortified.

That kind of practical problem is a symptom of the fact that mother-blame limits your freedom: you can't be an adult who freely considers all of life's possibilities. You restrict yourself to certain activities, interests, and friends to prove how different from Mother you are. You can't look honestly at who you are, because you might discover ways that you are like her! Frantic to avoid what you consider her failures, you overreact, throwing

1

out the good with the bad: you grow tough because you think she's sentimental, or you become a doormat because she wasn't warm enough. All that reaction against her, that desperate drive to prove your difference, restricts and damages your relationships with the other people you love—your mate, your children, your other relatives, and your friends. You offer them only a part of your true self, a caricature.

Angel in the House or Wicked Witch?

If you feel sadness, irritation, anger, or even outright fury toward your mother, I suggest that you stop right now and let yourself experience it. Look at it. Cry. Scream. Hit pillows. Make a list of the five worst things she's ever done to you. Then consider this: the biggest reason daughters are upset and angry with their mothers is that they have been taught to be so.

Most women sincerely but mistakenly believe that anguish in their relationships with their mothers is inevitable because their mothers are so limited, so dependent, or so terrible. Largely unaware that our culture's polarized mother-images create barriers between mothers and daughters, we have held each other responsible. Mothers are either idealized or blamed for everything that goes wrong. Both mother and daughter learn to think of women in general, and mothers in particular, as angels or witches or some of each. Our normal, human needs, feelings, and wishes are distorted in ways that erode our relationships by making us expect too much of each other and by making us exaggerate the bad or mistake the neutral and positive for negatives. As many mothers and daughters admit, one minute they can overflow with love and admiration, thinking of each other as positively perfect, and the next minute they can be overwhelmed with rage and contempt.

The polarized images have long and complicated histories. In part, in Anglo-American culture, for instance, the idealized ones stem from our Victorian heritage, in which the mother was supposed to be the "Angel in the House" who soothed husband's and children's tired feet and fevered brows, spoke sweetly and gently, and considered meeting their needs her life's mission.

The "Wicked Witch" mother-images familiar to most of us come partly from fairy tales about horrid women. Although they're rarely called mothers, they are often stepmothers or characters who harm children while filling mother-type roles, like the witch in "Hansel and Gretel" who lures children with food or the stepmother who offers Snow White (poisoned) nourishment.

Both extremes cause trouble. How can you have a relationship with a perfect being who's way up on a pedestal? And who would want to get closer to a person she believes has caused all her problems? Even without these images, other problems in mother-daughter relationships would still exist—problems of communication, of sibling rivalry, real individual psychological problems. But each of the two images is supported by a number of troublemaking myths or beliefs; for example, if we believe the "Perfect Mother myth"—that a mother meets all her children's needs—we feel cheated and angry when our mother doesn't measure up, and if we believe the "Bad Mother myth"—that it's wrong for a mother to stay closely connected with her adult daughter—we fear and resent our mother's offers of help or advice. These myths create avoidable problems that make dealing with the inevitable ones much harder.

The Angel/Witch, Perfect Mother/Bad Mother myths are rooted in a powerful tradition of mother-blame that pervades our culture. Most mothers are insecure about their performance as mothers and desperately need the approval of other women, including their daughters. Yet tragically, as daughters we are taught to belittle the work of mothering and blame our mothers for almost everything that goes wrong. We too easily point out our mothers' failings, without ever examining how much our negative view was shaped and intensified by the myths that lead to mother-blame. As daughters and mothers, for generations we have been trapped in a dark web we did not spin. But once we are aware of the myth-threads that form the web, as we tell our mothers' stories and our own, we can begin to pick apart the web. Daughters have to go beyond both kinds of images, taking away the masks of motherhood, as they try to see who their mothers really are.

At some level we all know how hard it is to be a mother, and most of us sense how hard our mothers have tried to do right by us, even if they didn't always succeed. Understanding societal barriers to good mother-daughter relationships frees you to see your mother's good and bad points in all their complexity and subtlety, rather than as examples of stereotypes—guilt-inducing mother, demanding mother, needy mother, overwhelming and judgmental mother, cold and remote mother. When you look at your list of the worst things your mother has done to you, after you've read *Don't Blame Mother*, you'll probably understand more about why she treated you the way she did, and as a result you'll feel differently about both her and yourself.

Relationships based on myths and stereotypes have no chance of improving. But when you look at your mother realistically, you begin to break down barriers and reduce the energy you waste on anguish about each other. This book is based on my experiences as a therapist, my research and the research of other people, women's responses to my earlier writing about mothers and the mother-daughter relationship, my university course on mothers, and feedback about this book's first edition.

The women described in this book vary by race, religion, class, age, sexual orientation, and such factors as whether the daughter is an only daughter or an only child, or has or does not have children of her own. But my primary focus is on commonalities in mother-daughter experiences, because in so many respects we women are treated alike, regardless of our differences and membership in other groups.

As you read stories from my life and from those of my friends, family members, students, workshop participants, and patients, I hope you will see that you are not the world's worst daughter, nor is your mother the world's worst mother—and, conversely, you are not the world's worst mother, nor do you have the world's worst daughter. These stories should also help you decide how to apply the principles and research presented here, so you can plan what to say the next time your mother calls or the next time you feel a fight with your daughter coming on.

The Emperor's New Clothes: Seeing through Mother-Blame

Mother-blame used to come easily to me, and it continues to come easily to most therapists, because that is how generations of therapists have been trained. I spent years seeing therapy patients before I realized how common mother-blame is and how much damage it does. Mother-blame is as rampant today as it was when I

began my graduate training in 1969. In fact, it was and is so common that for years I hardly noticed it.

When I worked in the United States and Canada with psychiatric patients of all ages in a general hospital, delinquent teenagers who were mental hospital inpatients, children who had school problems, and various families, I heard my colleagues lay at mothers' feet the responsibility for most of the patients' problems. If anyone in the family was depressed or aggressive, the mother was usually blamed: "She's overprotective," "She makes her kids so nervous," and so on. If the mother herself was the patient, she was blamed for her own problems—"She's a masochist" or "She comes on so strong—no wonder her husband hits her!"

In many settings, we therapists saw patients together and then, in case conferences, heard each other describe them and attempt to identify the causes of their problems. Most of what I actually saw most mothers do ranged from pretty good to terrific; but my colleagues usually described their actions in negative ways. I tended to leave case conferences feeling vaguely ashamed but not knowing why. One day, I realized that it was because, as a mother, I was a member of the group that my colleagues seemed to think caused all the world's psychological problems. I felt like the child in the fairy tale who knew the emperor was naked while everyone else praised his elaborate clothing.

A most distressing characteristic of mother-blaming among mental health professionals is how few of them seem to be aware they do it. Even when therapists are alerted to mother-blaming attitudes and comments, they usually deny that they themselves could do such a thing. After I became conscious of the clash between what I saw with my own eyes and what my colleagues said they saw, I began in each case conference to ask a simple question: "In addition to the mother's influence, what could have contributed to this person's problems?" When I asked my question, my colleagues said I was "soft on mothers" and "overidentified" with them. Their focus remained not on whether the mother had caused the problem but on how she had done so.

In spite of these responses, I was inspired to continue my questioning by the growing literature on mothers, although only a few books—Adrienne Rich's *Of Woman Born,* Judith Arcana's *Our*

Mothers' Daughters, and parts of Phyllis Chesler's *Women and Madness* and *With Child*—offered positive views of mothers. Most writers continued primarily to find fault with mothers and describe how they ruined their children's lives. Some began well, pointing out that all women have a rough time in our society, but mother-blaming was still present in essential threads of their writing: mothers can't let go of their children, keep daughters too dependent on them, are never satisfied, profoundly disappoint us, and burden us with unbearable guilt.

In 1977, in her enormously popular book *My Mother/My Self,* Nancy Friday presented such a pessimistic view that many women found themselves more hopeless after reading it than before—and thought that meant something was wrong with their mothers and with them, rather than with the book. (Even books from the late 1980s and the 1990s often have this tone. As one reader of the 1989 *Don't Blame Mother* wrote to me, the 1990s book *When You and Your Mother Can't Be Friends* "purports to give advice on how to deal with mother-daughter rifts but is laced throughout with mother-blaming and mother-hating passages," and is "dripping with hatred for her own mother," which the author was in many ways unable to go beyond. In my own reading of this book, I found little analysis of the way society sets mothers and daughters up against each other. Other recent writings are less mother-blaming but are largely theoretical and include little in the way of practical solutions.)

Despite this continued focus on mothers' limitations, I noticed the beneficial effects of all the loving, empowering things that mothers were doing—they rocked babies, cooked nourishing meals, soothed hurt feelings. These things were hardly mentioned. For all the inspiration of books by Rich, Chesler, and Arcana, little or nothing changed among mainstream psychotherapists. From my own experience, I saw that simply voicing objections to mother-blame had no positive results. I needed to document systematically the scapegoating of mothers by mental health professionals. In chapter 3, I describe some of the documentation that I gathered, which revealed that mother-blame had not abated, even in the face of the modern women's movement.

To document the problem and its effects on mother-daughter relationships was one thing; to figure out what to do about it was

another. Rich, Chesler, and Arcana had begun to describe what it feels like to be a mother and to be a daughter, and Jean Baker Miller—in her classic *Toward a New Psychology of Women*—had clearly described the nature of the subordination of women in general. A number of writers had begun to look at relationships between women. But still missing was some idea of where or how to begin to mend the rifts between daughters and their mothers.

Ways to avoid mother-blame and mend mother-daughter relationships still constitute largely unexplored terrain. In fact, until the past decade, almost no *systematic* research had been conducted on woman-woman relationships of any kind. The focus of nearly all psychological research until recently has been on male-male relationships (competition, achievement in the workplace, aggression, etc.) or male-female relationships—in other words, on any relationship that includes at least one male.

Almost everything said about mother-daughter relationships by experts consulted by women whose daughters range from young adults to old women came not from research but from individual speculations; this lack of research created a vacuum that mother-blame quickly filled. And sadly, even the 1990s surge in research about mothers and daughters has done little to stem the mother-blaming tide (see the preface). It is hard to avoid the influence of stereotypes when we look at the realities of mothers and daughters, and Ph.D. and M.D. degrees do not immunize us against those biases. It is time to cut a path through the myths and toward the truth. We owe it to ourselves, to our mothers, to our daughters, and to other women to accord mother-daughter relationships their due—to declare that they are worthy of our time, our effort, and our respect.

Mothers and Other Strangers

If we can temporarily think of our mothers as strangers, we can more easily put them and their treatment of us into perspective; even when we become very angry at strangers, we can see them in a new light more readily, since we have no long, shared history, we may have no common future, and certainly we do not have the intimacy and complexity that characterize our relationships with our mothers.

I once became impatient because an iron I had left in a repair

shop still wasn't ready six weeks later. I called and told the store manager that I needed to pick it up even if it wasn't ready. She spoke curtly to me and slammed down the telephone. Dreading an unpleasant encounter, I went to the shop the next day and found that not only was the iron repaired but the manager was also pleasant. I then recalled something I had heard years ago: the manager, a woman probably in her sixties, keeps the shop running so that her ninety-year-old father can keep working. I realized that she must have a terrible time keeping him happy by running the business, while also trying to hold on to some clientele in the face of her father's slow (but excellent) repair work. When I remembered this, my irritation with her vanished. My perspective changed.

Much of the work of mending the mother-daughter relationship involves placing mother-daughter problems in similar perspective, by looking at the forces that shaped our mothers and the pressures our culture puts on mothers and daughters to have a particular relationship. We owe it to our mothers and ourselves to consider our relationships with the same compassion as we do our business relationships with the neighborhood fix-it store manager. Furthermore, our feelings about our mothers have profound effects on our relationships with our daughters and with women in general. Those of us who believe we are supportive of women but deeply resent our own mothers are probably not as wholeheartedly benevolent toward women in general as we think we are. The better the connections we have with our mothers, the better our connections with other women tend to be.

In thinking through their problems with their mothers, most daughters find that their mothers have seemed worse than they really are; motherhood myths have badly distorted their view. Some daughters, however, have a very different experience and find that their view of themselves changes even more than their view of their mothers. As one woman told me,

> Although my mother really did some bad things to me, I now realize that it was not my fault. She hardly paid any attention to me when I was a child, and I thought I was to blame. When I was about thirty, she told me for the first time that my father had been so jealous of her love for me when I was a baby that she felt she had to downplay

our closeness. I'm still upset that she buckled under his childish jealousy, but I no longer believe that I was—or am—unlovable.

Some mothers are so difficult or hurtful that changing them is beyond anyone's power; but even in those cases, a daughter's understanding of the motherhood myths can strengthen her own self-esteem. I saw this happen gradually over two years to an eight-year-old daughter of divorced parents.

Ginger needed to believe—as most children do—that her mother was perfect. Her mother was an emotionally brittle woman who had been seriously disturbed from early childhood and still has trouble in close relationships. The mother told me, "The year my husband and I split up, Ginger was in first grade. A few times, she called me from school in the morning and begged me to let her come home for lunch. But I wasn't going to let her manipulate me. So I just took to putting my answering machine on first thing in the morning."

Since Ginger was six, she has assumed that she is undeserving of love: "Mom doesn't seem to love me, so I must be a bad child. In fact, I know I am," she told me at age seven. But during the next year, as she spent more time in other children's homes and saw how their mothers treated both them and her, Ginger began to see that the problem was her mother's, not her own. Recently, she told me, "It's been really hard to see that my mother is mean to me and even lies to me, because mothers aren't supposed to do that. But each time she's mean, I think about how many times she's been like that before. At least now that I know that she treats everyone that way, I don't feel so much like a rotten kid anymore."

If eight-year-old Ginger can gain this insight, adult daughters can do as much.

Some of you may be so angry at your mother that you can hardly speak to her. Some of you may feel overwhelmed or intimidated; still others may simply feel remote or detached from her. Not all mothers and daughters have constant trouble, but nearly all have trouble sometimes. And although mother-daughter relationships are no worse than mother-son, father-son, or father-daughter ones, several unique features characterize them.

Because mother-daughter relationships tend to be very close, they combine the potential for much joy and much pain. The joy comes because most women have been taught to develop their interpersonal sensitivity and skills, so mother and daughter have a good chance to make their relationship flower, once they see how to do it. Despite their problems, mothers and daughters usually find ways to show that they care about each other and share some interests, values, or jokes. In general, women are more willing than men to work on relationships, so when mother and daughter clash, they are likely to seek a solution rather than focus on winning the battle.

Part of the special pain between mother and daughter comes about because they feel that anger and alienation are not supposed to be part of the mother-daughter relationship. According to our cultural ideals, a mother is always gentle and loving—and so is her daughter. But precisely because of women's skill at understanding other people's emotions, many mothers and daughters can both wound and heal, both hurt and delight, each other better than anyone else can.

Learning the Stories

In more than thirty years of studying and practicing psychology, I have found that most mothers and daughters mistakenly believe that their problems with each other are mostly the result of their own, individual craziness, or each other's, or both. Those beliefs help neither one of them. In fact, most mother-daughter relationships improve once the women understand that they have both been duped—daughter into mother-blaming, mother into self-hate—and divided against each other by the myths.

When someone asks, "What causes the trouble between you and your mother?" most of us are ready with an explanation. We have our stories to tell—stories about her, and stories about our relationship. But some stories are closer to the truth than others. We need to get as close as we can to the real story about our mothers and ourselves. An old friend told me,

> All my life I had thought that Momma loved my sister more than me. I never questioned it, never asked about it, just believed it. When I turned twenty-one, Momma had a party for me, and I started talking about my childhood. As I said for the first time in my life the words, "Of course, Momma always loved Luisa best," I won-

dered for the first time whether or not it was true. Saying it out loud was such a definite thing to do. I suddenly felt a responsibility to Momma, to find out whether it was true before I kept on believing it myself.

When we tell the story of our relationship with each other, a mother and a daughter teach each other parts of the truth: "You felt scared then?! I thought you hated me!" When we strip our stories of the myths and then retell them, we begin to mend our rifts, learning what we have in common and experiencing the joy of discovering both great and tiny jewels of facts and feelings we hadn't known before.

Changes

Although some fortunate mothers and daughters can talk openly to each other about the problems between them, many women are daunted by the thought of doing so, or of trying to do so again. But these problems can be worked on successfully, and it needn't require years of expensive psychotherapy. It is striking how often, once a daughter is educated about our mother-blaming culture, she takes off rapidly.

Sometimes, naturally, it takes longer. At the end of the one-semester course I teach on mothers, the students write about how their feelings about and relationships with their mothers have changed during the course. The following are typical comments: In September, a woman described her mother as "cold," "distant," and "in pain," and said that she wished that "it could have been different between me and my mother, so I wouldn't have had to struggle so hard by myself in the past"; in December she wrote that her perspective had broadened: "I have hope for further changes in myself, and I'd like to meet with other women concerning these issues. This is new for me and it feels good."

Another woman wrote, "I have more respect for my mother than when we began this course, and I feel closer to her. . . . I am more tolerant of the things about my mother that bother me. . . . I no longer feel I am competing with my mother—but have more of a sense that we are both on the same team."

These changes did not require the daughters to suppress feelings of anger behind a smiling facade. Once some myth-based guilt, anger, and anguish are gone, the remaining feelings are easier to accept, understand, and work on, especially when mothers and daughters feel they are on the same team, working out problems together, rather than on opposite sides of an insurmountable brick wall.

Sharing, Listening, and Learning

Not all mothers are saints, nor are all daughters automatically wrong for thinking their mothers made mistakes. Mothers are human; they do make mistakes, and sometimes the way our mothers brought us up wasn't very good. Few mothers, though, are complete monsters. However, we easily believe they are monsters if we don't know how else to think about them—and that is where talking to other women comes in.

Most women want to talk about their mothers and, for some, about themselves as mothers. Nearly all women are filled with anger, guilt, fear, and uncertainty about aspects of their relationships with their mothers and/or daughters. Through patients and students I have learned that it is often easier to look clearly at someone else's dilemma than at our own stale anguish. Without a fresh look, simple and obvious ways to talk or to think about how we interact just don't come to mind. The daughter continues to blame her mother and fear her disapproval, and the mother continues to blame herself and agonize about the distance or conflict between herself and her daughter. Thus, both of them feel guilty. Each becomes entrenched in her own agony about their relationship and finds it harder and harder to understand the other's point of view and think of constructive ways they can be together.

Two activities have been especially helpful in my work with women. The first is simply to hear other women describe painful and infuriating feelings similar to their own. The second is to describe their own experiences as mothers. Every time a woman has told how angry she has been at her mother, sure that only she had ever felt this so intensely, she has found that many women have felt the same—and done the same "horrible" things because of it. One woman, for instance, described a wild tantrum she threw when her mother brought store-bought cupcakes to her third-grade Halloween party.

Hearing what others have to say helps daughters feel less crazy and mean. This releases energy they have been using to cover up what they regarded as their craziness or viciousness; they become freer to find better ways to deal with their mothers.

In classes and workshops, I ask participants to listen to other women's complaints about their mothers in new ways. Rather than feeding each other's mother-blame, they first acknowledge the daughter's frustration and then ask whether she might be misinterpreting or mislabeling the mother's motives and behavior. For example, when a woman describes her mother as overprotective, the participants ask whether it might be more accurate to describe her as loving and nurturing. The new, less angry labels don't always fit, but amazingly often they do. When women see how apt the new labels are, they realize how deeply the culture has ingrained in us the lesson, "When something is wrong, just blame mother." Through descriptions of their frustrations as mothers, women can provide each other with insights into their mothers' situations. Several women in one group described enjoying their careers but feeling torn apart when leaving their clinging toddlers at the daycare center. This discussion inspired some women to ask their own mothers how they had coped during those years.

Another woman talked movingly about her feelings when the hospital nurse said that her newborn was jaundiced and would have to be placed under special lights that would make him very listless. She was ashamed of both her terror about what the jaundice might signify and her powerlessness to help her baby. Watching him under the lights, she found that the only way she could maintain some semblance of calm was to take dozens of photographs of him. She believed that her worries were overblown but felt guilty about her ability to distance herself through taking pictures. She was doing her best to cope but felt simultaneously pathologically attached and pathologically detached. Her story helped other women gain new perspective on what had seemed to be their mothers' detached behavior. Instead of seeing this detachment as a sign that their mothers didn't care about them, they began to consider what else might have been behind such seeming unconcern. They began to wonder about the bigger picture.

The Goals of This Book

The goals of this book are simple:

- To reduce the pain felt by both daughters and mothers in their relationships with each other.
- To help daughters and mothers to feel better about themselves, by understanding the nature of the barriers between them.
- To give daughters and mothers a wider range of choices about how to conduct their lives by freeing them from myths that limit their vision of their options and teaching them new techniques and practical skills.
- To heighten both daughters' and mothers' awareness of how they have been kept apart by the ways they've been taught to think about each other.

To keep track of how you think and feel about your mother, keep paper and pen nearby as you read the following chapters. Jot down anything that comes to mind that might help in the unmasking process—things you realize you don't know about your mother and want to find out; a word or phrase that rings a bell for you, even if you're not yet sure why; stories that match your experience and stories that seem totally different from yours; questions that come to your mind. If you don't find the answers here, chances are you'll want to find them by talking with other people or reading other works, such as those in the bibliography.

Some of you will find that as soon as you read about a particular problem or issue, you will know how it applies to you and your mother, and you'll throw down the book in midchapter to do something about it. Others will want to read the whole book, think about the issues, talk to other people, and do further reading before even considering taking any action. Many readers will be in the second group: after a lifetime of being socialized into mother-blame, even a full chapter's worth of antidotes will be only a beginning. And if you gave up hope years ago, you'll have to work to get your engine revved up again.

Even daughters whose mothers have died have a great deal to gain from imagining, as vividly as possible, what they would say to their mothers if they could, and what they think their mothers might answer. Talking to your mother's close friends or other family members can be helpful, since one or more of them will have somewhat different perspectives on her, and other information about her, than you have. Some women in my course on mothers looked carefully at the books their deceased mothers had owned, noticing passages their mothers had underlined and notes they had written in the margins. Others inspected photographs of their mothers throughout their life spans, trying to read what they could from facial expressions and postures about how their mothers might have felt at different times in their lives.

Daughter's Move, Mother's Move

Initiating changes in your relationship with your mother—or in the way you think about her, if she has died or if you decide not to discuss these issues with her directly—may be mostly up to you. For that reason, this book is largely addressed to daughters. But mothers may find it useful, for knowing what has shaped her daughter's view of her can help a mother understand the way her daughter treats her. Because mother-blame is more deeply ingrained than daughter-blame, daughters are more often aware of anger at their mothers than vice versa; so a daughter may need to do more work, peeling away of layers of blame and myths, than a mother. But a mother who reads this book will probably understand more about her own mother (and their relationship), and this can shed light on her relationship with her daughter.

Usually, when a daughter is angry at or alienated from her mother, the mother is also suffering, for mothers tend to be excellent sensors of emotional distance. Despite their pain, though, most mothers of adult women come from generations taught that mothers haven't the right to ask for much (although some of them founded the Second Wave of the women's movement in the late 1960s and early 1970s or feminism's recent Third Wave); daughters in each generation are more likely than their mothers to feel comfortable questioning the roles our culture expects mothers to play and their perceptions of their own mothers. This is not to say that the taboos about questioning motherhood have disappeared. The night I finished writing my first major effort about mothers, I woke in terror, feeling that I had blasphemed and would be punished—not because of what I had said, because my view of mothers was generally sympathetic, but just for looking at mothers.

Our mothers generally feel this taboo even more: for them, even more than for most of us, society expected that they would become mothers (whether or not they also worked for pay) and would try to fit the self-sacrificing, uncomplaining mold of ideal motherhood. Indeed, this mold for young mothers exists even today. When their children reject or criticize them, most mothers feel that they have no right to complain, that the failure must have been their own—they themselves have internalized mother-blame. When their daughters are grown, hauling old wounds into the light for examination or reexamination is too frightening—unless and until they know that they will not be attacked for doing so.

Furthermore, mothers know that one generation has difficulty understanding another. A mother is skeptical that her daughter could understand how hard growing up during the Great Depression or World War II was or just how badly an unwed mother was treated even twenty years ago. Comments like, "But Mom, the Depression ended decades ago! You're rich now!" or "It was easier for you! In the 'sixties there was no AIDS!" quickly seal a mother's lips. Mothers need to know that their daughters are moving off the team that points an accusing finger and onto their mutually respectful and supportive team—not blindly or totally but thoughtfully.

Most women want to form close relationships and work out whatever interrupts that closeness. Most mothers and daughters, no matter how furious at each other, don't want to stay angry after the immediate release or empowerment of anger is over. We'd rather reestablish the closeness. We are sad and wistful when a bond is broken.

I hope to provide some tools for repairing that bond. Understanding how myths hinder a rapprochement—for it's hard in different ways to reapproach an angel or a witch—mothers and daughters will be prepared to reevaluate their history of problems, retell their shared story in a more truthful way, and begin their next chapter with a clearer vision of both the bridges and the gaps between them.

2

Such Love, Such Rage

"My relationship with my mother is so emotionally resonant—my feelings about her echo throughout my lifetime," a thirty-year-old graduate student told me, and for most adult daughters that rings true. We find ourselves thinking about our mothers in the middle of the night, first thing in the morning, in the midst of a crowd, while arguing with or hugging our daughters.

What are we thinking? We are longing for closeness with our mother; we are hating her for her power to make us feel infantile, ridiculous, and inadequate; we are chewing over what we said to each other last Thanksgiving in a horrible argument; we are trying for the thousandth time to think of just the right way to talk to her about a subject that we never seem to address calmly together.

All of this effort reveals our deep conflicts about our mothers. But it also shows us how much we care. We may often think our best bet would be to move to the opposite ends of the earth, but our struggles signal that we need to find less anguished ways to interact. Deep down, most daughters don't want to stay totally away from their mothers; they want to have an easier, more enjoyable time together. Madrona, a forty-four-year-old woman, felt this need. She had spent years resenting her mother—and didn't like herself for feeling that way:

> My mother had some wonderful characteristics: she was warm, loving, bright, and witty. So I wanted to enjoy my time with her, and I wanted to be a loving person when we were together. But my mother's negative features loomed so large in my view, and so infuriated me, I couldn't be the kind of loving woman I like to be.

I hated myself when I was with her—I hated my criticalness, my withdrawal, my anger. So I ended up hating her and me.

Dealing with this dilemma and growing beyond some of our anger requires first that we explore some of our most upsetting feelings about our mothers, as we do in this chapter; then, that we look at how and why we get stuck in these emotional ruts (chapters 3, 4, and 5), and finally, that we consider how to make productive changes (chapters 6 through 9). There is a way out of the mother-daughter stalemate. And finding that way is profoundly important, because in order to accept ourselves fully, we need to learn to understand more about our mothers and to accept—if not always to forgive—them.

You may not find in this chapter all of the upsetting feelings you have about your mother, but as you read about some of the most common negative feelings daughters have about their mothers, you will probably find some that apply to you. Although recognizing and exploring these feelings can be painful, they are essential steps toward mending mother-daughter relationships. The more you understand about your negative feelings, the better prepared you will be to start making positive changes.

Ambivalence about Mothers

Mother Wonderful, Mother Horrible

Most mother-daughter relationships involve a great deal of ambivalence. In the most loving mother-daughter relationships, the difficult times can be excruciating, partly because we know or can imagine how wonderful they could be. My relationship with my mother is basically very good, and she's a wonderful woman, but we do have our painful clashes and periods of alienation from each other. Just ask me—and just ask her. Even in more troubled mother-daughter relationships, the situation is rarely all bad; both mother and daughter usually think wistfully of good times they have shared and long for better times in the future.

Most women are very disconcerted when asked if they love their mothers: "Of course I do—she's my mother!" Not to love your mother seems unthinkable at best, inhuman at worst. Ask the average woman to describe her relationship with her mother, however, and the qualifications start to pile up: "Well, she's never really understood me. . . . She's always comparing me to other people, and somehow I never measure up. . . . She still treats me like a little kid." Resentments build: "I'm not on the phone two minutes with her before she starts trying to run my life. . . . I don't think there's one man I've gone out with that she's approved of!" Now, suddenly, rage: "It's no wonder I'm so screwed up! She's passed all of her neuroses on to me. Oh, I know she thinks she did the best she could, but if only she had [choose one]: (1) paid more attention to me; (2) paid less attention to me; (3) encouraged me more; (4) not pushed me so hard."

Why is it that in the space of a moment or two, we move from "Of course I love my mother!" to blaming her for everything wrong in our lives? The very word *mother* elicits a wealth of conflicting, ambivalent feelings—protectiveness, a desire for approval, need for her love versus rage at the terrible damage we feel she's done to us, however unwittingly. We feel justified in blaming her. After all, who had greater control over our lives when we were most vulnerable? Where did we learn our first rules about the world, about life, if not from her? We have heard that the first three (five, six?) years of life are the most important, the time when our basic personalities are formed, so we think it's obvious that the woman who influenced those years the most is responsible for what has gone wrong since then. How powerless we were! We don't even remember what our mothers may have taught us at this crucial time, how they may have planted the seeds of our neuroses. Once we are adults, when we think about it, rationally, we know it's not exactly her fault—but we still feel, somehow, "If only she had. . . ."

Women have ridden this exhausting merry-go-round for generations, to our own and our mothers' immense pain and misfortune. The love and fun we've shared (fed by the cultural idealization of mothers) combines with our anger and disappointment (fed by the cultural denunciation of mothers) and results in profound ambivalence. We know how best to please and to wound each other.

Coping by Blocking

Living with such powerfully loving and intensely painful feelings at the same time often seems impossible. Sometimes we try to cope by focusing on one feeling at a time, blocking out the rest.

When I was invited to speak about mother-daughter relationships to a young mothers' group, I asked them to tell me about their mothers. Nearly all expressed love, gratitude, and admiration for them. They denied having conflicts or problems with their mothers. But when I asked about how they were raising their own children, nearly all of them spoke with strong feelings—of fear, of awe, of hope—about their difficulties.

It is remotely possible that a whole roomful of women had perfect mothers but were encountering many difficulties in raising their own daughters and sons. More likely, these women were suppressing their negative feelings. Sometimes we feel it is not nice to say nasty things about our mothers. Blocking out negative feelings is one way that daughters deal with their ambivalence, especially publicly. But privately, or given the least encouragement, daughters often do a complete reversal, ventilating their worst feelings, and the positive ones are overwhelmed. Zenith Henkin Gross found that the adult women she interviewed "drew . . . shockingly rejecting portraits of their mothers." Workshops and seminars on mothers and daughters often degenerate into orgies of mother-trashing as soon as the first critical comment is made: when the socially created and culturally fueled mother-blaming bandwagon pulls up, women rush to hop on. They may even use mother-blaming to bond with each other.

Living with powerfully ambivalent feelings about our mothers is hard. We feel insincere when we pretend our mothers are all-good, and we feel vicious when we focus exclusively on their faults. And yet, the Perfect Mother/Bad Mother myths push us from one extreme to another.

Some ambivalence is present in any close relationship, but in mother-daughter ones it often seems more intense. Part of that intensity comes from a good feature of the mother-daughter inter-action: both members of this relationship are female, and, regardless of whatever other skills they might have, girls and women are far more likely than men and boys to have been taught to be emotionally expressive and sensitive to the feelings of others. (As a general rule, males are more likely to suppress, ignore, or deny many of their feelings.) So both mother and daughter are immersed in the realm of emotions and more likely to be aware of a variety of strong feelings on both sides.

In a study of woman-woman relationships, psychologists Lorette Woolsey and Laura-Lynne McBain documented this ambivalence through direct questions and observations. They found that relationships between women are emotionally richer than those between men but that the former include the potential for both strongly positive and strongly negative emotions.

The dramatically polarized mother-images of Angel and Witch, described in chapter 1, fuel daughters' ambivalence about their mothers. The Perfect Mother myths are a source of pressure not just to love but to adore our mothers. The Bad Mother myths transform our irritation and disappointment with our mother into fury and a sense of betrayal. Because the one feeling our culture prohibits women from expressing openly is anger, both mother and daughter suppress negative feelings, creating a pressure-cooker atmosphere and, ultimately, explosions of rage.

These intensely ambivalent feelings generally surface on the first day of my graduate school class on mothers, when I ask the students to (anonymously) (1) write down the first three things they think of when I say the word *mother*; (2) expand a bit on those three things or write anything else that comes to mind about their mothers; and (3) complete the sentence, "In regard to my mother, I wish that . . . "

One woman wrote that her first three thoughts about her mother were "warm," "friendly," and "colorful." But immediately afterward she wrote, "My mother's influence on me has been one of strict guidance. I always felt as if she were hovering over my shoulder, watching my every move." She wished that her mother "had had more children so that her focus would not have been so singularly on me. Perhaps then, more of the good qualities of our relationship could have emerged and less of the petty squabbling would have taken place."

Another woman also began with three positive images—"warm," "large," and "giving." But her next words were that her mother had "made me hopeful, but guilty; not provided a role model and had low self-esteem." She wished her mother "could feel stronger in herself; I wish I didn't get so triggered by her insecurity." A woman who found her mother "opinionated," "loving," and "sad" went on to write that she felt very close to her mother, despite feeling harshly criticized by her. And one whose first images of her mother were "cold," "distant," and "in pain" also said she was "courageous," "intelligent," and "generous."

A healthy range of ambivalence in a close relationship is normal; we usually see and respond to the other person's good and bad points. But the pressure on women to be perfect mothers and perfectly accepting daughters can make them uncomfortable when their ambivalence is in fact normal, and despondent when it is more intense.

Despair and Betrayal

Polarization of mother-images leads to two other feelings adult daughters commonly have about their mothers: despair of ever pleasing them and a sense of betrayal about their mothers' failure to nurture them enough. These feelings originate in the expectations that mothers should be perfect and produce perfect daughters. During those times when you think your mother is perfect (or she's thinking she should be perfect), you may feel that you can never satisfy her, from your choice of clothes to your decision about whether to have children. Somehow she seems to do everything right, and you can never catch up. Since she's supposed to be perfect, you're also likely to feel betrayed when she's unable to meet your needs, instead of regarding her as an average, imperfect human being. At such times, you usually feel disappointment or even rage, followed by guilt about those feelings. The mother who is on the receiving end of this despair and sense of betrayal feels understandably helpless, for she cannot be an ordinary person; in her daughter's eyes, her strengths put her on a pedestal, possessed of apparently unmeetable standards, but her human limitations are construed as dramatically letting her daughter down.

My friend Chava and her mother, Sue, had an experience that elicited these feelings. When Chava left her husband, she and her three teenagers moved back to her hometown. Chava's parents had lived there since before she was born, and they were loving and supportive while she learned to cope with single parenting and being divorced in a city with small-town attitudes. Toward the end of the year, she fell in love with someone new. When he invited her for a week's vacation, Chava told her mother and said she considered her kids (aged fifteen, sixteen, and seventeen) old enough to stay on their own. Sue chided Chava: "It's terrible for you to travel with this man. My friends will be shocked. How can you do this to me?" Chava was floored. She had been so sure that her mother would be happy for her. Sue also said, "Since you're determined to go on this trip, I don't think you should leave the kids alone. Please let them stay with me."

While Chava was away, her kids repeatedly broke the curfew their grandparents set, which drove Sue crazy with worry. Finally, she told them she was too old to put up with their nonsense and sent them back to Chava's to take care of themselves for the last half of the week. When Chava came home, Sue yelled at her, "Don't ever ask me to take care of those kids again." Chava felt betrayed: her mother had asked to have the kids stay with her but then acted as though Chava had imposed it on her. At such times, Chava despaired of reestablishing the loving relationship that she had as a child with her mother.

Many daughters recognize this all-too-familiar trap, feeling betrayed by their mothers but wanting to be closer to them. They wonder if greater closeness is possible and worth the trouble or if they should just give up. If not, they feel stuck—they don't know how to begin and feel they have tried everything. Despairing, they wonder, "Why attempt again the approaches that seem to have failed miserably for years?"

Anger

Our cultural idealization of mothers makes our anger at Mother almost inevitable; if you expect someone to be perfect, sooner or later you'll criticize them for having any faults. A young patient had this liberating insight:

> Mom needed so much for me to think she was a perfect mother—
> and I bought it. You can imagine how furious I was any time that
> image cracked! If I hadn't felt that she ought to be perfect, my fury
> about her imperfection wouldn't have been so boundless.

Judith Herman and Helen Lewis suggest that mother-daughter anger results from the contradiction "between women's inferior status and their special power as mothers." Thus, on the one hand, daughters feel, My mother is so powerful! because within their relationship she probably is; but on the other hand, mothers have little or no power and receive little respect from the rest of the world for their mothering work, and daughters may join in that lack of respect and easy criticism. A woman who seems in some ways very powerful is a ready target for the anger of a daughter who longs for her to be powerful enough to protect her from all danger and harm.

Energy spent in angry blaming of our mothers (and ourselves as both daughters and mothers) blocks our growth. One of the world's biggest sources of misdirected emotional energy is the rage millions of women feel toward their mothers. Major works of art could be created, social problems solved, and identity crises resolved if the force in this obsessive mother-blaming were more productively channeled. But such a rechanneling is blocked by powerful messages we get from professionals, from popular culture, and from each other, telling us that our worst problems stem from our mothers—while at the same time, at some level, we've learned that a good mother is a perfect mother. No wonder we get angry.

The Uses of Anger

Anger is a secondary emotion. We don't go from feeling nothing to feeling angry. Anger is usually the feeling we have when we don't like having an earlier feeling. For example, someone ignores us, we feel hurt, and because we don't like the hurt feeling, we get angry at the person who caused it. Similarly, we become angry at bureaucrats because they make us feel powerless; impotence is an uncomfortable feeling to have. Suppressing, denying, or ignoring anger doesn't make either the anger or the primary feelings go away, but expressing only the anger usually doesn't help much.

Anger can help us overcome feelings of powerlessness: when we see that we don't deserve to feel powerless (or humiliated or hurt), showing some anger can be empowering, a way to say, "I deserve better than this and can speak up. I don't have to wait quietly, hoping I'll be treated better." In the words of a friend of mine, "I was formerly a very angry and attacking daughter, and I think that to some extent that was how I survived—it kept me sane by separating me from my mother's impossible demands." Her mother's demands may or may not have been impossible; she may have been wrong in thinking of her mother as a witch. But since that was her image of her mother, her anger felt empowering. It was a way of maintaining her integrity, of refusing to attempt to meet unreasonable demands. And once she knew that she could protect herself in this way, she didn't feel as angry at her mother and was better able to accept her.

Accepting one's anger at an exceptionally abusive and/or rejecting mother is justified and can be empowering, making the daughter feel less unworthy: if her mother's unreasonable demands are the problem, then the daughter is not deficient for failing to satisfy them.

Going Beyond the Anger

We have to go beyond just expressing anger, however; anger usually doesn't change the other person's behavior or prevent a repetition of the original, hurtful events. If I just tell you, for instance, that I'm angry because you were rude to me, you will probably leap to your own defense by attacking or criticizing me. That can start an unending cycle of anger. Furthermore, you may not be aware of having done anything rude, so even if you want to avoid making me angry in the future, you're not sure how to do that. But if I explain to you the underlying feelings that made me angry—and tell you specifically what provoked those feelings in me—that gives you the power to improve our relationship by changing your behavior. If I tell you, "When I walked in, you finished talking to Dad before you spoke to me, and that hurt my feelings, so I got angry that you had hurt me," then if you care about me, you know how to prevent my feeling hurt—and then angry—the next time.

No matter how bad she is, seeing your mother as a person rather than a demon is helpful. If, after reading through this book, you believe your situation is one of those rare ones in which your mother is profoundly damaged, unusually hurtful, or abusive, then keeping your interactions with her to a minimum, or deferring contact until you feel stronger or clearer about how you want to conduct yourself—even if that takes a long time—may be the best route to your well-being (see chapters 6, 7, and especially 8). In the meantime you can continue to learn more about your mother, yourself, and your relationship. At least you'll know that you did your part and are not responsible or at fault. Furthermore, finding out what feelings underlie the anger helps in three ways: (1) a daughter who realizes she's sad, guilty, or afraid of her mother, rather than just angry, no longer thinks of herself as simply an angry person; (2) identifying these feelings in herself makes the daughter feel less the villain than anger does, since it's more acceptable to feel sad, guilty, or afraid of an idealized mother than to be angry at her; and (3) sadness, guilt, and fear can diminish as we become aware of them.

We also have to go beyond the anger because women tend to feel guilty, much more than men, about being angry, especially at our mothers. Twenty-four-year-old Liv described the vicious cycle of anger and guilt:

> After I've gotten mad at my mother, I feel guilty and ashamed of myself. Then I get mad at her because she's the reason I feel guilty and ashamed: the guilt is because I don't want to hurt her, and the shame is because she's the one who always said I should learn to control my anger.

So anger can lead to guilt, and guilt can lead to anger. Women are good at feeling guilty any time they think they've hurt or disappointed anyone, all the more so with their mothers. Daughters know that their mothers receive little respect for mother-work; since daughters are supposed to be sensitive and supportive, we feel, how can we—of all people—let mother down? But guilt is a heavy burden, and when enough piles up, daughters get angry and often depressed. Sadly, this anger is usually aimed at mother rather than at the social arrangements that caused the daughter's guilt.

Most of us want our mothers' approval; when we don't get it wholeheartedly, we may automatically respond by attacking or blaming them. But this response damages the relationship and intensifies our self-hate. I am not suggesting that all anger should be wiped out; but attack and blame are not healthy or productive. We'll feel less guilty once we understand why we're angry—both the feelings that underlie the anger and the way mother-blaming promotes the anger.

Anger and Self-Confidence

A common cause of a daughter's anger is what seem to be her mother's assaults on her self-confidence. This is what happened to Madrona—the woman mentioned at the beginning of this chapter whose resentment of her mother prevented her from being the kind of woman she wanted to be. She deeply desired her mother's approval but felt continually criticized by her. This made her feel insecure and increased even more her need for her mother's approval. She was all the more devastated, and then infuriated, when the approval didn't seem forthcoming.

Until we eradicate sexism, most women will lack self-confidence, and this makes our mothers' approval especially important to us. When we don't get it—or don't get enough—we may defend ourselves by saying, "Nothing's wrong with me! She's impossible to please." But our lack of confidence and need for mother's approval can lock us into our often-buried anger. In addition, insecurity makes us exaggerate the slightest criticism from other people; even if our mother mostly loves and admires us, we won't see it. Listen to Betty, who in her midfifties had enrolled in law school after raising three children:

> After I graduated from law school, my first job was with a huge law firm that had never hired a Black woman before. The senior partners were especially tough on me, and my self-confidence—which had never been terrific but had improved when I did well in law school—just plummeted. One evening, after one of the senior partners had taken me to task for what was really a minor error on my part, I dropped by to see Ma. When I told her my troubles, she said, "I guess you have to expect to be monitored closely, when you're the first Black woman to do something."
>
> I hit the ceiling. I had wanted her sympathy, and I thought she was being really hard on me. I flounced out and drove home. When I walked in the door, the phone was ringing, and it was Ma. She didn't know why I was so upset, because her comment was meant to be sympathetic—"It's hard being the first Black woman and have people watching you like hawks." I had been so afraid she wouldn't support me that I mistakenly believed she wasn't.

This is a vicious cycle: insecurity and a sense of inadequacy intensify our need for mother's approval and our belief that she generally disapproves of us; we get angry and become hypercritical of her, and our self-respect plummets even more because our interactions are angry and painful. We become less and less the women we really want to be.

Fear

Three of the major fears a daughter has in relation to her mother are the fear of losing her love, the fear of her death, and the fear of being like her or repeating her mistakes.

Fear of losing a mother's love is related to being unable to please her, of being unable to live up to her goals for us. As a fifty-five-year-old secretary named Silvia told me, "Fear is that hollow feeling I still get in the pit of my stomach when I've displeased my mother. If I don't please her, she might stop loving me."

Women who feel they haven't met their mothers' standards or have not made some sort of peace with their mothers develop an intense dread of their mother's death. They sense how guilty they will feel about their unresolved conflicts, lingering anger, and guilt about that anger. Daughters have come to me, frantic with worry, saying:

> I'm terrified to think about the fact that my mother will die some-day. I can't think about it—when I try to, my heart pounds and I start to cry. It's partly because we're not as close as we used to be, and we argue a lot. I'm not sure why that is or what to do about it, and my fear that we won't ever get anything resolved, that we'll still be fighting and alienated when she dies, is so overwhelming that I can't think calmly about how to try to work things out with her.

Advice columnists such as Ann Landers and Abigail Van Buren have frequently printed letters from daughters overcome with remorse after their mothers have died. Because dread of our mother's death has such power, few of us can simply write our mothers off, put them out of our minds. Yet here is the positive side of that fear. Fear is an emotional parallel to physical pain. As pain is the body's way of telling us something is physically wrong, so fear and apprehension signal that important emotional work remains undone. If we can recognize this, we needn't just dread our mother's death; our fear can propel our search for ways to overcome the barriers between our mothers and ourselves in this life.

Fear of Repetition

If we weren't deeply affected by mother-blaming, we wouldn't fear being compared to our mothers; we could even be proud. Blaming our mothers harms us, because what we believe about our mothers, we often suspect about ourselves. It's hard to find a woman who does not spend time thinking she acts just like her mother, or that she is very different from her mother, or both. In all of those thoughts, her mother is the standard, so what she believes about her mother matters a great deal. Even women who say they adore their mothers often fear that they have picked up their mothers' bad qualities. Among women of my generation and young women, this is a common worry—in some, an obsession. Here is a typical comment:

> Everyone loved my mother, because she was so sweet and had such a great sense of humor. It's true that she was very kind and generous, and I loved her for that. But her sense of humor was sometimes shockingly bawdy, and that used to embarrass me no end. I love to tell jokes myself, but I never tell any joke that's the least bit off-color, because I'm so afraid I'll seem as crude as she did. It's as though I can't figure out how to tell a sexy joke without sounding exactly like her.

If we regard our mothers as masochistic, rejecting, demanding, guilt-inducing, or embarrassing, we usually begin to suspect that we are too. Most daughters try hard to avoid repeating what they consider their mothers' specific mistakes, and many are determined to dress differently, choose friends differently, and have different values from those their mothers have. At the same time, we often believe almost superstitiously that we cannot avoid that repetition. We secretly fear that we are exactly like our mothers in all the ways we dislike.

Since we tend to believe that we are like our mothers, deprecation of them usually leads to self-deprecation. Hatred not only hurts the person who is hated; it is destructive also to the person who hates. Ultimately, hatred and blame keep us tied to and preoccupied with the target of those feelings. Our behavior is controlled by the need to get revenge on her, "show" her, react against her, ostracize her, or prove her wrong. At one of my lectures, a woman called Maram said, "I used to feel that everything my mother did reflected on me. I was embarrassed by her looks, the way she dressed, the way she talked, and I hated her for it. But then I also hated myself for hating her. I wasn't proud of letting my mother's appearance bother me so much."

To a disturbing degree, we don't want to be like our mothers.

Why should we want to be like them, we might ask, since so much of what they do is ignored or devalued? Isn't that like wanting to be a welfare recipient or a kid in the slow reading group? But in our mothers' eyes, our wish to be different seems one more sign that no one values the way they've spent their lives.

A telling manifestation of the persistence of mother-blame is how often the increasing numbers of mothers with paid jobs are faulted—and encouraged to fault themselves—for both inadequate mothering and inadequate performance in the workplace. When more women were stay-at-home mothers, some optimistic souls believed those women would be held in higher regard if they also worked for pay and certainly if they had high-powered, highly paid careers. But as women with dual roles bemoan, they are now often accused of shortchanging both the people at home and the people in the office. As a result, young women who want those dual roles are frightened by the rarity with which their mothers' work in either place is valued. Is it progress for society to have moved from disparaging full-time mothers for spending their days in "easy, lazy work" to driving mothers with paid jobs crazy with guilt for not giving their all in either arena? As I've often said, "In a sexist society, anything that *can* be used against women *will* be used against women." In a mother-blaming society, whatever mothers do will be used against them. This observation is not a statement of hopelessness about society; it is a note of caution about a society that clings to its mother-blame and other forms of sexism.

Daughters, then, often believe that they want to avoid taking on their mothers' individual, personal characteristics. But a little probing usually shows that what daughters really want to avoid is anything connected with women's devalued and limited position: her mother's weight doesn't fit the slender feminine mold; she gets no respect outside the home or at home; she is intimidated by her husband.

Sadness, Numbness, and Alienation

Sadness is the predominant feeling many adult daughters have about their mothers. For some, the sadness comes from Mother's failure to match the idealized mother image. As one woman said, "I still can't stop wishing she will love and protect me completely and tell me—as she did when I was a child—that everything I do is wonderful. I really feel that I have lost something."

When I encouraged this woman to think back over her child-hood, she recalled some occasions when her mother had not been completely loving and supportive; after all, her mother is just a human being. So this daughter's sadness came not so much from changes in her mother as from the contrast between reality and her distorted memories. And those distortions came from the ide-alized side of mother-images.

For other daughters, sadness about their mothers comes from the emotional distance between them. When anything goes wrong in the relationship, they are acutely aware of a sense of loss. Something that's usually there is missing, and that something is the closeness; the daughter feels sadness or alienation. After one of my lectures about mothers and daughters, a woman told me this story:

> As you spoke today I realized that my mother and I grew apart when I got promoted to an executive job in the department store where I had worked for eight years. Until then, my mother always told me how proud she was that I was a buyer for the women's clothing department. But once I got my promotion, she started falling silent whenever I was around. And just today I understood that that is because, in her eyes, my executive job puts me in the same world as my father. As long as I was a women's clothes buyer, I did work she knew something about, because she is a dressmaker. But my father is a business executive, so now Dad and I have some-thing in common, and Mom feels left out.

For some daughters, the sadness comes from sorrow over the closeness they lost during their rebellious years. For sons, a fair amount of rebelliousness is often encouraged, especially in the name of breaking away from Mom. For daughters, rebellion is harder to carry out, partly because it's not in keeping with the accepted feminine role and partly because—in the idealized ver-sion of mother-daughter images—daughters are supposed to want to stay very close to their mothers. So daughters' rebellion is likely to be more painful, more in danger of being misinterpreted as betrayal of their mothers, than is sons' rebellion. Thus, daughters are more inclined to believe their rebellious times were indeed a betrayal. This is even more pronounced in families of immigrants who moved from cultures with strong prohibitions against par-ent–child conflict to ones where such prohibitions are more lax, such as Hispanic, Portuguese, or Asian families who move to the United States.

Perhaps even more worrying than ambivalence, anger, guilt, despair, fear, and sadness about Mother is the emotional numbness or sense of alienation that some daughters feel. Sometimes numbness and alienation set in when other feelings are overpowering. One can only endure so much anger, guilt, and despair before emotionally shutting down. A well-known politician whose visits with her mother begin well, become upsetting, and end with feelings of alienation has said that her mother likes the idea of her visiting but not the reality. She thought she should just let her mother meet her at the airport, then catch the next plane back.

When numbness or alienation predominates, a daughter's first question to herself should be whether that is masking other feelings. If the answer is yes, she can begin to identify those feelings, using the framework and methods suggested in the rest of this book. The block against feelings can be removed, although it should be removed with care, so the onrush of bottled-up feelings isn't overwhelming; after all, the intensity of those feelings in the first place was so great that they had to be suppressed. A woman who attended one of my workshops explained a few weeks later:

> I realized that the feeling of deadness I had about my mother was a safe cover-up, to protect me from my strong feelings of powerlessness to change the misery that's in her life because she never went beyond grade four in school and is afraid to go back to school. And then I was knocked out by how much sadness and rage I felt. I felt sad for her, and I felt enraged because nothing I could do seemed to help. She sits at home all day, watching TV and feeling useless, but she's clearly just too frightened to go back to school and get enough upgrading to get a job. Even my offer to go with her didn't make any difference.
>
> It was a good thing I had talked to other women in similar positions at the workshop, because after my initial burst of sorrow and rage, I felt the old numbness setting in. I found that I started thinking of ways to avoid seeing Mom. But then I remembered what other daughters had said about their feelings of powerlessness when they couldn't save their mothers, and how our group had decided that even if we can't save them, it doesn't help us or our

mothers for us to run away. It's a struggle to acknowledge how helpless we are to change our mothers, but only when we've done that can we stay close to them and offer what will help them, which is our continuing love and support. My mother needs my love and support, even if she can't use it to do what I wish she could.

Emotional numbness can also set in when a relationship seems to have reached an impasse. When Dvora told her parents she was lesbian, her father said he hoped she would find a love that would make her happy. But her mother wailed, "Oh! I never thought I'd have a child who would do things to people with her mouth!" and said she would "sit shiva" (the Jewish ritual for mourning the dead). In the face of her mother's repeated refusals to talk with her, Dvora's hurt was so piercing that she said, "I felt wounded, cast out, powerless. To stay sane, I had to stop feeling anything for her." Not until her mother told Dvora's brother that she felt Dvora's sexual orientation was a sign she had failed as a mother did Dvora find a place to begin her efforts to reconnect, at which point the numbness began to subside.

Occasionally, a daughter goes emotionally numb to protect herself from a truly unlovable, vicious, or very sick mother, or one who has been toughened up by a very different culture. Creating a wall may be the only way the daughter can stop blaming herself and feeling unlovable because of her mother's treatment of her. It may also stem the tide of guilt that she feels for not loving her mother. A young adult woman said:

> My mother has always been unhappy. Her family immigrated to this country when she was twelve—a terrible age to make such a big adjustment—and she never felt at home here. When I hit adolescence and started doing all the typical adolescent things like talking on the telephone for hours or worrying about what clothes were "in," she turned on me and tore me down at every turn. She'd accusingly say things like, "In my country, girls didn't worry about such superficial things. We took life seriously and worked hard." I knew she was afraid that as I got more "American," I was growing farther and farther away from her, and I felt bad about that. But I couldn't take her vicious criticism and humiliation of me. She made me feel totally worthless, even though at some level I knew I

was just normal. The only way I could cope was by tuning her out completely. As soon as she'd start to speak, I'd think about something else. For all practical purposes, she vanished from my emotional life. I stopped counting on her for warmth or approval. I stopped feeling anything for her. I didn't want to hate her, so feeling nothing was my only option.

Because the Perfect Mother images exist, daughters feel guilty for not regarding their mothers as perfect; but if they don't, a whole culture out there is ready to pounce, to encourage them to see Mother as a miserable failure. No matter what a mother has done to her daughter, the chances are that sometime she did something good, so that her daughter feels guilty about branding her as a failure. In addition, no matter how bad a mother is, her daughter usually senses that either within or outside the family, people identify her with her mother. So if she is going to regard Mother as thoroughly horrible, what does that make her? A society that encouraged us to see our mothers simply as people would diminish daughters' need to go emotionally limp.

Pent-up Love

We are used to believing that pent-up hostility is dangerous; but the real tragedy for daughters is pent-up love. When mother-blaming attitudes overshadow our view of our mothers, it is far too easy to believe they deserve only our scorn and blame; but bottling up our loving feelings makes us feel inhuman, mechanical, cold. We feel better about ourselves when we are free to show love, warmth, and respect. So the release of pent-up love and respect for our mothers brings the added gift of love and respect for ourselves. Furthermore, as many experienced therapists agree, digging around in our past in order to find the cause of current problems has only limited value. What works much better—and is more empowering (perhaps the most important aim of therapy)—is to focus on what we can do now and how we can go beyond mother-blaming. Ruth's story illustrates this process. Like most adolescents, Ruth had serious self-doubts. At first, she was relieved to believe that her mother was deficient, not she herself, "I believe that prior to blaming my mother for not loving me enough or for disappointing me in various ways, I blamed myself for being unlovable and the cause of her failure as a mother."

For Ruth, mother-blaming was one step away from self-hate and self-blame. As an adult, Ruth realized that neither she nor her mother was so terrible. Recently, raising her own daughter has made her appreciate her mother more.

Sue and Chava, the mother and daughter described earlier, found a way to go beyond their stalemate about Chava's trip with her boyfriend to release some of their pent-up love. Chava felt despair, because nothing she did seemed to meet her mother's standards: her divorce was an embarrassment to her mother, as was her new relationship. Leaving her teenagers alone for a week was not acceptable to Sue, nor was leaving them with her. Chava also felt betrayed and unsupported, because Sue was not thrilled at Chava's chance to travel with her new man.

Chava could have simply blamed and chided her mother for being unreasonable, but that would have meant ignoring her own wish to be more loving with her mother. Wisely, Chava thought to ask Sue why she was so upset. Sue explained that she was terrified that her friends would disapprove of Chava's traveling with a man to whom she was not married and would consider it a mark of Sue's failure as a mother. She had friends who considered her a failure because Chava "hadn't managed to keep her marriage together." Sue had wanted to help Chava but felt embarrassed and worried; when the children misbehaved, she was overwhelmed and unable to cope. Furthermore, Sue was afraid that Chava was vulnerable, having recently left a difficult marriage, and would have her hopes for a romantic adventure dashed. Sue had loved Chava's husband like a son, so Chava's divorce involved a loss of a relationship for Sue, too. Understandably, Sue held back from getting her own hopes up about this new man.

As Sue and Chava talked, Sue managed—at least for the moment—to stop feeling she should be Supergrandma. She described how taking care of Chava's children, though well-intentioned, had proven to be more than she could handle. As she talked, she realized that her failure wasn't Chava's fault, and Chava realized that her mother was neither perfect nor totally unreasonable but an ordinary person. Sue was relieved to hear that her daughter wasn't horrified by her inability to handle the teenagers—after all, who could sympathize with the frustration of that task more than Chava? Together, Chava and Sue saw that they had both been controlled by the unreasonable expectations that if Sue were a Good

Mother she would immediately and wholeheartedly approve of everything Chava did and would manage to meet the needs of Chava and her children with grace and ease. Most of all, their improved mutual understanding lowered the barrier between them and replaced it with a bridge.

It Needn't Be So Hard

Mothers and daughters have not always been plagued by enormous anguish in their relationships with each other. In her article "The Female World of Love and Ritual," historian Carroll Smith-Rosenberg notes that in the eighteenth and nineteenth centuries, women relatives "assumed an emotional centrality in each others' lives," "hostility and criticism of other women were discouraged," and "Women, who had little status or power in the larger world of male concerns, possessed status and power in the lives and worlds of other women." Writing about mother-daughter relationships during the past two centuries, Smith-Rosenberg describes great intimacy and shared sympathy and joy; expressions of hostility were rare, she believes, not because they were suppressed but because such feelings were uncommon.

Guilt and agony have not always characterized mother-daughter relationships in the past, so perhaps they need not characterize our relationships today. And if cultural and social changes have magnified mother-daughter problems, understanding the nature of those changes can take us a long way toward overcoming our difficulties.

In order to see our mothers as they really are, and really have been, we have to understand the very fabric of mother-blaming, to think about a variety of its manifestations, to learn how it works so that we can catch ourselves doing it. Chapter 3 begins this exploration.

3

Mother-Blaming

If you really want to know why this child is a mess,
just look at its mother!
—*frequent, informal assessment by both
real and armchair psychologists*

Mother-in-law in Trunk
—*seen on hundreds of bumper stickers*

Start with this fact: in our society it is acceptable to blame Mom.
Then add the Perfect Mother and Bad Mother images, which lead
us to blame Mom for not being perfect when she doesn't live up
to our idealized image, and, when she does something not so terrific, to blame her for being horrible rather than only human. In
view of the intense social pressure placed on girls to be "little
mothers," it is troubling that their most salient model is not
regarded as a worthy one.

Mother-blaming is like air pollution. I live in a large city with
moderate pollution I rarely notice—until I get out into the fresh
country air, when I suddenly recall how good it feels to breathe
really well. My students and patients swear that getting away
from mother-blaming helps them breathe more freely.

The essential foundation for improving our mother-daughter
relationships is a thorough understanding of mother-blaming, for
only when we see how easy blaming Mother is will we have a
chance of doing otherwise. Only when we see the pollution can
we clear the air.

We need to explore the fabric of our prejudices with care. We
daughters can't expect to forget the irritating or infuriating things
our mothers do and just focus on the wonderful ones. But we
need to realize that our culture encourages us to focus only on

our mothers' faults and to let their good points slip our minds. Blaming our mothers is so easy that we rarely stop to consider whether anyone else might be to blame, or even whether no one is to blame. For us mothers, understanding how mother-blaming operates can lighten our load. After all, untapped energy is bound up not only in the daughter's mother-blaming but also in the mother's self-blame and self-hate.

The less a group is valued and respected, the easier it is to target its members as scapegoats. The undervaluing of mothers is revealed not just through anecdotes but also by hard facts. According to a 1998–99 U.S. Department of Labor report, the average child-care worker and home health aide (requiring many of the same skills as being a mother) were paid only 73 percent and 81 percent, respectively, as much as a nonsupervisory animal caretaker.

This undervaluing is largely a product of our times. Before the technological revolution, mothers did most of their work at home. Their children could see them tending chickens, cleaning, laundering, preparing food, sewing, hauling water and firewood—"all obviously hard work," explains sociologist Jessie Bernard. Now, however, mothers spend much of their time and energy trying to meet their children's emotional, psychological, and learning needs; they have nothing concrete, visible, and immediate to show for it—no woven shawls, no fresh eggs.

How easily does mothers' work become invisible! How easily do stay-at-home mothers face the accusations of husbands who assume women have nothing to do all day! "Why isn't dinner on the table? Why isn't the house in order? Why aren't the kids in bed?" Many men still want their needs met and discount the fact that mothers—even the huge majority with paid jobs—do most chauffeuring of children to and from school, activities, and doctors' appointments; entertaining of them and their friends; refereeing siblings' and neighbor children's conflicts; empathizing about minor and major tragedies; and trying to give to and receive support from other women who are also trying to be terrific mothers and terrified they aren't.

For women raising children today, the undervaluing of mothering work has become more complex. Those of us with paid employment may feel valued in work environments but often wind up feeling unappreciated for the enormous weight of the double load. Mothering tasks, after all, are still believed to require little or no skill or effort. And hand in hand with mother-blaming goes a taboo against father-blaming.

My friend Raquel is a busy psychologist, whose husband Stefan is a surgeon. When Raquel tired of planning all of the family vacations, she informed Stefan that she would leave all plans for their next annual family ski trip to him. He made no plans. When she told him how disappointed she was, their six-year-old son said angrily, "Don't get mad at Daddy. He is a surgeon, and he works very hard. He's so busy and important that he has to have a nurse and an assistant. He doesn't have time to make travel plans." And another son added, "That's right. And Daddy's so important he even has a dictaphone. You don't have a dictaphone!" Many people hear such stories and just laugh, not recognizing how much the devaluation and blame can hurt.

Motherwork is not only undervalued but often unnoticed. Even an assembly-line worker in a factory receives a regular paycheck, which carries the message, "Someone values the work that you do." In contrast, not only is motherwork not paid but most of mothers' boring or difficult work is actually unnoticed or made light of. What mother has had her children or husband say, "That was a great week's worth of dusting you did! Thanks!"?

You may feel that your mother doesn't go unnoticed. Many women tell me their mothers are "strong women," as though that means that they are appreciated. That may be true in some cases, but if you think of your mother as strong, be careful: that image is often another way to brand mothers negatively—"Don't worry about my mother. She comes on like a Mack truck!" (See chapter 5: perceiving a mother as powerful often means perceiving her as dangerous.) When we unthinkingly describe a mother as strong, we often focus on her power to make us put our dirty clothes in the hamper or make us feel guilty; we don't recognize that she might have little power outside the home. Quite possibly, she receives no respect or appreciation even at home, only mockery and fear.

People whose eyes tear up when they talk about "mother-hood" or their mothers often treat their mothers with disdain when they are face-to-face. Paradoxically, motherhood in principle and in general is described in glowing, all-important terms—and as a result, mothers feel ashamed to complain about their low status in fact and individually.

During the 1950s, an era now infamous for the popularity of the image of happy-little-wife-at-home, author Philip Wylie pulled together every demeaning image of mothers and gave them ugly, vicious form. In his book, *Generation of Vipers,* his loathing of mothers vibrates with intensity, and although this book is painful to read, we need to know that it was popular when mothers were raising the children who are now in their forties and fifties. Furthermore, Wylie's writing is not all that different in tone from the jokes of many comics in the year 2000 or even recent writings by therapists. Wylie wrote:

> Megaloid momworship has got completely out of hand. Our land, subjectively mapped, would have more silver cords and apron strings crisscrossing it than railroads and telephone wires. Mom is everywhere and everything and damned near everybody, and from her depends all the rest of the U.S. Disguised as good old mom, dear old mom, sweet old mom, your loving mom, and so on. . . .
>
> . . . nobody among [American sages]—no great man or brave—from the first day of the first congressional meeting to the present ever stood in our halls of state and pronounced the one indubitably most-needed American verity: "Gentlemen, mom is a jerk."
>
> . . . [Mom used to be so busy with child-raising and housework] that she was rarely a problem to her family or to her equally busy friends, and never one to herself. Usually, until very recently, mom folded up and died of hard work somewhere in the middle of her life.
>
> . . . Nowadays, with nothing to do, and all the tens of thousands of men . . . to maintain her, every clattering prickamette in the republic survives for an incredible number of years, to stamp and jibber in the midst of man, a noisy neuter by natural default or a scientific gelding sustained by science, all tongue and teat and razzmatazz.

Wylie's words continue to be widely quoted to justify mother-trashing, make men feel ashamed of loving their mothers and refusing to revile them, make women feel that mother-love is sick, since who in their right mind could love the kind of creature Wylie so vividly described? Even people who never read Wylie's actual work are familiar with the essential features of his mother-images.

The term Wylie coined, *momism,* became widely used to refer scathingly and fearfully to mothers' allegedly excessive domination. To this day, mother-blaming perpetuates "momism" in a different sense, one that parallels other isms: sexism, racism, ageism, classism. Perhaps it is time to use the word *momism* to label mother-blame and mother-hate explicitly and succinctly as a form of prejudice as virulent as the other isms are acknowledged to be.

There is a lesson about the treatment of mothers in one aspect of the history of racism. Fortunately, by the late 1960s publicly expressing antiBlack sentiments had begun to become déclassé (although racism itself persists, of course); but it has remained acceptable to say venomous things about Blacks as long as they are Black mothers—or about Jewish mothers, Italian mothers, funny old grannies, or mothers-in-law. Racist statements about Blacks or other ethnic groups have been on their way out, like anti-Semitic comments—but only when they are about groups (sex unspecified) or about males. In this new century, just as racism has not vanished but has taken subtler forms—becoming harder to pinpoint and attack—so has sexism taken subtler forms. Blatantly woman-hating jokes are considered inappropriate in some social circles, yet mother-bashing ones are not. Jokes about mothers and mothers-in-law are far more common than jokes about fathers and fathers-in-law. It is terrible to be a mother and know that you are expected to find them funny, that to be hurt instead is to seem overly sensitive—or ridiculous.

Once we're aware that mother-blaming comes easily and distorts our view, we can begin to catch ourselves doing it. A friend who knew that I was writing this book explained,

> I couldn't sleep last night. I kept thinking about my eighty-five-year-old mother, who is in a nursing home and may not live much longer. Every time my sister and I talk, we moan and groan, "Do you know what she said to me today!? She asked me why I'd had my hair cut! Why doesn't she leave us alone?!"
>
> I kept thinking about the things she says to me that make me crazy, and about the things I wanted her to do that she'd never done. Then I thought about your book, and I sat up in bed and

asked myself why I always focus on the ways she has failed or upset me. Why do I never think about the good things she's done for me? And I started remembering how, after my husband and I split up, she came and stayed with the children and me and helped take care of us. I thought of all the things she had done over the years to make my life easier or to make me laugh.

This woman has begun to see the mother-blaming mold in which her experience has been shaped, and she understands that it has thrown her mother's love and humor into shadow while turning the spotlight on her mother's weak points. Whether or not she suspects it, she may be using mother-blame to avoid her fear of her mother's impending death.

Mother-Blaming All Around

If you are a daughter, don't think that it's only you—or other daughters—whose view of mothers is distorted. Mother-blaming is interwoven throughout our daily lives. At every level of conversation and discussion, in every conceivable arena, mothers are ignored, demeaned, and scapegoated—in jokes (often unfunny), on bumper stickers, on television and at the movies, in works by popular authors, in our own families, in the research literature, in the courts, and in psychotherapists' offices.

Our everyday language reflects this pattern: try to think of terms that are as demeaning to fathers as everyday terms like "son of a bitch." Even for expressions that are not profane, such as "mama's boy," the parallel "daddy's girl" is not really equivalent. "Mama's boy" calls up images of a smothering, overprotective mother whose "boy" seems psychologically sick, or at least un-manly and ridiculous, through his association with her. A "daddy's girl," on the other hand, is the lucky, feminine daughter who has been singled out by the high-status parent. At worst, she might be thought of as overly reliant on her "feminine wiles."

Toronto social worker Ruth Goodman told me the following story: At the Toronto Festival of Festivals a filmmaker was asked why his film included so much violence. He replied, "If you knew my mother, you'd understand." The audience snickered. This glib response allowed him to disown responsibility for his actions by switching the focus to his mother. Ironically, the only sins of the mother in the movie were that she had corny wallpaper and liked Muzak, whereas the father was a very disturbing person.

When I speak about my book *The Myth of Women's Masochism,* in which I carefully avoid mother-blaming, I learn that many readers manage to work it in anyway; strikingly often, one or more people approach me and say: "I read your book and really understood what you said, and now I agree that women are not masochists, they do not like to suffer. Except one: my mother." Apparently, untold numbers of otherwise thoughtful people believe that their mother is the world's only living masochist, a sicko.

The most poignant instances of mother-blaming within the family are those in which the mother blames herself for whatever goes wrong. Mothers of misbehaving kids blame themselves for "not setting enough limits" if they are slightly less rigid disciplinarians than average, and if they are slightly more rigid, they blame themselves for "coming down too hard" on the child. Mothers whose children get many colds are far more likely to berate themselves for failing to dress them warmly enough (even when they haven't failed to do so) than to blame the pediatrician for not suggesting that the coughs and runny noses could be caused by food allergies or that colds are hard to prevent when kids spend all day in groups. Hearing ourselves and other mothers blamed from all sides, we naturally learn to do it ourselves.

I am still surprised when I hear successful, well-educated women putting themselves down as mothers, even when they might not be totally responsible for all of their children's suffering. One such woman was a frequent face on the lecture circuit. Upon learning that one of her daughters was bulimic, she stopped her media tour and rushed home to nurse her daughter back to health—which she succeeded in doing! But she concluded that she was to blame for her daughter's bulimia; she believed that she had neglected her daughter's emotional needs for years because she had been preoccupied with her own career and had hungrily fed on her daughter's admiration for her work.

Although the typical father, even today, is preoccupied with his work and wants his children's respect and approval, such fathers are not blamed for their children's problems. Furthermore, the lecturer was divorced from her daughter's father, so what preceded or followed the divorce, perhaps even something in the father's treatment of the daughter, just might have contributed to the bulimia. So might a host of other factors. But the mother never mentioned any of this in her lecture. Hearing this woman publicly offer her "guilt" as proof of mothers' failures and culpability was tragic—and frightening. She doing an injustice to herself and reinforcing the blaming of other mothers and their self-blame.

Even when we're not faulting ourselves, other family members often do it for us. Essayist Nancy Mairs said that when her sixteen-year-old daughter Anne went to Central America as a volunteer worker, Mairs's parents-in-law chided her for allowing Anne to go:

> [George's parents] never mentioned the matter to him. I was at first hurt, angry, feeling picked on; later I came to understand that I was the natural target of their misgivings. George couldn't be counted on to know what girls should or shouldn't do, or to communicate his knowledge if he did. But I could. I was Anne's mother.

Mother-blaming among laypeople is well nourished by the words of mental health researchers and practitioners, whom our culture considers experts on human behavior. We often forget that their theories and their research are influenced by the same tendency to scapegoat mothers that pervades the whole society.

Mother-Blaming among the Experts

If Researchers Say It, It Must Be True

In chapter 1, I mentioned my study of mother-blaming by mental health professionals. My documentation came from their own writings in scholarly journals, and the results show that they generally make little or no attempt to hide their mother-blaming; apparently they feel no need to conceal it. This was revealed in my initial research, and it continues today.

My student Ian Hall-McCorquodale and I read 125 articles published in nine different major mental health journals in 1970, 1976, and 1982. Some articles were single case studies, and some were reports of research on large numbers of people with emotional problems. We categorized each article according to sixty-three different types of mother-blaming. These ranged from "number of words used to describe mother" and "number of words used to describe father" to the repetition of earlier mother-blaming claims without questioning whether they apply in the current case. We found that, regardless of the author's sex or occupation as psychoanalyst, psychiatrist, psychologist, or social worker, mental health professionals overwhelmingly indulged in mother-blaming. In the 125 articles, mothers were blamed for seventy-two different kinds of problems in their offspring, ranging from bed-wetting to schizophrenia, from inability to deal with color blindness to aggressive behavior, from learning problems to "homicidal transsexualism."

Two articles reporting our findings were published in 1985, and the responses were gratifying. In a typical letter, one woman wrote, "My husband and I are both practicing psychiatrists, and I have been trying to convince him for years that mothers get blamed for everything. Now I have documented proof!" Her letter illustrated an important point that is still true today: most therapists, like this woman's husband, are not even aware of how much mother-blaming they and others do. The rare negative responses we received were all from people who were worried that reducing mother-blame meant increasing father-blame, though we never advocated the latter. The alarm at the possibility that father-blaming might increase somewhat starkly contrasted with most therapists' comfort with mother-blaming.

The degree to which mother-blame persists in therapists' publications is disturbing. The blame at times takes the form of pathologizing mothers and their mothering behavior, and at other times of holding them disproportionately responsible for their children's problems. Therapist Jane Knowles discussed the pathologizing of mothers: "The psychiatric world is gradually realizing how many young mothers are unhappy and their response to this is to see it as illness in the individual." She also notes that, when mothers come to her seeking therapy, she is struck by how "normal" they actually are, how understandable are the ways they struggle to deal with the stress of being mothers, yet how likely they are to regard themselves as "sick" because of their inability to mother with ease and serenity.

A particularly poignant example of therapists' ongoing overemphasis on mother-blame when children have psychological problems was published recently in the very journal that published our original documentation of mother-blame in clinicians' articles, the *American Journal of Orthopsychiatry*. Researchers studied children over a sixteen-year period to see if they could find early behavior that might lead to assaultive behavior in adolescence. Although most of the children came from two-parent, heterosexual families, the researchers studied only the children's interactions with their mothers. It is not surprising that they found a relationship between what they called mothers' "negative" treatment of their children and those children's later assaultive behavior. Their exclusive focus on mothers was not the only problem with this study. They also failed to consider the possibility that the mothers' "negative" behavior might have been a *response to* trying to care for a difficult child, rather than a *cause of* the child's problematic behavior.

In other, recent writing, enlightened authors showed that the alleged mental illness referred to as Borderline Personality Disorder (BPD), which is usually blamed on mothers, is in fact a combination of behavior usually resulting from severe child sexual abuse, which is disproportionately often perpetrated by men. Thus, mother-blame is unfair to mothers, is confusing to the incest victim, and, appallingly, takes the focus off the perpetrator.

The biases in research and theory are not new. They pre-date the time when our mothers were raising us. One sixty-five-year-old mother of three told me that she remembers learning in a university course that the severe emotional disorder called infantile autism was caused by cold mothers who rejected their infants (a claim later found to be untrue). She said, "Every time I felt a little tired or distracted when I picked up one of my babies, I was sure I was going to drive her into an autistic state!"

One parallel contemporary example is making it mothers' responsibility to provide technical help for their children who have learning disabilities. I spent years working with such children and writing about their problems. Even though by definition learning difficulties are not caused by motivational problems or lack of exposure to learning, I often heard mothers held totally responsible for dealing with their children's disabilities. One mother told me, "I read all the books about how to teach your child to read, and I tried to use them to teach Jessica. But we just haven't gotten anywhere. At the end of every tutoring session, she and I both feel like failures. The teacher says I should keep working with Jessica, but I don't know what else to do."

As sociologists Dorothy Smith and Alison Griffith have found in their research, school systems depend heavily on mothers to help them accomplish the work they are supposed to do. This is true not only for children who have problems but right down to the expectation that kindergarten and first-grade students will come to school already knowing their ABCs because their mothers have taught them.

Child Abuse: A Case in Point

One of the most sobering examples of mother-blaming interpretations of research is in the area of child abuse, both sexual and nonsexual. Conducting good research about child abuse is difficult because abuse tends to be hidden, especially among wealthier, better-educated people. For this reason, research on the question Who abuses children? has given us a skewed picture of the truth. Many so-called authorities on nonsexual child abuse claim that mothers are more likely than fathers to abuse their children. This comes as a surprise to people who think of mothers in idealized terms as the "Angels in the House." But it fits the darker cultural stereotype about mothers: that they are "Wicked Witches," unable or unwilling to control their unlimited rage.

Researchers who make these claims rarely ask how much time each parent spends with the children. In general, mothers spend far more time than fathers with children, and many of the fathers in studies of abuse have left their families or are rarely home. So for each hour spent with the children, the mothers actually abuse them far less than the fathers do. But many "experts" continue to believe that mothers are more likely than fathers to commit child abuse—a belief that is a serious distortion.

This distortion affects every mother; nearly everyone who has taken care of children has sometimes felt so frustrated, exhausted, and helpless that they have used some physical punishment or abused a child outright (then felt horribly guilty for doing so). Although child abuse is wrong and damaging to children, my own work in this area has shown that the misinterpretation of research findings takes the focus off important issues that contribute to the abuse, like mothers' lack of support and their sometimes desperate circumstances. It feeds the fear that mothers are dangerous, especially compared to fathers, and can create a self-fulfilling prophecy: when a woman believes that she is a horrible mother, her self-esteem plunges and her sense of isolation grows, increasing the likelihood that she will be abusive.

Some researchers who say that child welfare workers should use their findings to identify abusive parents also focus on mothers. A press release from a major university conveyed the impression that only mothers abuse their children. Although the release was headlined "Study of Family Interaction Leads to New Understanding of Abusive *Parents*" (my italics), the entire section reporting the study's results describes only mothers. According to the release, researchers produced a profile of abusive "parents," but in fact they studied only mothers—one hundred of them! Then, reporting their results, they described various kinds of abusive mothers—harsh/intrusive, covert/hostile, and emotionally detached:

"Harsh/intrusive" mothers are excessively harsh and constantly badger their child to behave. . . .

A "covert/hostile" mother shows no positive feelings towards her child. She makes blatant attacks on the child's self-worth and denies him affection or attention. . . .

An "emotionally detached" mother has very little involvement with her child. She appears depressed and uninterested in the child's activities.

Thus the blame is placed on the mental illness or just plain nastiness of individual mothers, as though fathers are never abusive, as though more complex family and social factors play no role in leading to abuse.

In the 1980s the women's movement demolished the myth then purveyed in psychiatric textbooks that the so-called incest taboo made incest extremely rare. Millions of women revealed that they had been sexually abused as children. Mental health professionals were quick to blame this abuse (which, as noted, is nearly always perpetrated by men) on the victims' mothers, claiming that mothers are usually aware of the abuse but allow it to continue anyway, that they may see the abuse as a relief for themselves ("Now I don't have to have sex with him"), that they organize time for the husband and daughter to be alone, and that they may have refused to sleep with their husbands. Even when the mother is absent, seriously ill, or disabled, she is likely to be blamed for her husband's assault on their daughter. In the words of Mary DeYoung in the *Journal of Family Violence,* "Even those women who indeed do believe, support, and protect their daughters cannot escape criticism." DeYoung also points out that mothers themselves are rarely even asked what they did when they learned about the incest.

Because professionals—and the larger society—blame mothers when their daughters are incest victims, the daughters often blame their mothers far more than the men who victimized them. This pattern of blaming the mother and ignoring or even absolving the perpetrator of blame is effected by describing abusers as "sick" and therefore having diminished responsibility. But as Carole Ann Hooper points out, "women are commonly accorded *sole* responsibility" although "they lack the resources to exercise it effectively." Women who do seek help, Hooper notes, often receive none at all from child welfare agencies, and the only outcome in some cases is that the mothers are put under surveillance! In the *Journal of Child Sexual Abuse,* Ila Schonberg reports that mothers who are clearly upset when reporting the incest are likely to be described as "hysterical," and the court is likely to give the perpetrator unsupervised child visits.

The distribution of blame is unforgivable, in view of what is known about father-daughter incest. Dr. Kathleen Coulbourn Faller of the University of Michigan School of Social Work concludes, based on more than three hundred cases, that the mother usually does not know that it is happening. When she does know, she usually brings it into the open and tries to stop it; when she doesn't report it, it is often because her husband threatened to harm her and their daughter further if she tells, or because she has been taught that a good woman must keep the family together (perhaps even obey her husband no matter what). And the discovery of abuse often does destroy the two-parent family. Furthermore, one reason some mothers do not suspect incest is that many perpetrators do continue having sex with their wives at the same time that they are abusing their daughters. And even when the mother knows about the incest, the perpetrator is often simultaneously battering the mother (and children), leading to her terror that he might maim or kill the children or herself if the abuse is reported.

Some daughters who try to inform their mothers about the abuse do so in such vague or unclear ways—because they feel afraid or guilty—that their mothers don't understand; and since sexual abuse is unthinkable for most people, often a mother genuinely never realizes what her daughter is trying to tell her (maybe all the more true if the abuser is the mother's own partner). As one highly educated, loving mother said, "Before I found out that my ex-husband was abusing my daughter, if you had asked me, I would have said, 'He's selfish and ruthless and sneaky—but sexual abuse? That he would never do.'"

It has been well documented that men who perpetrate incest are sneaky about it. In general, they are like alcoholics in the lengths to which they will go to deny and conceal the incest. And of course, a mother who does not "organize time" for father and daughter to be alone risks being called possessive and smothering.

Even in extreme cases of mother-blaming for abuse, however, there is hope.

One incest survivor, a woman in her twenties, disclosed at her survivors' group meeting that an adult male neighbor sexually abused her when she was a very young child. She said that when she told her mother about it at the time, her mother never said a word, never reacted at all. She had always felt that her mother had betrayed her and failed to support her because of this. Her group leader urged her to talk to her mother about it, and the woman gathered up her courage and did so. Her mother's response was, "When you told me I was so afraid that I would say or do the wrong thing, something that would be bad for you, that I tried not to react at all. So I went to the psychiatrist to ask him what I should do, and he said that for your sake, the best thing I could do would be never to mention it again."

Naturally, the daughter had spent years blaming her mother; it's what we all are taught to do.

Mother-Blaming among Therapists

Psychotherapists had begun acquiring an aura of authority by the time our mothers were raising us, and that aura persists to this day. In popular books and articles and on talk shows, mental health professionals convey the mother-blaming messages they learn in their training. Psychotherapists have had tremendous influence ever since the 1930s, and many people consider them experts who reveal objective, scientific truth—an erroneous assumption.

Some fair and sensitive psychotherapists have been enormously supportive and helpful to distraught mothers and daughters. But for decades, all too many—knowingly or unwittingly—have intensively promoted mother-blaming, and this has often been even more devastating to mothers than mother-blaming research. A psychotherapy patient reveals her most intimate feelings and shameful secrets to her therapist. She goes to the therapist seeking both to feel better and to learn more of the truth about herself and her life. This gives the therapist enormous power. Because the training for most therapists involves so much mother-blame and woman-blame, only the unusual ones help the patient to go beyond mother-blame and self-blame. Traditional therapists tend to believe sincerely that mother-blaming fits reality, and they regard themselves as helping their patients to accept this reality. Thus, women are primed to accept the therapist's descriptions of themselves and their mothers—or themselves as mothers—as manipulative, overprotective, intrusive, cold, rejecting, and so on. Let us look at some examples of therapists' demeaning descriptions of mothers.

Since the 1960s, therapists' attitudes toward mothers have been widely influenced by Margaret Mahler's work on the child's psychological "separation and individuation" from its mother. (Although Mahler did important work on profoundly disturbed children, her writings have been widely applied in mother-blaming ways.) Mahler advised therapists to watch carefully when a mother entered the consulting room. They were to note whether she carried the child "like a part of herself"—revealing her inability to separate from the child—or "like an inanimate object"—showing her to be cold and rejecting. Imagine being observed by a therapist who used such a pigeonholing scheme, in which each pigeonhole is a different form of bad mothering! Even more painful to imagine are the messages such a therapist will convey to the mother about her relationship with her child.

The names of Mahler and some of her like-minded colleagues have never become known to most laypeople, but many theories that share this mother-blaming foundation have become familiar as presumed truths. In one currently fashionable type of psychotherapy, the wives of alcoholics, drug addicts, compulsive gamblers, and womanizers are said to make life hard for their children, because they support their husbands' addictions and compulsions. Proponents of these theories use the terms "codependent" and "enabler" to describe the wife/mother and say she "needs" her husband's problems to continue: "She loves playing holier-than-thou" or "She gets her jollies from how abject and disgusting he is when he is drunk."

In fact, however, if you ask these women how they would feel if you could magically take away their husbands' problem behavior, they sigh with relief at the thought. Men who try to stop their addictive behavior find it physically and/or psychologically difficult, and all too many take out their frustrations on their families, including subjecting their wives and children to beatings or verbal abuse. When the wives bemoan this worsened behavior, many therapists say, "Aha! She doesn't want him to stop drinking!" They ignore the fact that the wives wish the men would stop both the drinking and the abuse.

Other recovering men are humiliated to face the wives who knew them when they were drunks, so they want to leave them. No wonder some women are frightened by the prospect of their husbands' recovery—but this is a far cry from wanting the drinking to continue. The irony is that mothers who leave such husbands are blamed for breaking up the family and depriving the children of their father, but women who stay are given the demeaning, pathologizing term "codependent" and are accused of "loving too much" and failing to save the children from their father's addictive behavior.

You don't have to be a mental health professional to absorb the cultural propensity for blaming Mother for Father's alcoholism. Television star Suzanne Somers has described the anger that she and her siblings felt toward their mother because of their father's drinking. Sensing the danger in confronting their abusive, alcoholic father but trying to find a way out, they directed their disappointment and rage toward Mom. The happy ending to Somers' story is that their father is sober, and she and her siblings appreciate their mother's strength and love, which enabled them to overcome the bad times.

As I have mentioned, when the patient is not the mother's husband but rather her child, mother-blaming knows no bounds. A friend described for me her experience as the target of psychiatrists' mother-blaming, in a situation in which she already felt helpless and frightened because her child was sick. Kumiko's ten-year-old daughter, Laurel, had what seemed to be a stomach virus. For weeks after she stopped vomiting, Laurel was extremely tired and said she could not eat anything without feeling nauseated. Kumiko used many gentle techniques to induce her to eat, but the listlessness and nausea persisted. The family doctor ordered numerous, expensive medical tests, which revealed no physical problem; so the doctor sent Kumiko and Laurel to the state university's hospital, a three-hour drive away.

The university's regular medical staff found no physical cause for Laurel's problems and transferred her to the psychiatric ward. The psychiatric staff instructed Kumiko to leave Laurel there for three weeks and have no contact with her during that time. When Laurel wept from loneliness, the psychiatrists concluded that "her relationship with her mother is too close, symbiotic." After the three weeks, they shipped her home, still physically ill and depressed. Both Kumiko and Laurel were now psychiatrically labeled, and Kumiko felt guilty and ashamed. Months later, on a friend's advice, Kumiko gave Laurel a commercially available medication that eases digestion. Laurel's nausea vanished, she began to eat normally, and with nourishment, her depression disappeared.

Of course, there are many variations on this limited set of examples. In my own investigation of mother-blaming, I found an article whose authors' stated purpose was to study whether children of male prisoners of war suffered because of their fathers' experiences. They found these fathers to be distressed and emotionally distant and the children to have a high incidence of emotional problems. They blamed the latter on the mothers! Their reasoning was: the women were upset at seeing their husbands' anguish, and this interfered with their ability to mother their children properly! Similarly, as Aphrodite Matsakis documents in her book about Vietnam veterans' wives, they are blamed for the ill effects their husbands' psychiatric symptoms have on their families.

Usually, women who are able to go beyond mother-blaming do so on their own or with the help of other people, not their therapists. A forty-year-old professional woman told me that her therapist had helped her to get angry at her mother but not to go beyond that:

My mother was intimidated by my father, and she did use me to stand up to him, from the time I was four years old. She and I both knew that I had the guts to say things to him that she didn't dare say. And it wasn't fair to put me in that position. My therapist helped me feel my anger about that, but then he just left me there, furious at my mother for being so manipulative.

What changed this woman's view was her own later experience, not her work with her therapist:

Only after I became a mother myself did I put her "manipulations" in perspective. First of all, I realized that, yes, she had been somewhat manipulative, but mostly she had been a terrific mother. And all my therapist wanted me to do was talk about the bad side of her. Having my own children and seeing how hard it was to work toward that impossible image of the perfect mother made me appreciate how much she had done for me. Instead of just being stuck thinking of her as getting me to stand up to Dad, other memories started to come back to me: the time she volunteered to drive two hours to pick up the Girl Scout cookies for four hundred Scouts to sell—and then at 2:30 in the morning, as we continued stacking them all through the house, said, "Well, the night is young! And we've only got the mint ones left to do!" She had a wonderful sense of humor and was totally supportive of me and of everything I did. And in the course of my therapy that had slipped my mind.

It may seem hard to believe that therapists do so much mother-blaming, but we must understand that they do and why.

Therapists Aren't Held Accountable

We don't tend to question the opinions of high-status people very energetically; for that one powerful reason, therapists get away with unjustifiably increasing women's alienation from their mothers. At a conference on mothers and daughters, a woman therapist showed a videotape of an interview with a mother, a father, and their young adult daughter. The therapist and the audience joined in groaning, laughing mockery of the mother for "not participating" when the father and daughter were interacting and for "sitting there, looking left out and pitiful." But in fact the daughter might be considered a classic "daddy's girl" who showed an unhealthy adoration of her father, a Real Man who went out into the Real World and made a great deal of money! The father treated his daughter like a pampered doll, and neither wanted any part of the mother, because the mother knew their faults, and they needed to keep up their charade of adored, adoring, perfect father and adored, adoring, perfect daughter. The therapist didn't seem to realize that the mother was the only family member whom no one held in high esteem. The father was respected because he was male and the financial provider for the family. The daughter was valued because she was young, attractive, and prepared to worship her father unquestioningly. But the mother was "only" a housewife. When an audience member objected to the mother-blaming inter-pretations, the therapist ignored her comments. And because the therapist was considered the expert, her mother-blaming attitude shaped most audience members' interpretations of the family.

All too rarely are therapists' pronouncements questioned. Most laypeople mistakenly regard themselves as too little versed in the "science" of psychiatry and psychology (little of which is actually rigorously scientific) and are afraid of sounding foolish if they question therapists' claims. In fact, most high school students could find serious errors of logic, research design, and interpretation of data in the majority of mental health research reports, as well as errors of reasoning and attribution of the causes of patients' prob-lems in case reports. But few people read such reports, relying instead on what they hear from their own therapists, on therapists' comments on talk shows, and on therapists' incomplete or inaccu-rate descriptions of evidence for claims they make in their books. Thus, therapists' mother-blaming practices often go unchallenged.

Mothers in Court

In the justice system, mothers are often rendered completely pow-erless. Phyllis Chesler has documented the way that judges have long been ordering the unwarranted removal of child custody from mothers who range from acceptable to wonderful. In the words of Rickie Solinger, in recent times mothers have lost custody because of being "disabled, a political activist, too young, unmar-ried, . . . divorced and had sex, too old, the wrong race, an atheist, a Native American, deaf, mentally ill, retarded, . . . lesbian, reported to speak Spanish to her child, enrolled full-time in college, a drug user, poor." Renee Romano reports that in the past several decades, "approximately twenty-five child custody disputes arose on the state appeals court level after local trial courts had denied white women who had married black men custody of their white children from previous marriages." Good mothers have been denied custody of their children both because they have paying jobs ("they care more about their careers than about their children") and because they don't have paying jobs ("they don't love their kids enough to contribute to their financial support"), both because they are living with a man ("they are promiscuous") and because they are not living with a man ("they are isolated or cannot provide a stable, heterosexual child-rearing environment").

With regard to this last point, although in the past twenty years the numbers of lesbian mothers (previously heterosexually married ones, single ones, woman-partnered ones, both birth mothers and adoptive mothers) has been on the rise, and despite the considerable research literature showing that—contrary to some people's assumptions—people raised by lesbians do not differ in their emotional adjustment and functioning or their sexuality from people raised by heterosexuals, the courts have not rid themselves of their antilesbian bias.

Another expression of antimother bias takes a different form: Judges rarely consider a man's sexual or physical abuse of his children, or of his wife in front of their children, to be legitimate grounds for refusing him custody of his children. So mothers who are abused or who watch their husbands abuse their children feel understandably helpless.

Katha Pollitt points out the hypocrisy of the courts when dealing with pregnant women who are substance abusers. Admittedly, the first response of many people upon hearing that an addict is pregnant would be, "That woman does not deserve to keep her child." Going beyond that knee-jerk reaction, however, Pollitt notes that the courts do not genuinely seem to care about the welfare of either the child or the mother-to-be, because "judges order pregnant addicts to jail but they don't order drug treatment programs to accept them [such programs tend explicitly to exclude pregnant women] ... let alone order landlords not to evict them, or obstetricians to take uninsured women as patients, or the federal government to fund fully the Women, Infants, and Children Supplemental Feeding Program, which reaches only two-thirds of those who are eligible." Pollitt's article dramatically shifts our perspective from simply blaming the usually poor pregnant women who are addicts to the shocking recognition about how many ways our society, through the courts and otherwise, *could* help these women and their children but chooses not to.

Therapists commonly bring mother-blaming into the courtroom when they appear as "expert witnesses" in custody battles. The justice system and the mental health system provide a double whammy of mother-blaming. Many mothers who thought psychiatric assessment would help them get custody of their children, especially if the father was violent, irresponsible, or disturbed, have been sorely disappointed to find themselves pathologized, whereas the husband was praised for "caring enough about his children" to sue for custody.

As noted, within the past twenty years or so, hundreds of thousands of adult women who were incest victims have come forward and told their stories—in therapy groups, where they went to try to heal their aching emotional scars; in family gatherings, where they bravely confronted the men after learning that they were abusing members of the newest generation; in books and articles they wrote to try to heal themselves and let other women know they were not alone; and in court, where they went to prevent abusers from hurting others. For a while, since these survivors were now adults and could command a little more respect than when they were being victimized, people listened and believed them. Sometimes.

More recently, there has been a dangerous shift. Reports of now-adult victims are treated as though they have little or nothing to do with current abuse. Disrespect for mothers' and children's reports has resurfaced, and the fashion is to say that mothers coach their children to claim falsely that the mothers' ex-husbands abused them. What is said to be the mothers' motive? That they are vicious ex-wives out to take revenge on their husbands—and that they manipulate incompetent or unethical therapists into falsely persuading the children that they were abused. There are occasional false claims, and the unjustly accused often receives a great deal of publicity. To be one of those men must be awful. But some innocent people are falsely accused under every law, yet we don't hear clamoring to strike down laws designed to punish thieves or murderers. In fact, most reports of sexual abuse of children are true.

Father-daughter sexual abuse puts mothers in a catch-22 situation: a mother who does not report the abuse is said to be complicit, even to have consciously or unconsciously instigated the abuse, and a mother who does report it is said to be man-hating, lying, or hysterical.

I have been shocked to learn how much the antiwoman backlash is promoted by lawyers. A group of family lawyers asked me to speak to them about how, as their leader's invitation went, "women get shafted by our legal system." I soon saw that the lawyers (one woman and about twenty men) had no interest in hearing about women's mistreatment in the justice system. They wanted to talk about scheming, vengeful ex-wives who construct false reports of sexual abuse to keep their ex-husbands away from the children.

Experienced and fair-minded therapists such as Dr. Peter Jaffe, director of the London, Ontario, Family Court Clinic, present a more accurate picture. Dr. Jaffe explains that he has seen more than five hundred cases involving custody and access disputes in the past six years; only two involved false allegations of sexual abuse, and in both of those cases the mothers genuinely believed that abuse had occurred.

Sadly, too few people care about the facts. In a typical case, a social worker who had extensively assessed a family was asked whether the father had sexually abused his nine-year-old daughter. The worker concluded: "It wasn't clear whether or not he had sexually abused her, because this was brought up in the context of a custody dispute, so the mother's bitterness toward her ex-husband was her motivation." When reminded that there was no custody dispute (during the seven years since the parents' divorce, the mother had had custody of the child, and the question of custody had not been mentioned even after sexual abuse was reported), he backtracked only slightly. The primary issue—the sexual abuse of a little girl—was lost because of the social worker's insistent mother-blaming.

Skepticism about mothers prevents proper attention being given to abused children all over North America, even when the husband and wife still live together. The attorney for a southern state's Department of Social Services claims that some mothers really are responsible for their husbands' sexual abuse of their daughters. His evidence? "A woman went back to get her Ph.D. and got a part-time job, leaving her husband and daughter alone together." One woman called me after seeing me on a television program. She had recently learned that her husband was sexually abusing their young daughter, and she had gone to her local hospital's sexual abuse clinic for help. The only recommendation the sexual abuse team made, even after she told them that her young daughter had said, "Daddy puts his thing in my pee-pee, and it hurts a lot," was for the mother to take medication because they thought she might be manic-depressive. Period.

Such stories are hard to believe, but they are not uncommon. Why would members of a team whose purpose is to stop child abuse be so insensitive? One reason is that, despite their heightened awareness of abuse, most of them were trained in traditional, mother-blaming programs; they and their supervisors are often skeptical of sexual abuse reports. Furthermore, even members of abuse teams are not immune to social pressure coming from the antiwoman groups who claim that sexually abused children and their mothers fabricate their stories.

With such "experts" constructing false, negative pictures of mothers, no wonder mother-blaming becomes second nature to so many people. Not only is mother-blaming untrue; it also creates unproductive, misdirected anger toward mothers.

As the end of the twentieth century approached, some lawyers and therapists worked together to create an appalling and breathtakingly effective method for discrediting ex-wives who report that their ex-husbands are sexually abusing their children. It is now common practice to claim that the woman's belief that her child is being abused is prima facie evidence that she suffers from a mental illness called Munchausen syndrome by proxy (MSBP), said to be an attempt to attract attention by saying that terrible things are happening to her child. Compassionate lawyers have told me how it pains them when an honest client now reports that her child is being abused, because they don't know how to advise her. It is no longer a simple case of saying, "Tell the therapist and the court this, and justice will be done. Your child will be protected." Now, they feel duty-bound to warn her that if she accuses her ex-husband of child sexual abuse, the courts are likely to find that she has MSBP and therefore should lose custody of her child.

Mother-Blame Serves a Purpose

The general purpose mother-blame serves in our society becomes evident when we start to examine the myths about motherhood and discover that even mutually exclusive myths coexist. For instance, the myth that mothers need experts' advice in order to raise healthy children coexists with the contradictory myth that mothers naturally know all they need to know about child rearing. Similarly, the myth that mothers are endlessly nurturant coexists with the contradictory myth that mothers are endlessly needy and emotionally draining. These conflicting myths serve an important function: they are all ways to justify demeaning and mistreating mothers. As my son Jeremy and I have written, "Any society that wants to keep a group in a scapegoated position has to worry: 'What if members of that scapegoated group do some good things? Won't that make it harder to keep laying blame on them?'" Scapegoating allows people who hold the reins of power to maintain their power, because they can claim that they deserve to stay on top; it's the members of the scapegoated group who cause all the trouble, they argue. Therefore, ways must be found "to take *any* good or even neutral things members of that group might do, and transform them into further proof of the group's inferiority, evil, or blameworthiness." For the power distribution to remain as it is, there must be a mother-myth for every occasion.

Mother-blaming perpetuates the unequal distribution of power between men and women in other ways as well. First, it does so by keeping women down, ashamed, frightened; we are the judged, not the judges, so insecure about our mothering behavior that we "focus intensely on being better mothers than before—even competing with our own mothers—rather than trying to make things easier and less oppressive" for ourselves and other mothers. The anger toward us that our sons and daughters are encouraged by society to feel adds further to our powerlessness, as does the seemingly endless task of defending ourselves (and mothers in general) against the attribution of all society's ills—delinquency, divorce, drug abuse, and the like—to mothers.

Coping with mother-blame also leaves us less energy for working toward achieving more power for mothers and other women and toward greater sharing of power between women and men. Why should men object to women's—or mothers'—power? Much could be said about that, but I want to focus on two parts of the answer: fear and envy.

Fear

Men are afraid that if women were freed from shame, anxiety, and fear, they could wield enormous power. That frightens many people, especially men who don't want to share their power. Many women do pack the potential for great emotional power, because they have been encouraged to stay in touch with a range of feelings and to express them. Many men, having learned to be uninterested in or uncomfortable about emotions, fear this unfamiliar strength. Their fear is of the unknown.

Furthermore, many men fear the power their mothers had over them when they were young. Now, as adults who believe it is unmasculine to be controlled by someone else, losing power reminds them of their relatively powerless childhood days. Back then, Mother likely had daily control over them, so now they must avoid mother's power to prove their manliness. Because mothers can make children feel both so good and so bad, they seem powerful to children of both sexes. But men feel more pressure than women to show that they are beyond mothers' influence and are thus both adult and masculine.

Although being loved, especially by our mothers, can empower us—by giving us support, self-confidence, and strength—many men are so afraid of being "engulfed" by love that they don't learn about its positive qualities. Then their mother's love comes to seem dangerous.

If just one mother seems too powerful, how much more threatening is a group of mothers! No one feels threatened when women work in groups as men's auxiliaries or as advocates or helpers of the poor, the ill, the disabled—anyone except themselves and other women. Men who consider women's emotional power a threat are led to contemplate the economic, social, and political power that women wield when we get together.

In any society, the forces that maintain the status quo are usually stronger than those that push for change. Supporters of mother-blame belong to the former group. Those who aim to keep mothers in their place use anything that mothers do as evidence that they deserve blame; the Perfect Mother myths and the Bad Mother myths are excellent "evidence" (see chapters 4 and 5). After all, if we stopped blaming our mothers for all our problems, we would see that to combat many of our social problems, we would need to make major changes (e.g., pay equity, respect and pensions for housewives), and women would find it easier to band together to press for those changes. So, even when we are tempted to praise or appreciate our mothers, supporters of the status quo find ways to keep us stuck in mother-blaming.

Envy

Men fear mothers' power because womb envy is alive and well, though often disguised. Partly as an antidote to Sigmund Freud's claim that all women have penis envy, men are said to have womb envy. Many people have laughed at this idea, but as men become more open about their feelings, many are acknowledging their envy of women's capacity to give birth and breast-feed. Men's eagerness to participate in the childbirth process, to write books about their participation, and to videotape it attest to that fact as well.

The magic and power associated with these functions are substantial in themselves; they are also associated with the emotional power that adheres to women. Womb envy is not just literal, not just a wish to be able to become pregnant and nurse an infant; it also symbolizes men's envy of women's freedom to be nurturant and to express a range of feelings. Many so-called New Men write long treatises about the pain of being called "effeminate" or "wimpy" when they show their tender side, and much of the world is not ready for expressive men. So most suppress their feelings, have trouble knowing how to express them, and wish that they were as free as women to do this.

Because of their fear and envy of women's power, many men have exaggerated mothers' bad behavior and mislabeled the positive as negative. They have said that up is down, plus is minus, mothers are bad. It is time for us to notice that up is up, plus is plus, and mothers are often good.

Internalizing Mother-Blame

Who among us has managed to escape the social pressure to blame our mothers for whatever goes wrong? The pressure is so pervasive that eventually most of us internalize the attitude and the techniques. We initiate mother-blaming ourselves, without waiting for pressure from outside, and then are reinforced by others for doing so. We can really get and keep each other going. A fifty-year-old friend told me recently,

> I just got back from a dinner with three women I've known for decades—and we spent the whole meal going after our mothers. I tell you, we ripped them apart. When I got home, I felt very unsettled, and as I thought about what we had done, I realized to my horror that we had just joined the big mother-hating conspiracy! And all of us are mothers ourselves! Our fathers got off scot-free.

These women acted like most people in our culture: they allowed even the most vicious or unfair mother-blaming remarks to pass unquestioned. Chances are, they had been egged on in the past when criticizing their mothers.

Blaming our mothers gives us temporary relief from self-examination and self-doubt. As one of my students put it, "I simply found reasons to blame my mother for every wrong that befell me. In this way, I would not have to look at what was happening between my mother and myself." Painful though it is to be angry at our mothers, it is less threatening than acknowledging that we need to take a good, hard look at ourselves. But in the long run, being angry is a destructive way to cope: when someone dies, the mourning process is harder if we had mixed or angry feelings toward the deceased than if we had a basically good relationship. Once they are dead, it is too late to make amends; our guilt can never be truly assuaged. As long as we take the trouble to hate, we are connected. Guilt, blame, and hatred are powerful glues, binding us to the object of those feelings; but little good comes from them. Furthermore, most women get no pleasure from having negative feelings: they are not productive, we have been taught that nice people (especially women) don't have them, and they release chemicals in our bodies that make us continue to feel bad.

Conflict can be either constructive or destructive. An argument can be a sincere effort by two people to thrash out differences about which they have strong feelings or fears, or it can be a chance to release hostility or wield power in destructive, demeaning ways. When we think about a problem, we can try to understand its causes, or we can simply assign fault. The difference is between knowing who's responsible and laying blame. Blaming is a way of saying, "It's not my fault. It's all hers." Assigning blame may make you feel temporarily better because it helps you believe that you are the good person of the pair; but if you have any interest in a continuing relationship with the blamed one, or in changing yourself, you'll need to do something else. No one reacts well to being blamed—so if you insist on blaming your mother, you can probably forget about improving your relationship with her. Blame is a conversation stopper; it obstructs the pursuit of insight. It promotes estrangement and anger rather than mutual love and respect for our own and our mothers' autonomy.

It Doesn't Have to Happen

In the face of all of this mother-blaming, we are heartened to know that it's not inevitable. As Gloria Joseph wrote in *Common Differences: Conflict in Black and White Feminist Perspectives*,

> Black daughters learn at an early age that their mothers are not personally responsible for not being able, through their individual efforts, to make basic changes in their lives or the lives of their children. This recognition enables daughters in later life to be more appreciative, understanding, and forgiving of their mothers when they are unable to fulfill and meet the daughter's expectations and needs for material and emotional comforts.

Although racialized women have to cope with the additional burdens that racism places on mothers' shoulders, all mothers in our culture care for their children in an environment in which the work of mothering is devalued and demeaned. The following story is about my mother's struggle against a self-described expert's efforts to demean both my grandmother and her relationship with my mother.

Fighting Back: Daring to Love Your Mother

Daughters who have problems are often urged to cut themselves off from the alleged source of their problems—their mothers. Friends, relatives, advice givers in the media, and therapists freely dispense this advice, and it can be tempting to follow a recommendation that is offered as the way out of all our troubles. But ignoring such advice is possible. A psychiatrist made such a recommendation years ago to my mother, Tac, who had consulted him for reasons unrelated to her mother.

When Tac was in her late thirties, she resented the repeated offers of her mother, Esther, to do her grocery or butcher shopping for her. "With the therapist's urging," she says, "I interpreted this as an attempt by my mother to control me. I told her, 'You're making me feel like I don't know anything, like I can't choose decent food for my family.'" Her psychiatrist advised her to refuse to see her mother for six months, in order to "break away from her need to control you." Even in the late 1960s, a psychiatrist's word was considered golden. But my mother found the strength to reject his advice, because, she said, "My mother was very friendly and warm and fun-loving, and basically I did feel very good about her and wanted to feel good about her. I had a good relationship with her, and there were lots of times we did have a good time together." In light of that, my mother was certain that not seeing her mother for six months was, at least, serious overkill. It involved both an undue emphasis on the problems and a failure to acknowledge the strengths of their mother-daughter relationship.

My mother was able to resist the therapist's directive because, as she grew older, her previously low self-confidence improved. She felt better about herself and trusted her own perspective. She realized that "if I put [my mother] down, I felt momentarily better, but it really wasn't working. I felt better about myself when I took some positive action." These changes enabled Tac to think for the first time about whether her mother's motives might include anything other than those she considered to be direct insults to her.

As she thought about her mother's life—and then asked Esther about it—she realized that the grocery offers had nothing to do with her mother's lack of faith in her. Instead, her mother had been brought up to believe that a woman's value lay primarily in providing for others. Esther did not have a paying job, her children were grown, and except when she cooked for her family and cared for her grandchildren, she felt useless. Shopping for her daughter was her desperate attempt, within her familiar framework, to convince herself that she was still a needed, and therefore a worthwhile, person.

As Tac came to this understanding, totally without her psychiatrist's help, she underwent a transformation from a resentful child lacking in self-confidence to a compassionate adult in a more egalitarian relationship with her mother. And this happened none too soon, for shortly afterward Esther was found to have cancer, and she died within six months. When she was in the hospital, she and Tac talked about how happy they were that Tac had ignored her therapist's advice and had started the process of understanding her mother.

My mother told me that this experience showed her how understanding our mother can reduce the need to blame and pull away from her; it can instead decrease the estrangement and increase the love and respect on both sides. As Tac no longer resented her mother, Esther no longer felt that the one bit of help she was able to offer was scorned. Each realized that she was loved and appreciated by the other.

How many years of mother-daughter estrangement could have been avoided, how many chasms bridged, if instead of simply blaming them, daughters had known to ask why their mothers did what seemed to be intrusive, insensitive, or uncaring? When we stem the tide of our own mother-blaming, some of our anger at our mothers abates; our insecurity and self-hate subside as we realize that our close relationships to our mothers are not always cause for alarm and may even be cause for pleasure and pride.

Mother-blaming is so pervasive that it's almost a wonder that women choose to become mothers and that daughters ever speak to their mothers. If someone offered you a job, saying, "If anything goes wrong, even sixty or seventy years from now, you will be blamed," you'd tell them to forget it. But that is what motherhood is. Millions of mothers throughout the world feed, bathe, heal, and talk to their children every day, filled with anxiety, guilt, and fear.

They know that if anything goes wrong, they will be held almost totally responsible.

In the next two chapters, we shall see how the general attitude of mother-blaming harms mother-daughter relationships through the Perfect Mother myths (chapter 4) and the Bad Mother myths (chapter 5), which impede our views of who our mothers (and our daughters) really are. Then, in the last chapters, we'll see how we can go beyond mother-blaming and the myths and begin to mend our relationships with our mothers.

4

Mother–Daughter Barriers
The Perfect Mother Myths

To understand what has happened between our mothers and ourselves, to tell our true mother-daughter stories, we have to see clearly how our inner needs and fears have interacted with society's needs and fears.

As daughters, we need to feel like decent, acceptable people; some of that feeling comes from acceptance by our mothers and society in general, and some from our sense of integrity and honesty. (Although we also need to feel accepted by our fathers, my focus is on the mother-daughter issues, and we are less likely to blame fathers for our low self-esteem.) We also need close, loving relationships with our mothers. We fear rejection by our mothers and by society; since Mother often does society's bidding, we hope that if we can please her, we can please society. When we have to choose between pleasing our mother and pleasing society, we are caught between her enormous control over our daily lives and the message from our culture that our mother's opinion isn't important or worthwhile. (Ironically, often the mother whom we believe to be society's minion is in quiet or vocal rebellion against social pressures.)

What are society's needs? They include the needs for women—both mothers and daughters—to fit the traditional feminine stereotype, for mothers to train their daughters to fit that stereotype, and for mothers and daughters to be divided against each other and so anguished about their relationship that they don't notice that societal expectations cause the problems, instead blaming themselves and each other. Myths about mothers meet these needs. Myths, by definition, are not real, but the barriers they create between mothers and daughters certainly are.

At least ten major myths help keep mother-blaming alive and strong. Listing the myths is an important beginning, for the process of solving a problem begins with giving it a name. We shall see how each myth produces mother-daughter barriers—in the form of the kinds of painful feelings described in chapter 2—and what we can do about it. This chapter is about the Perfect Mother myths, and the next is about the Bad Mother myths.

Each myth rests near either the Angel or the Witch pole of mother-images described in chapter 1; in the daughter's eyes, the Perfect Mother myths make all mothers' good efforts seem inadequate because they're imperfect, and the Bad Mother myths highlight mothers' failings and even make some of their strengths or neutral points seem harmful.

As we daughters realize that we may have mislabeled and misinterpreted our mothers' motives and behavior, we can learn how the myths have led us to do that. In addition, when we keep the myths clearly in mind, we can see how they shaped our mothers' behavior as well as our own; we stop feeling that our mothers have hurt, rejected, or confused us willfully.

Mothers are familiar with the Perfect Mother myths; even before their children notice, they see where they fall short and fear their children's disappointment. Mothers are as frightened of matching the Bad Mother myths as of failing to match the Perfect Mother ones; in both cases, they fear their offspring's (and other people's) rejection and scorn. You'll notice the absence of a set of Reasonably Good Mother myths (despite a few mental health professionals' attempts to speculate about the "good enough mother"). A mother is not allowed to make many good efforts but be humanly flawed; she has to be perfect, because so much is at stake—the physical and mental health of her children, for which she is assumed to be totally responsible.

The myths discussed in these chapters may not be the only ones that support mother-blaming, and you may think of others. But these ten will be familiar because we have been raised among them.

The four Perfect Mother myths I've identified establish standards that no mother can meet:

- Myth One: The measure of a good mother is a "perfect" daughter.
- Myth Two: Mothers are endless founts of nurturance.
- Myth Three: Mothers naturally know how to raise children.
- Myth Four: Mothers don't get angry.

Myth One: The Measure of a Good Mother Is a "Perfect" Daughter

> Daughters feel anger for many reasons: they see their mothers pressuring them to conform to society's expectations of girls and women, or they find their mothers paying too little attention to those expectations and offering scant emotional support to daughters attempting to conform. Mothers grow angry at daughters either because daughters don't fulfill their expectations or because their daughters expect too much of them.
> —*Susan Koppelman*, Between Mothers and Daughters: Stories across a Generation

Every culture has molds into which it wants to fit each new generation. In our culture, the responsibility for that molding is mainly delegated to families, which in practice usually means that mothers mold their children into the cultural pattern. For most of us, our mother, more than anyone else, said: "Do this." "Don't do that." "Pick up your toys." "Don't talk to strangers." Daughters hear many additional "Dos" and "Don'ts" that our brothers escape: "Cross your legs." "Smile." "Be nice." Girls are thought to be naturally tidy and restrained, but when a daughter is not, her mother is blamed for not teaching her well enough. We might well ask, "Why does something that comes naturally have to be taught?" We shall see this pattern repeatedly as we examine the myths of mother-blame: in a culture that subordinates women, glaring contradictions can persist, as long as they help keep women down by restricting or demeaning us. In this case, women's behavior is restricted by our diligent efforts to be tidy and restrained, and thus feminine. All women are demeaned when anyone believes that a daughter's untidiness or lack of restraint is the fault of a woman—her mother.

Society has perched on our mothers' shoulders, whispering, "If you want us to think you are a good mother, you'll teach your daughter to be sweet and to cross her legs." (For mothers today, the message is more likely to end with the words, "you'll teach your daughter to get an education, develop herself, and be sweet and cross her legs.")

Many young daughters sense that the "feminine" pattern they are following at Mother's direction is the very thing that often makes Mother unhappy, and they feel that she is betraying them by urging them into the patterns that are the source of her own misery. Claudette told me she hated sweeping the kitchen floor and cleaning the bathrooms when she was a child: "It was partly because they are crummy jobs but also because my mother was constantly complaining she was exhausted from cleaning our house. I didn't see why she made me do the things she hated. It didn't seem fair."

The frightening flip side of the myth that a "perfect" daughter is the sign of a good mother is that a "bad" (or atypical) daughter is the sign of a "bad" mother. This equation causes mothers and daughters a great deal of unnecessary anguish. Every mother wants to be considered a good mother. But not every mother thinks that her daughter should have to follow the traditional feminine model, nor does every daughter take to such a prescribed role, especially if her mother seems unhappy in that role. Should a mother carry out society's orders to secure her reputation as a good mother, or should she act in her daughter's best interests? How can a mother choose between her daughter's welfare and her own need for approval? And what are her daughter's best interests—to develop her full potential and risk being a "misfit"?

When daughters describe to me their wish to please their mothers, their tension is often palpable. Some haven't even understood why so much was at stake in relation to following their mother's rules. But they have sensed that society's opinion of their mother's worth depended on the daughter's display of the right behavior. Which of us wants to bear the guilty burden of being the public signboard of our mother's failure?

Furthermore, since the only good mother is a perfect mother, no amount of rule-following seems enough. No daughter feels she's done everything society—through her mother—wants her to do, since it's impossible always to be nurturing, self-denying, sweet, and slim. No wonder many daughters feel unable to please their mothers.

As daughters, we assume that the urgency in Mother's rule-making comes from her individual, critical, controlling nature; we don't often recognize that the rules come from a fundamental cultural belief, and Mother is just its transmitter—or that some rules come from a mother's attempt to protect her daughter from the common criticisms of or violence against women. What the daughter thinks she sees is a neurotic, uptight, or heartless woman who has generated a host of prescriptions to torment her.

In my work with women, I often find that a daughter's belief that her mother uncompromisingly disapproves of her is actually a misinterpretation of her mother's role as rule enforcer. Sadly, instead of daughter and mother getting together, seeing that the source of their problem is a set of impossible cultural standards, and trying to change that culture, mother gets trapped into trying to produce a perfect specimen of a daughter (for both their sakes), and daughter hates mother for being unreasonable. A huge wedge is driven between them. A ninety-two-year-old woman named Belmira told me that she was worried about her daughter's failing, forty-year marriage. She said,

> I told her I knew her husband has a terrible temper and lashes out at her for no good reason. But I said that my husband was the same way, and a woman has to learn to overlook that. But I felt bad for doing that, because overlooking my husband's temper never helped me, and I knew it wouldn't do my daughter any good either.

One particularly tricky set of rules involves those that growing girls are supposed to learn about emotional control. We are assumed to be extremely emotional by nature (certainly more than growing boys), but we are carefully taught that our emotions must not interfere with other people's comfort. By the time we reach young womanhood, we are supposed to be emotional enough to meet men's and children's needs for love and support without "burdening" them with our feelings. Women are assumed to keep feelings under control only with great difficulty—although a woman who is emotionally reserved is in danger of being called cold and unfeminine. Thus, women are expected to remain in touch with our feelings only for the purpose of helping our men and our children. Mother and daughter each sometimes find it disconcerting for the other to be warm and expressive, because we're not quite sure whether that's okay. If we get too comfortable allowing our feelings free rein when we are with each other, then won't that make it easier to slip up and be "inappropriately" or "intrusively" expressive when we go back to our men and our children? Furthermore, some men regard a close mother-daughter relationship as a threat to their wife's allegiance to them.

Mother as Enforcer, Daddy as Darling

A daughter tends to resent her mother as most people resent the imposers of rules but even more so because there are more rules for daughters than for sons. She also resents her mother for being so tough on her—after all, Daddy isn't. (The familiar warning of a mother, "Wait till your father gets home," is rarely translated into actual punishment by the father for the behavior that leads to the mother's anger. Fathers' physical or sexual abuse of their daughters is usually quite separate from these types of warnings by the mother.) Daddy's greater leniency is usually a side effect of his generally lesser involvement in child rearing than his wife's. But all the daughter knows is that Daddy treats her better. (Of course he does—when you don't have the major responsibility for someone's behavior, you can afford to be more lax about discipline!) Thirty-year-old Latoya recently told me in an interview,

> Until last year, I always thought my father loved me more than my mother did. The reason I thought that was that he never punished me when I was growing up. In fact, when Mom announced punishments for me, he always persuaded her to make them more lenient.
>
> But last year, when my kids were four and six years old, I suddenly realized that the same thing is happening in my own family now: my husband tells me I'm really great with the kids, but that's just his way of staying out of the nitty-gritty of parenting. I have to be the heavy, I'm always the one who disciplines the kids, and then once the punishment is over, my husband sweeps in and takes

them out for ice cream. Naturally, they think he's terrific, and I'm the one they're scared of. You can bet that I appreciate my mother a lot more, now that I see how I ended up preferring my father over her!

Do We Ever Stop Fearing Mother's Disapproval?

The highly competent and polished host of a radio phone-in show told me about her most recent visit with her mother. She had flown from California to Florida, where her mother lives, and as she walked off the plane, her mother told her that the color of her dress was all wrong for her:

> Here I am, forty-eight years old, and I still care so much about what she thinks! I receive compliments all the time on my good fashion sense, but not from her. And one note of criticism from her is enough to undermine all the self-confidence about my appearance that it's taken me years to build up.

We are so vulnerable to what our mother thinks of us; when she seems to have reservations about us, we are devastated, whether we are children, teenagers, young adults, or middle-aged or old women. Our mother's power to make us feel inadequate often makes us angry—we may even hate her for it. Once, in reality, she had enormous power over us, could lock us in our rooms or, by withdrawing her love from us, ensure that we received little love at all from anyone. When you're six years old, it's harder to run out of the house to look for a friend or relative who'll say they like your clothes if your mother doesn't. Even as adults we can't just run away and never see or call our mothers again—and most of us don't want to. What most of us want is not to banish our mothers from our lives but to end both their power to make us feel bad and our guilt over our power to make them feel like failures.

Now that we are adult, we can see that our mother was not so much the rule maker as the rule enforcer, and many of the rules she enforced constrained her own life, too. One of my students, who is in her late twenties and specializes in counseling mothers and daughters, says she knew when she was a child that her mother felt trapped in her housewife-mother role:

My mother had been forced to quit school after the eighth grade, since attending ninth grade would have meant going to a school in another town. Her mother had told her that it was a lot more trouble to raise a daughter than a son, and she was pretty much pushed into a kind of arranged marriage to the only member of their church who was of marriageable age. Then the kids started coming—eight of us, and oh, did she feel trapped.

While my student knew deep inside that her mother felt trapped, she still grew up resenting her mother for her stifling upbringing. Only when she began to think about how limited her mother's options were did she begin to see her in a different light:

Both my uncle and my father used to scream at her for putting us girls in jeans rather than dresses. She didn't think we should have to wear dresses, though, except to church, so that was one rule of femininity we often got to break. But she had to make us follow a lot of rules, because the only thing she had was being a mother, and she couldn't stand to have my father and my uncle always telling her she was a failure.

Daughters should understand that Mother herself worries about being judged by her daughter's success—which partly depends on her appearance or behavior. A daughter understandably resents the fact that her mother's acceptance by society seems to depend so much on her. From childhood we have sensed our mother's fear that any misstep on our part could reveal her shortcomings as a mother. Once we know that the source of that feeling is society's withholding of approval from so-called inadequate mothers, we easily see that our dress doesn't signal her failure as a mother but that she is understandably afraid that someone will think so.

Each Other's Judges

Part of growing up female has meant that daughters, like mothers, are expected to take on the role of guardians of society's (largely man-made) rules. In other words, it is not just mothers who do the monitoring; daughters catch on early to society's expectations and begin to monitor their mothers' behavior as well. In this way, mother and daughter come to fear each other as their

harshest judges. A growing daughter who catches her mother failing to fulfill any social expectations often feels betrayed ("Why
don't you bake cookies for our class parties?") or superior to her
mother ("I'm more like Martha Stewart than you are!"), neither of
which endears her to her mother.

Furthermore, as a mother limits her daughter's exuberance,
assertiveness, and aggressiveness, she unwittingly conveys the
message, "This aspect of you is not good, and therefore I do not
accept, love, or cherish it," lowering the daughter's self-esteem.
When a mother makes a daughter feel bad about herself, she dri-
ves a wedge of resentment between them.

The problem is cyclical. Many mothers are especially anxious
to keep their daughters from breaking the rules because the mothers recall how unhappy they were when they, as children, were
punished for doing so. Forty-eight-year-old Ashley described to me
in a therapy session the effect an incident in her childhood had on
her treatment of her daughter:

> When I was twelve years old, a teacher caught me climbing a tree.
> In a disgusted voice, she chided me, "Don't you know the boys can
> look straight up your dress when you climb?" I wasn't sure why
> that was so horrid, but I felt totally ashamed. She made me feel
> like a slut.
>
> When my daughter, Janice, started sixth grade, and started devel-
> oping physically, I became very tense. I wanted to protect her from
> sexual insinuations like the one my teacher had aimed at me. What
> really upset me, though, was that the only way I seemed to be able
> to do this was by sounding like my teacher myself. To my horror, I
> found myself saying things to Janice like, "Don't talk so loud," as
> though she were committing a major crime rather than just doing
> something unfeminine. But I was doing it to try to protect her from
> other people's disapproval. The tragedy was that, in so doing, I
> made her the butt of my disapproval, and that probably hurt her
> more than harshness from strangers would have done.

In such situations, the daughter usually senses her mother's
fear and anxiety, and she surely feels her mother's disapproval.
Since we tend to stay away from people whom we make anxious
or who disapprove of us, the wistful distance between mother
and daughter grows. No mother purposely inflicts such anxiety

or harshness on her daughter, but few daughters can help feeling hurt when their mothers have those feelings. These childhood hurts can stay deep and sore throughout our lives if we never go back and hear from our mothers why they behaved as they did.

Myth Two: Mothers Are Endless Founts of Nurturance

> Woman needs to give. She cannot help herself. . . . This flow of life is not intended only for her children but also for her mate. . . . [Woman's primal driving force is] love and the service of those she loves.
> —*Irene Claremont de Castillejo,* Knowing Woman

> That reflexive maternal guilt . . . emerges at the infant's first wail: "I'm sorry. I'm sorry. . . . I'm sorry I can't keep you perfectly full, perfectly dry, perfectly free from gas and fear, perfectly, perfectly happy."
> —*Nancy Mairs,* Plaintext

Myth Two is that women are born nurturers, capable of giving endlessly. Being a warm, generous person is not a bad thing; the "endless" part is what causes the trouble between mother and daughter.

The Cinderella story may be the most familiar example of this womanly ideal. Cinderella represents goodness because of her unhappiness, suffering, deprivation, and toiling for others, in contrast to her stepsisters' selfishness. Cinderella's lesson is that a woman's selflessness, suffering, and passivity earn her a fairy godmother and a prince.

The story of Snow White and the Seven Dwarfs is also about this role. To become ripe and ready for marriage, Snow White must take care of seven little men. The fact that the dwarfs are both little and male prepares her to nurture both children and husband. She does this—as most of our mothers did—alone and isolated.

Through the centuries, women have been expected to fill a nurturing role. In a book called *Letters to Mothers,* the popular nineteenth-century author Lydia Howard Sigourney suggested how mothers should raise their daughters:

Inspire her with a desire to make all around her, comfortable and happy. Instruct her in the rudiments of that science, whose results are so beautiful. Teach her, that not selfish gratification, but the good of a household, the improvement of even the humblest dependent, is the business of her sex ... especially, if you visit the aged, or go on errands of mercy to the sick and poor, let her be your companion. Allow her to sit by the side of the sufferer, and learn those nursing services which afford relief to pain.

This was our grandmothers' and our mothers' heritage. Books mothers read while raising daughters now in their thirties and forties offered similar advice.

Contemporary personality theorists have also reinforced the myth. Jungian theorist Irene Claremont de Castillejo writes that the basic feminine attitude involves "acceptance" and that women need to give in order not to feel empty. Toni Grant makes a similar claim in her book *Being a Woman.*

Fortunately, some writers call attention to the danger of this myth. Psychologist Harriet Goldhor Lerner writes, "Women have been taught that they must be non-threatening help-mates and ego-builders to men, lest men feel castrated and emasculated." And in *The Mermaid and the Minotaur,* Dorothy Dinnerstein explains that woman is "seen as ... the being so peculiarly needed to confirm other people's worth, power, significance that if she fails to render them this service she is a monster, anomalous and useless." Underlining this danger to women, Sheila Rowbotham writes that girls learn to feel they are truly women only when they are self-denying: "Self-affirmation can only come through self-abnegation."

Research shows that women live up to the nurturance myth, spending far more time than men taking care of the younger generation, the older generation, their spouses, their siblings, and their friends. So resilient is the nurturing-woman myth that even when men lose their jobs, they don't tend to take on more household tasks; instead, the women carry on with those chores and also find paid employment.

Because the woman-as-nurturer myth is so deeply ingrained in our notions of female identity, it is hard for us to stop expecting endless giving from both our mothers and ourselves. When we ask ourselves, "Who am I?" a large part of most women's answer is, "A helper, a giver, a nurturer. If not, then I don't know who I am." As Huong, a twenty-eight-year-old pharmacist, told me,

> I was brought up to say "I'm sorry" when someone in a store stepped on my foot. And I felt very feminine and womanly because I was able to do this. So asserting myself, or seeing my mother assert herself, was very disconcerting. It meant something was not right with the world—and certainly not with us.

Where Lies the Harm?

Our mothers' imperfections are often magnified because we expect so much from mothers. We expect less from our fathers, because being masculine doesn't require being nurturing. Some scientists even claim that women are born nurturers but men are not. (Ironically, many people believe that fathers are capable of loving children as much as mothers, but then they say that mothers are naturally better at the routine, boring, or difficult parenting tasks like diaper changing, food preparation, or teaching the facts of life.) We don't give mothers much credit for what they do for us, but we condemn them as withholding and unnatural when they don't completely meet our needs. Theorist Mary O'Brien has said, "If you're not a good mother, you're deviant. If you are a good mother it's because you can't help it."

Because of the differing expectations, we tend to feel our fathers are terrific when they are even a little bit nurturing, but when our mothers don't quite give us all that we want, we feel that they have let us down. This simple double standard is so common that we don't even notice it. Since motherliness means being all-giving, we think, Mother could have met all my emotional needs. Yet who among us can give unceasingly? And who should have to? In fact, considering the many ways that women, and especially mothers, are unfairly treated, most mothers are remarkable to give as much as they do.

I remember what a major expedition grocery shopping was when my son was a toddler and my daughter was an infant, as I tried to meet their emotional needs while juggling the parcels. It seemed like a major crisis, because the following dilemma went through my head each time:

I can't carry the groceries and Emily and hold Jeremy's hand while he clambers up the stairs. Now, if I leave Emily in her infant seat in the car while I take Jeremy and the groceries upstairs, even if I lock the car so she won't be kidnapped, she might feel abandoned. But if I leave Jeremy in his seatbelt while I take the baby and the groceries upstairs, then Jeremy might feel abandoned, and he's old enough that he just might be able to unlock the car door and run away before I get back.

Not until years later did I realize that that was an insane way to have to live, that it was natural and healthy for me to wish their father would do the grocery shopping, and that I wasn't selfish and inadequate for finding the total responsibility for everyday life with children so difficult.

The nurturance myth causes other mother-daughter troubles: nurturing involves making the other person's life better—and women's power to do that is so limited. Our mothers can talk and listen and offer us love and emotional support, but they cannot prevent much of the damage done to us by the unjust treatment of girls and women by our society's institutions or by individuals— even, often, by Mother's own husband. Unfortunately, instead of recognizing the culture's responsibility for those limits, we act as though our mothers had no such limits and blame them for "their" limitations. As daughters, we can't undo or make amends for the many sources of sorrow in our mothers' lives. Because of this, mother and daughter often face each other wanting to do more to heal each other's wounds but feeling frustrated and ashamed because they cannot.

The Deepest Wounds, the Sharpest Pains

I believe that the myth of women's endless nurturance, more than any other, may be the source of the deepest, sorest wounds and sharpest pains that daughters feel in relation to their mothers. Why? To open ourselves up, to pour out our hearts, makes us vulnerable. Will the recipient of our outpouring both really listen to us and accept what she or he thereby learns about us? If both these happy things occur, we are strengthened; if either or both do not, we are stabbed in a vulnerable spot.

In general, when we open up to our fathers, we do so with some caution, not expecting their full understanding and support. So when we are imperfectly understood, our tenderest places are less likely to have been exposed, and the hurt is less deep, less blood is shed. But since we expect full understanding from our mothers, we're more likely to lay ourselves wide open to them— the risk is great, but if we fully show our real selves and she does accept us, what bliss, what security, that provides! And when she does not fully accept, what devastation. Magda, in her late thirties, told this story:

> When I was about thirty-five, I was visiting my parents, and my father came in to wake me up. I had just been having a terrifying nightmare, and as I floated up out of sleep I told Dad about it. When I had finished, he just said, "Well, it's time to get up." I was a little hurt, but mostly I just felt that next time I wouldn't even try to tell him how I felt. I also remember thinking that he loved a lot of things about me and that he loved me in a different way from Mom. I knew that Mom would probably have been more sympathetic about my nightmare.
>
> There have been times, though, when I tried to tell Mom about something that mattered a lot to me, and usually she was pretty receptive. But when she wasn't, I felt that she had seen the deepest core of my being and didn't find me lovable. What despair I felt then!

Turning to Daughter

The myth of endless nurturance can also feed a mother's resentment of her daughter: just as everyone expects nurturance from girls and women in general, so a mother expects such nurturance and support from her daughter. A mother is supposed to train her daughter to be a nurturer, in accordance with the nurturance myth. She believes the myth that a perfect daughter is the measure of a good mother: what more tempting place to begin than by training her daughter to take care of her mother, her closest companion? Such training may seem like the right thing to do. A daughter who takes good care of her mother will be well prepared to fit the ideal: a woman who can nurture her husband and sons. If she begins to feel in infancy or early childhood that such behavior is an obligation, then so much the better for society, for the girl will feel that it "comes naturally." She may even feel uncomfortable or unnatural behaving otherwise.

Leah, a forty-three-year-old divorced mother of two, told me in an interview that, after working at her nine-to-five job, picking up her kids at day care, cooking their dinner, and then spending an hour of "quality time" with them, she was ready to collapse:

> I have a bad back, and the pain gets worse when I've been on my feet all day. At night, my lovely seven-year-old daughter sometimes asks if I want a back rub. I always feel a little guilty, because I'm supposed to be taking care of her—but I am glad she's learning to be good to others, and she does like helping me.

That is a nice story, but when I asked Leah if her nine-year-old son ever rubs her back, she replied that he loves to play with his friends, and she doesn't feel she has the right to interrupt that playtime. In spite of the changes women have made, the difference in comfort levels between having a daughter and a son help out remains significant. Although one might expect that some changes in sex-role stereotyping of behavior since the 1970s might have altered this pattern, a wealth of research even in the decade before the milennium shows that it persists. Mothers and daughters of all ages tend to have closer, warmer, more emotionally expressive relationships with each other than mothers do with sons, or fathers with any offspring.

Some mothers of infants seek nurturance in wishing the baby would behave well, not cry, let her get a good night's sleep, smile at her, and be cuddly. Some mothers need this nurturing because of their unusually lonely, deprived, or upsetting early lives; they hope that at last they will get some affection, some peace, or both. For other mothers, the wish for nurturance from the daughter comes from the usual difficulties most women in our culture face—the responsibility and isolation of motherhood, the various forms of sexist treatment to which women are subjected, the exhaustion from the double workload of mother and worker, and so on. Any of these experiences can leave women feeling intensified needs for love and support.

When a baby girl or young daughter does not do what is expected, a mother who doesn't get or can't accept support from other people may feel like a failure and develop a lasting resentment of her daughter. Maggie's infant daughter was extremely colicky, had sleep problems, and wasn't cuddly "the way you hope your baby will be." Maggie's mother was chipper, but not warm or supportive; her father was extremely formal, distant, and preoccupied with his business. Maggie considers herself a deprived child, who lost what shreds of parental affection she had when her younger twin sisters were born. "Their birth destroyed my life," she claims. Feeling deprived, she has always lacked confidence in her ability to give love to others. Maggie never wanted a baby, and now she had one who not only required a lot of giving from her but seemed to offer no affection in return. Her daughter Sara's failure to be close and cuddly was devastating, Maggie says. Even now, eight years later, although Sara has shown that she can be warm and loving, Maggie treats her coldly and irritably.

We find forgiving our mothers particularly difficult when their failure to nurture us as much as we want is because their nurturance of our brothers, our fathers, their fathers and brothers, their male bosses—any male—takes priority. As I shall discuss in chapter 5, most of us have been trained to regard men as the prime needers of our care: "Men are such children. He's lost when I'm not there for dinner. He can't really cook, and he hates microwaved, frozen dinners. He has such trouble dealing with his feelings, unless I help him." Such common remarks reflect women's learned belief that men need our help more than women and girls, since the latter more likely can open cans of beans or deal with feelings. But blaming Mother for her learned sexism is no more fair or helpful than blaming her for being less than totally giving. Putting her sexism into action is what she was taught was right.

Once daughters become aware of having different expectations for nurturance from our mothers and our fathers, our anger at our mothers usually diminishes. We should not demean our fathers' nurturance (and some fathers are deeply loving and nurturing) but rather show equal appreciation for what our mothers do for us. When Mother gives only 90 percent, we may perceive it as 80 percent or as 10 percent or as nothing, because it was not all that we wanted. Then we create an unnecessary rift between our mothers and ourselves; furthermore, in this way we shut ourselves off from the good that our mothers do have to offer.

Because of the double standard, we often focus on what our mothers have failed to do, without considering why they might have failed. All families have their own challenges. Sometimes a mother fails to meet her daughter's needs because other family members need her, too. Or she may be a single mother, an immigrant mother, or a mother coping with the consequences of racism; she may be a disabled mother, a mother on welfare, a mother who is physically ill or depressed or anxious, a mother juggling paid work and housework, a mother with a depressed, alcoholic, or abusive partner, or a mother with many children or with a young, ill, or disabled child. And all mothers sometimes fail simply because we are human. If a mother doesn't play with her children as often as she might, then she should be regarded as not playing with them as often as she might, rather than as miserably failing to meet an impossibly high standard.

Myth Three: Mothers Naturally Know How to Raise Children

Myth Three is the widely believed notion that mothers instinctively know everything that's necessary for raising physically and emotionally healthy children. It is closely related to Myth Two, since women's allegedly innate capacity for nurturance is said to be part of our natural fitness for child rearing.

According to the myth, the hormones coursing through a mother's body during labor and delivery cause her to love her newborn immediately and totally, and suddenly she has the million and one bits of information she will need to be an excellent mother. Unfortunately, it isn't true. In her book *Mother Love*, historian Elisabeth Badinter painstakingly documents the evidence that giving birth is not the same as being able to mother, and that one does not lead inevitably to the other. Compelling evidence from psychologists contradicts the claim that mothers bond immediately to their babies and that they must do this for babies to grow up normally. But because mothers have heard that that is what we are supposed to do, we believe we have failed if we feel anything else instead. As writer Jain Sherrard has said,

Women do not have a handy gland called "mother" which is myste-riously activated upon giving birth. Contrary to every myth perpe-trated on us throughout history, not all women make good mothers, just as all men don't make good plumbers. That we can give birth does not guarantee that we can also mother successfully.

Feeling less than immediate and total love for one's newborn is not uncommon. According to one mother's description,

> Eventually, after twenty-two hours of labor, this daughter whom I had wanted so desperately . . . was born. I remember looking at her, looking at my husband with the tears in his eyes, and wondering if I could love her. He certainly did, but after it was finally all over, I wasn't so sure.

Once a mother gets baby home, her enjoyment of her child is limited by the endless nurturance myth; since the standard is to be naturally happy and serene, every time a mother feels fatigued or resentful because of the amount of nurturance her baby needs, she believes she is a failure as a mother. A mother's feelings include rapture but also panic, fear, rage, and despair. Sometimes the baby's needs seem unmeetable, the meanings of her wails are unclear, or she needs something just when her parents are exhausted or about to leave her for the first time ever. When a woman has these normal feelings, she doesn't feel like a natu-ral mother.

Hillary Rodham Clinton has described how upset she felt when, as a new mother, she had to ask the nurses to help her learn how to breast-feed Chelsea because, like many of us, she did not know what to do. Hillary was understandably upset, but a mother who is Black, poor, and unmarried is actually in danger of being severely punished for being unable to "do what comes naturally" as a moth-er, even when it is patently not her fault. In 1999 Tabitha Walrond was convicted of negligent homicide in her seven-week-old baby Tyler's death from malnutrition. Tabitha tried unsuccessfully to breast-feed him and sought help at Albert Einstein's Outpatient Clinic but was turned away because she had not yet received Tyler's Medicaid card in the mail. When she complained to a social worker, she was told the card would get there soon. But Tyler died a short time later.

As her child grows up, a mother continues to worry; her negative feelings don't disappear, and she never feels she immediately, naturally knows what to do for the child. When she doesn't intuitively know what her son needs, she is less distressed; after all, he is a member of a different sex. When she is perplexed about what to do for her daughter, she is more upset because she feels she has no "excuse."

Roxanne, whose daughter is now fifty years old, was trained as a surgical nurse before she was married. She vividly recalled, as most mothers do even decades later, how new motherhood felt to her:

> Wouldn't you have thought that the combination of being a woman and having been a nurse for eight years before my daughter was born would have made me the perfect mother? No such luck! When she cried, not only did I feel sorry for her because I didn't know how to help her, but I also felt ashamed because all of this understanding of my baby wasn't coming naturally. I was embarrassed to tell anyone how little I felt I was doing right for my daughter.

When Roxanne's daughter was six weeks old, Roxanne left her with a baby-sitter for the first time and went to her bridge club. Two members of her club had slightly older infants, so Roxanne hoped they could give her some good advice:

> I described my daughter's late afternoon spells of ceaseless screaming. The other new mothers said their babies didn't do that, and one explained, "When my baby cries, I can always tell whether he's hungry or needs his diaper changed." I was mortified. I felt so inadequate.

Later in the week, Roxanne's mother and mother-in-law came to visit. Although she was grateful for her mother's diagnosis of the baby's crying spells as caused by colic, she was ashamed that she hadn't known that herself. Fortunately, as Roxanne explained,

> Right after my visitors left, one of my bridge club members called to confess that her baby, too, cried every day at five o'clock, and

she had no idea what to do. She hadn't wanted to admit that in front of the other women.

Neither Roxanne nor her caller realized that for no woman does all of mothering come naturally. When not mocking mothers, television sitcoms portray them as knowing all the answers and striking the perfect balance between encouraging children's autonomy and setting limits, between loving and letting go. If mothers can be so wise, wonders daughter, why isn't mine? Why does she often say the wrong thing? Why does she make me crazy? As daughters grow up, feeling unhappy or confused or scared, we often blame Mother, who was supposed to protect us from pain and teach us how to be happy.

How does this myth create a barrier between mothers and daughters? At the simplest level, a daughter is apt to resent her mother for not doing everything right, not always instinctively knowing what she wants, not always being the perfect mother. After all, how is a daughter to know that her mother is no worse than others?—most mothers try so hard to conceal their weaknesses. For her part, a mother resents her daughter for having needs her mother can't meet, because that shows she is not a naturally terrific mother.

Precisely because mothering is supposed to come naturally, few mothers tell their children how difficult it can be. This has concerned me for many years—since I first had children—and I have taken some pains to tell my children that I don't always know what's right and don't always know what to do for them. Even so, they are surprised every time I say, "Well, I sure messed that up. I really made the wrong decision there." In a culture in which mothering is generally undervalued, chances are slim that anyone other than their mother is going to teach children how much effort and uncertainty are involved in the job. So both daughters and sons grow up thinking mothering is supposed to be easy. We don't see her human struggle, imperfections, and uncertainties; we only see a woman who doesn't measure up to the standard of the naturally selfless, serene, and sage mother. And often, we resent her for that failure.

As adult daughters, when our mothers don't have all the answers, when they can't make things "all better," we either decide they are shamefully deficient or believe they did know what to do but let us down by not doing it for us. A daughter called Cyndi described her experience:

> When my kids were three and four years old, my former boss offered to give me back my old job. I was thrilled—but because it was full-time, it would mean putting my children in day care. I asked my mother what she thought, and I really desperately wanted-ed her to tell me the right choice to make.
>
> She said, "You'll be happier if you're working, and that would be good for the children. But you may miss a lot of important times with them if you're away eight hours a day."
>
> She just presented the pros and cons but wouldn't tell me what to do. I was furious at her. But then I realized that I wasn't mad at my husband for refusing to make the decision for me. Because she was my mother, I expected *her* to know the right choice.

Myth Four: Mothers (and "Good" Daughters) Don't Get Angry

Anger presents a special problem in relationships between mothers and daughters. Anger is a natural part of any close relationship, but anger is considered unfeminine. Mothers and daughters are not supposed to get angry, certainly not at each other; if they do, at least one of them is bad. According to the myth, the mother-daughter relationship is a mutually loving, supportive one with no room for anger. In contrast, showing anger is consistent with the male image, even enhancing it. Father-son hostility is considered healthy or masculine, but a daughter's anger at her father is even more taboo. In a seminar, 52-year-old Mary Ellen acknowledged, "Looking back, I can see that my husband and I always came down harder on our daughter when she mouthed off at me than on our son when he talked back to my husband. It just seemed so much more inappropriate when she acted like that."

The "women don't get angry" message helps ensure that women will nurture others: showing anger is not supportive. As with the other social rules, a mother is to teach her daughter to suppress anger. Sometimes she does it as an explicit order: "Don't get mad. Nice girls don't get angry." Sometimes she conveys her message through praise—telling a daughter she is terrific to skip a party, without complaining, to baby-sit for her younger brother. Nietzsche wrote, "Praise is more obtrusive than a reproach," and that certainly applies to the mother-daughter relationship: the mother's praise may make her daughter feel good but irritates her because she earned it by accepting limits on her freedom.

While a daughter may feel like a true woman for not getting angry and for focusing on other people's needs, she will likely resent her mother for taking away her ability to defend and protect herself through anger when necessary. The conflict between maintaining her integrity by expressing justified, self-protective anger and keeping her mother's approval tears the daughter apart.

Because women's anger has been forbidden, it often becomes the center of mother-daughter relationships. Arguing with your mother about clothes and haircuts is a difficult though expected part of mother-daughter interactions; the relationship becomes excruciating when burdened with intense anger that isn't supposed to be there. So mother and daughter begin with the pain of hostile feelings between them; then they have to cope with the secondary problem of knowing these are forbidden.

Mother worries that a daughter who doesn't learn to suppress her anger is a sign that mother is a failure and that daughter will not do well in the world. A mother who has spent decades suppressing her own anger will be very unsettled to watch her daughter struggling to control similar feelings; her daughter's expression of anger tempts mother to express her own anger. Unfortunately, we want to stay away from someone who elicits our forbidden feelings; we fear they'll bring out the worst in us. A late-middle-aged mother called Judith said in one of my classes,

> For the first year after my daughter separated from her husband I couldn't stand to be around her, because she was so filled with hostility. I believed she had the right to be furious at him, because he'd been unfaithful to her many times, but I just didn't feel like being around her. One reason was that I became more irritable with my husband every time I saw my daughter. I just got so mad about some of the things men do to women, and that made it harder for me to ignore my husband's lack of warmth toward me.

When, as is inevitable in any relationship, anger arises between mother and daughter, they try to understand why they're not living up to the ideal. Each may blame herself, or they may blame each other. Neither is an attractive alternative, and both are misdirected, for the problem probably doesn't come from within them; it is thrust upon them by society. When we feel we have to suppress our feelings about another person, our time together is strained. But strain itself is inconsistent with the popular view of the ideal mother-daughter pair. The daughter in a typical mother-daughter pair who attended one of my public lectures described this experience:

> The first time I came home from college for a visit—at Thanksgiving—both Mother and I expected things to go smoothly. We'd fought like cats and dogs during my last year of high school, but we both blamed that on our sadness about my leaving home. Now that I lived in another state, we both assumed we'd finished our combative stage.
>
> No such luck! We fought horribly on that first visit, and we took turns blaming it all on each other and feeling guilty and blaming ourselves. It was so bad that I didn't attempt another visit home until the end of the next August, after my summer job ended. She didn't ask me to visit any sooner!

As we learn to suppress an emotion, we increasingly feel that if we ever do express it, some disaster will befall us. In the case of women's anger, we not only fear being considered unwomanly if we express that feeling but also believe that our anger is destructive: after all, if our mothers can't accept our anger, we feel, then how dangerous our anger must be!

Earlier in this chapter, I mentioned the mother's and daughter's fears that fully expressing our warm feelings toward each other will make it harder to suppress such feelings in the presence of men, who might consider us "overemotional" or be jealous of our closeness to each other. Mother-daughter anger endangers our relationships with men in at least two ways:

1. Many a man can't stand to see an angry woman, even if he's not the butt of her anger, because this clashes with his ideal of femininity.

2. Once mother and daughter get angry, that energy might be turned against men who mistreat them; so, for many men, the presence of a woman who is angry for any reason at all reminds them of how precarious their position would be if that anger were directed at them.

Women sense how uncomfortable their anger makes most men (that's one reason women smile so much, even when they don't feel happy), so women who want close relationships with men may feel frightened by anger they feel at their mothers. Thirty-one-year-old Dana felt that way, and in her not-atypical case, she felt two dangers: that her husband would be uncomfortable about her anger at her mother, and that her husband and mother would team up against her.

When my husband and I were engaged, I hated for him to see my mother and me together, but it took me a while to understand why. I finally realized that, when he was around, she was so anxious for us to get married that she played up to him, agreed with everything he said, had me serve him at the dinner table, and made an even greater show than usual of serving my father in all sorts of ways. I was furious at her for being so subservient, and I've only recently begun to forgive her, because I now understand that she was only doing what she had been taught a good woman should do.

But part of my anger at Mom was because I did not want to wait on my husband hand and foot, and when we were engaged he was already expecting me to do that. So there was Mom, doing what George wanted me to do but what I was trying to escape from. It was pretty complicated, because I wanted both Mom and George to love me, but I think I felt they were almost in league with each other against me. And when the three of us were in the same room, I'd get irritated with Mom, and then George would tell me that I shouldn't get so mad at her. Of course, part of the reason he said that was because, in a funny way, she and he were on the same side. If I had been able to articulate why I was so damned angry, it would have dashed his hopes of having an obedient wife.

To keep a proper perspective, we must realize that hostility between mothers and daughters is often exaggerated. In fact, in early adolescence the greatest decline in parent-child hostility is in the mother-daughter relationship, and even before the decline, most of these relationships are described as "less positive" rather than frankly negative. Research also shows that teenage daughters tend to confide "a lot" in their mothers and little or not at all in their fathers. Mother-daughter hostility is often exaggerated because even a little of what is forbidden looms very large.

Where Do We Go from Here?

Recognizing the myths about mothers and daughters, and the many forms they take in our daily culture, is essential to improving our relationships with our mothers. For most women, understanding that our mothers were unwitting vehicles for transporting cultural myths into our hearts and minds is much better and more empowering than believing that our mothers consciously, voluntarily, as individuals untouched by social pressure, chose to impose the myths on us. What mother would willingly teach her daughter such methods of self-destruction? And what woman would want to have to answer to her daughter for having done so? Yet so many mothers have been myth transmitters. The fact that mothers—most of whom are conscientious about doing right by their children—transmit these myths demonstrates the power of social pressure in a culture that keeps mothers under its heel. (Even when mothers transmit only a fraction of the myths, they are often blamed for transmitting all.)

Seeing how this process works makes it easier for us as mothers and daughters to become allies, to refuse to be divided against each other. When we see that the price of society's acceptance of us is our readiness to turn against and blame our mothers, we are less likely to pay the price of that acceptance.

Asking Questions, Seeking Answers

We need to raise questions—in our own minds, with our mothers, and with other people.

- Is a mother's success or failure gauged by the way her daughter turns out, rather than by the mother's efforts or by the forces that interfered with those efforts?

- Is a daughter to blame her shortcomings on her mother's inability to meet all her needs?
- Are mothers (or daughters) truly capable of giving of themselves endlessly? And is it right to expect that of anyone?
- Is any woman truly capable of naturally, instinctively doing all it takes to be a perfect mother? And is it fair to expect that of our mothers and ourselves?
- Is women's anger sometimes healthy, and should we expect mothers (and daughters) always to suppress their anger?
- Is it possible to look at what factors that impinge on a daughter's development are overlooked when a mother is blamed?
- How do all of the Perfect Mother myths damage mother-daughter relationships? And do those myths do any good at all? If they do, let's not throw the baby out with the bathwater; for instance, let's encourage mothers and daughters to be nurturing but stop expecting them to do so unceasingly.

The long history and power of these myths make them hard to overcome. However, mothers and daughters are encouraged to make the effort when they begin to see what a difference it makes to their relationship. A mother-daughter pair, Jasmine and Shelley, who learned how the endless nurturance myth created a barrier between them, jointly wrote me a letter in which they said,

Each of us had felt the other expected too much, but we hadn't realized that we ourselves did, too. Now, when either of us feels the other has let us down, we stop and ask ourselves—and then each other—"Was I expecting your total approval again?" And, usually, it's true.

Just asking the question solves most of the problem, because when you put it that way, you realize how unrealistic that expectation is. Also, we're both adults now and don't really need anyone's total approval. But somehow, being able to say, "I wanted your one hundred percent support" makes it better. For one thing, the other person can tell you she does support you wholeheartedly, even if you were too insecure to know that. Or, she can tell you what reservations she has about your lover or dress or job, and you can talk it out. Knowing what the other person is worried about is always better than just feeling she's not giving you her all.

Another example of a mother and daughter whose examination of a myth helped lower a barrier between them involves thirty-seven-year-old Stephanie and her mother, Ruth. Stephanie told me about a conversation in which the two of them discussed their fear of anger:

> When I told my mother that I was ending my career as full-time housewife and going to work as a market researcher, she grew very cold toward me. In fact, she seemed to be furious. So, for the first six months of my job, I never talked to her about it. Finally, she asked me how things were going at work, but I was so frightened of her anger that I got tongue-tied. Then she got mad because I wasn't answering her. All I could manage to say at that point was, "I don't think you really want to hear!"
>
> She looked stunned. "Wherever did you get that idea?" she asked. I told her I'd spent the past six months thinking she was angry at me for getting a job and not being home when my kids got home from school. Then she looked terribly relieved and explained that what I had interpreted as anger at me was really her anger about the time she had wasted by not having a job when my twin brother and I started high school. Dad hadn't wanted her to work, so she waited until we left for college, and when she finally did start work she had the time of her life. She had always been bitter about the four years she had sat at home, while my brother and I were out at school and extracurricular activities and Dad was at work, and twiddled her thumbs, doing charity work she didn't really enjoy and feeling useless.

As Stephanie and Ruth talked, they realized that Stephanie had felt that having her mother angry at her was thoroughly devastating. Ruth had had no idea either that Stephanie thought she was angry at her (when she was really angry about her own history) or that it mattered so much to Stephanie if she was. Talking about the unacceptability of women's anger in general, and about Stephanie's particular dread of her mother's anger, took away the myth's power.

The mothers and daughters in these two examples were able to legitimize women's basic humanity. We do this by believing—and helping other people to see—that no one can be a perfect mother, even the children of terrific mothers can go wrong, no one can be endlessly nurturing, and mothers and daughters can have a whole range of feelings, including anger. The Second and Third Waves of the women's movement have helped, partly by showing women the unfairness and impossibility of living up to traditional feminine stereotypes and partly by showing us that we have many legitimate reasons to be upset and angry. But although many of us now feel less ashamed and apologetic when we are angry or otherwise imperfect, lessening the taboo against women's anger and reducing the requirements for perfection in women in general hasn't reduced our expectations for mothers or weakened the taboo against anger at or from our mothers. The idealized view of the perfect, unalloyed love we are supposed to have for our mothers, plus injunctions to honor them, combine with genuine appreciation of what they have done for us, and all of this makes us feel ashamed of our anger at them. Conversely, the idealized view of how mothers should act—plus injunctions always to be the perfect, loving, kindly mother—makes mothers feel ashamed about what they regard as how they have "failed" us.

Daughters who want to see their mothers more realistically are also helped by contrasting their expectations of their mothers with their expectations of their fathers. Most daughters quickly recognize that they expect more nurturance and support, more good advice, and less anger from their mothers than from their fathers. Our relationships with our mothers can be improved once both we and they acknowledge the unfairness of that disparity and modify our expectations accordingly. (This double standard of expectations of mothers and fathers is discussed in chapter 5.)

As if the Perfect Mother myths didn't cause mothers and daughters enough trouble, there are also the Bad Mother myths, which are the subject of the next chapter and which also need to be understood in order to lower the barriers between mothers and daughters.

5

The Bad Mother Myths

Where the Perfect Mother myths establish standards every woman will fail to meet, the Bad Mother myths make mothers' ordinary behavior seem worse than it really is. With the help of the Bad Mother myths, we exaggerate our mothers' real faults and transform their neutral or not-so-bad characteristics into monstrosities.

No doubt there are others, but six major Bad Mother myths are:

- Myth Five: Mothers are inferior to fathers.
- Myth Six: Mothers need experts' advice to raise healthy children.
- Myth Seven: Mothers are bottomless pits of neediness.
- Myth Eight: Mother-daughter closeness is unhealthy.
- Myth Nine: Mothers are dangerous when they're powerful.
- Myth Ten: Both stay-at-home mothers and mothers with paid work are bad mothers.

Myth Five: Mothers Are Inferior to Fathers

That mothers are inferior to fathers is probably the most pervasive mother myth. In chapter 4, we saw how, because of higher expectations for mothers than fathers, we are quick to criticize our mothers for not being perfect but appreciate our fathers for merely trying. The myth of mothers' inferiority takes many other forms as well. For example, although traditional mother's work—child-rearing, housecleaning, cooking, and monitoring the family dynamics—is unpaid and largely unappreciated, the traditional father's major work is breadwinning, paid work. Even in families in which both parents are wage earners, the fact that men's parenting activities tend to involve more play, while women do more limit-setting and mundane activities like feeding and dressing children, helps perpetuate the relatively greater appreciation of fathers. (As mentioned, the respect and honor that are supposed to compensate a mother for her motherwork and household work are rarely forthcoming.)

The myth of mothers' inferiority leads to women being far more frequently the target of their husbands' and grown children's violent behavior than men are of their wives' or children's assaults. Furthermore, despite the public's increased awareness—through the O. J. Simpson trial, for instance—of the frequency of wife battering, when it comes to interpreting the motives of *victims* of abuse, women are still assumed to have "brought the violence on themselves," whereas men victims are thought to be undeserving targets who deserve sympathy.

Sexism Starts at Home

The myth of mothers' inferiority leads daughters to think disparagingly of both their mothers and themselves. Often, mothers themselves have helped indoctrinate their daughters in the myth, having been pressed to encourage daughters to accept their inferiority, to set "realistically" modest goals, to develop enough humility to avoid scaring off potential husbands. Trying to help daughters survive in a rough world, many mothers have schooled their daughters to ally themselves with men rather than with their mothers or other women, a pattern that in recent decades seems less changed in the home than in the workplace.

When I was a teenager facing a moral dilemma, my mother would discuss it with me and then say, "When your father comes home, ask him. He always knows the right thing to do." My father has always had high moral standards, but so has my mother; unfortunately, because of what my mother said, I grew up thinking of him, but not her, in that way. In spite of the women's movement, many young women today tell similar stories.

Flo Kennedy says that the men-are-better myth makes possible what she calls "horizontal hostility":

> If you have a sense of your own worthlessness, then somebody else from your class or race or religion is clearly not to be looked

up to. This is one of the bases for the pathology of women saying, "I don't get along with women. I get along with men; they're superior, so if I get along with them I'm superior; I've left all of my class behind."

As one woman wrote to me, "The parent who invests less effort in the family exposes less of himself to his family to be judged." The media are filled with stories of men's ongoing struggle to overcome their socialization in emotional illiteracy, reflecting the fact that this important struggle is far from won. Even today, and even in families parented by highly educated heterosexual couples who regard themselves as egalitarian, the typical father spends less time and emotional energy on the family, and his distance can lead his children and wife longingly to idealize him.

Even in families with strong mothers, the myth of female inferiority has been perpetuated, although substantial psychological contortions have been required. An old friend told me how this happened in her family:

> My mother was an amazing woman, She raised four of us kids virtually single-handedly, and that included knitting all our sweaters herself, doing all the housework and cooking, while starting a mail-order business that eventually did very well. Daddy was at work every night until after dinner and worked half-days on Saturdays. Thanks partly to Mom, I never thought of her as working, but she made it clear that Daddy worked very hard.
>
> When Daddy was due to arrive home every night, she'd get us to wash our faces and settle down. His nightly return home was an event—because she made it one. But no one did that for her. When Daddy fell asleep reading the evening paper, she made us keep quiet out of respect for how hard he worked. But on the rare occasions when she took a nap, he didn't do that for her.
>
> Not until my mother's funeral—when the minister talked about her remarkable strength and energy—did I realize what an unbalanced view of my parents' worth I had.

Even today, parents of both sexes often treat their sons differently from their daughters, setting fewer limits on boys' behavior and making fewer demands for them to take care of others. According to Judith Arcana, "[sons'] behavior may deviate from standard, appropriate behavior far more than that of daughters and still be acceptable," another message about daughters' inferiority.

If as a child you were undervalued because of your sex, you may later realize why you were not wholeheartedly accepted; but by then a great deal of harm has been done. The seeds of insecurity are sown with awesome firmness in the earliest years of life, when a child experiences herself as one who is not a source of pride, who is not cherished; then, angry about feeling inferior, she often turns her rage against her mother, who was there all the time and did not seem to value her.

The motion picture *Nuts,* in which the character played by Barbra Streisand has been sexually abused by her stepfather, reflects some of the worst harm that can be caused by the male superiority myth. Because of that myth, the mother believed she had to have a man in the family. Until the daughter grew up, the mother was unaware of the abuse, partly because her husband took extreme measures to keep it a secret. Furthermore, her first husband had abandoned them, and she was terrified of losing her second. She considered herself worthless because her first husband hadn't wanted her, and she believed her daughter needed a father-figure; to persuade her new man to stay with them, she tried desperately to please him and to protect him from all demands. When her daughter started skipping school, becoming promiscuous, and taking drugs, family counseling was suggested. But the stepfather feared that in counseling his secret would be revealed, so he made excuses to avoid it, saying the stepdaughter was the problem. To avoid angering him, the mother accepted his view.

This film was true to life. In families plagued by incest, the father's avoidance of responsibility and intimidation of mother and daughter are common. The same is true for fathers who tyrannize their families in other ways. In the course of creating and preserving a traditional nuclear family—that is, keeping an adult male in the home and protecting the father's reputation—the mother's and daughter's psychological and physical safety have often suffered. Sadly, this gives the daughter more reason to feel her mother has let her down.

Some of the serious consequences of the male superiority myth involve mothers and daughters being driven apart by the allegiance either or both of them feels to a man, no matter how much he may be in the wrong. A woman I'll call Maureen had worked diligently to overcome the emotional distance between her widowed mother, Pat, and herself, and she seemed to be having some success. Then Maureen learned that her brother, Ben, had become a compulsive gambler and was running his family deeply into debt. He didn't want his wife to get a job, so he was the sole breadwinner for himself, his wife, and their three sons.

Maureen went to great lengths to support her sister-in-law's attempts to take her children and leave Ben, but Pat refused to believe the truth about her son and angrily condemned Maureen's attempts to look out for her nephews. So great was Pat's need to safeguard her image of her son that she denied Ben was capable of serious wrongdoing. So profound was her belief in the superiority of men ("He's the only man I have left," she said) that, rather than live with the truth, she chose to believe the lies and scorn Maureen's attempts to restore their mother-daughter relationship.

Even when men are clearly inadequate—because of drugs, abusiveness, or extreme emotional withdrawal—mothers and daughters often seek men's approval even while they try to protect each other against the father's abuses of power.

Penis Envy and Penis Pity

In chapter 3 we saw how mother-blame is validated and reinforced by claims from the scientific world. Sigmund Freud's work was ingenious but not scientifically proven; nevertheless, his theory of penis envy has been skillfully used to support the myth of male superiority. According to Freud, all women wish they had a penis and believe that men's genitals make them superior. This idea has become part of everyday culture.

Freud said that women hold their mothers responsible for their lack of a penis. In the daughter's eyes, Freud argued, the mother is omnipotent; the daughter believes her mother could have endowed her with a penis but chose not to. Freud also suggested that the little girl's embarrassment over her own "inferiority" is connected to her contempt for her mother: "I despise my mother because she is just like me in this deficient way."

Because Freud's influence has been so great, we need to think carefully about penis envy. What Freud calls "penis envy" isn't just about penises: daughters' disappointment over their mothers' failure to give them a penis is less than their disappointment over their mothers' powerlessness compared to their father, their mothers' inability to empower them (compared to their brothers), and their mothers' preferential treatment of their brothers. Furthermore, daughters are often sad to see how limited their mothers' lives and choices have been and are alarmed by the poverty of possibility for their lives that they see mirrored there. As Kim Chernin wrote in *Reinventing Eve,* "When the daughter at the crossroads rejects her mother and chooses her father instead, it is because she cannot find within the mother-world a way to grow into the full promise of her original female being." For all these reasons, we may look down on our mothers and ourselves and look up to our fathers and brothers.

The danger of using the penis as a symbol of the inequities between mother and father, between brother and sister, is that it makes the inequities seem inevitable. Fathers and brothers will continue to have penises, and mothers and sisters will not, so if the penis is the real issue, we may as well believe that males will always be superior and females always deficient. But the penis only represents men's greater social, political, and economic power, a power imbalance that is not our mothers' fault and that can be changed.

Even when we think about penis envy in its literal sense, we need to know that not all girls feel this envy. Many feel what I have called "penis pity." Some people of both sexes think that penises are funny, strange-looking, wobbly, out of control, and vulnerable to harm. At the age at which Freud said penis envy appears, when two- to four-year-old girls notice their physical differences from boys, children have important concerns that lead to penis pity—issues of control and self-control, protecting their bodies, and privacy. Little girls at this age may regard themselves as lucky: they needn't try to control something that dangles and swings willy-nilly, nor protect something that is externally exposed, sensitive, and easily hurt, nor struggle to maintain privacy and avoid embarrassment about visible, easily observable genitalia.

For many little girls penis pity is quite real. As Simone de Beauvoir has written, "This tiny bit of flesh hanging between boys' legs is insignificant or even laughable; it is a peculiarity that merges with that of clothes or haircut. . . . It may even happen that the penis is considered to be an anomaly: an outgrowth, something vague that hangs, like wens, breasts, or warts; it can inspire disgust."

How does the concept of penis pity change our vision of the possibilities for the mother-daughter relationship? Believing in penis envy feeds our belief that all daughters resent their mothers for not giving them either penises or access to social power, that all women feel contempt for themselves and other women, and that this is natural and unavoidable. But once we realize that penis envy is not inevitable and that little girls may actually feel relieved not to have a penis, that justification for resenting our mothers is gone.

As we saw earlier, the myth of mothers' inferiority underlies many of the other mother-myths, and one of those is the notion that without the advice of experts—many of whom are male—mothers cannot raise emotionally healthy children.

Myth Six: Only the Experts Know How to Raise Children

The explosion of advice from child-rearing experts during this century has led mothers to believe that the truth about good child-rearing is out there somewhere, if only they can find and follow it. Mothers read the latest book or watch the latest talk show and find that they should be setting firm limits with their eight-year-olds, because young children feel secure knowing that their impulses won't have free rein. The next book hot off the press from another expert arrives. Mothers read it and learn that their limits should be very flexible, guidelines for their children's behavior should be set in democratic family councils, and children should play a substantial role in setting consequences for failing to keep to the guidelines. This expert says this method helps the child develop internal controls and feel that Mother respects the child's ideas.

Mothers think about the apparent disagreement between the two experts and conclude that both make sense. Children probably need some of each. But . . . how are they ever going to decide when their child needs how much of each? The answers to these questions matter desperately, because both the child's current and future happiness and the mother's success as a mother are at stake. Where is the superexpert who will tell them which expert to follow when? Conscientious mothers have made mistakes in trying to follow experts' advice, since no superexpert has been at their elbows to guide them, to say, "Now you're doing too much" and "Now you're not doing enough," and certainly never "Now you're doing it just right!"

The so-called experts carry on unending debates about bottle-feeding versus breast-feeding, feeding on demand versus feeding on a schedule, whether or not to teach your child to read before the first grade, whether or not to give immunizations, how best to discipline your child, whether or not having an only child is bad, whether or not to involve the child in a highly structured classroom, and so on. A contemporary of my mother's told me,

> One expert instructed mothers to stay home with their children until they started kindergarten, another said even teenagers need to know mother will be home if they get sick at school, and still another said we should go out to work so that we could feel better about ourselves as people. With the big shots disagreeing with each other, and us mothers feeling hopelessly inadequate, how were we supposed to make our decisions?

On the subject of children's psychological welfare, a great deal was discussed in chapter 2 about the experts' mother-blaming. Even when mother is not directly blamed, she is haunted by the experts' tendency to interpret children's behavior as indicating problems. Since the 1980s, Dr. T. Berry Brazelton has been a glorious exception; in his books he takes care to describe how wide is the range of normal behavior. However, few other child-care experts convey that message.

A hardworking professional woman I know took her four-year-old cerebral-palsied daughter for an educational assessment. The examiner administered a huge battery of intellectual and developmental tests and found that the child's scores ranged from above average to dramatically superior. Without asking for any background information, the examiner said accusingly, "You have certainly been pushing this child!" Until then, the mother had felt guilty for having a career, because she thought perhaps she ought to stay home all day, teaching her daughter. Now she was being criticized as though she had stayed home but overdone it. Always, it seems, mothers are told they are doing either too much or not enough, and it doesn't get easier as the children get older. Listen to Alexandra, the mother of a fourteen-year-old girl whose grades had dropped when she entered high school:

> My family doctor told me I wasn't pushing Sally enough. "You need to set up more structure for her, keep her to regular homework times, and so forth," he said. Because he felt I was intimidated by Sally, he sent me to a psychiatrist who was supposed to help me be a stricter parent. But the psychiatrist told me, "Sally picks up on your excessively high standards of achievement, and her lower grades are her way of protesting against them. Stay completely out of her schoolwork. Don't even ask her if she's finished her homework."

Another realm where experts' opinions interfere with mother-daughter relationships is that of sexual orientation. Despite the recent increase in numbers of women coming out as lesbian, many mental health professionals continue to claim that any sexual orientation other than heterosexual is a mental illness. Although the authors of the major classification system for mental disorders (the bible of therapists, the *Diagnostic and Statistical Manual of Mental Disorders*, or *DSM*) declared in 1974 that homosexuality was no longer a mental illness, the truth is that it remained in the next edition of the *DSM*. And even though homosexuality per se no longer appears in the *DSM*, the category of "sexual perversion" does, a term therapists may interpret as they choose. Furthermore, therapists continue to say publicly that there is something wrong with mothers who raise lesbian or gay offspring. Reading through the deeply moving book *Love, Ellen*, by Betty DeGeneres, about her struggle to accept the fact that her daughter Ellen was lesbian, one feels poignantly how important it would have been if she had not had to grapple with the views of "experts" that lesbianism is a form of mental abnormality and mothers of lesbians are at fault.

Still another realm in which the pressure of experts' opinions can cause harm is one that experienced a major surge beginning in the 1980s, that of putting enormous emphasis on early childhood and even infant intellectual stimulation ("Hold vocabulary flashcards over the crib"). More recently has come a focus on developing one's offspring's emotional intelligence and "multiple intelligences." Although the latter certainly have some merit, the point here is that mothers who fail to execute these tasks tend to be held—and to hold themselves—more responsible for children's failures in the areas of these various kinds of intelligence and achievements than do fathers, because most child-care work is still left to mothers.

Judges are experts whose power over mothers can be particularly devastating. Sometimes their own mother-blaming tendencies shape their decisions; and they base decisions on mother-blaming "explanations" presented by therapists who testify as "expert witnesses." In their book *"Bad" Mothers: The Politics of Blame in Twentieth-Century America,* Molly Ladd-Taylor and Lauri Umansky point out that courts have been biased against mothers who fit any of the following descriptions: they do not live in the traditional heterosexual married nuclear family; they have been unable to protect their children from harm; and their children have somehow "gone wrong." They give the example of Jennifer Ireland, who placed her three-year-old daughter in day care while she attended classes at the University of Michigan and lost custody of the child because the court found that that university was so academically demanding that she could not be a good parent.

The ironies involved in the myth that mothers need the advice of experts in order to raise children are many. First of all, as seen in chapter 4, honest experts freely acknowledge that human behavior is complex and that they usually cannot explain why a child from a problem-ridden home can turn out fine, but a child who seems to have everything can become a criminal.

Second, coexisting with and contradicting the myth that only experts know the answers is the myth that mothers naturally know how to raise children (chapter 4). The truth is that neither experts nor mothers know as much as each might wish; to a great extent, all of us fly by the seat of our pants and try to learn quickly from experience. But the proliferation of so-called experts on child-rearing feeds a Bad Mother myth, because they make already insecure mothers (that is, most mothers) feel that only the experts know the right thing to do.

Ironically, many real mistakes that mothers make are based on bad advice from "experts" or on their misguided attempts to follow that advice. Yet there's no shortage of experts willing to condemn anything a mother does, and she herself often feels woefully inadequate. Plagued by impossibly high expectations for their behavior and/or trying to follow "expert" advice, mothers develop intense anxiety and guilt. That children *are* harmed by parents' anxiety and guilt is one of the few principles on which mental health professionals do agree. Mother becomes unduly anxious around her children: instead of trusting her instincts and perceptions, she worries constantly about whether or not she is doing the right thing. But mothers cannot legitimately be held solely responsible for this harm, for they didn't set the unreachable standards. Ronni, a thirty-one-year-old mother, told me this story:

> When my children were three and five years old, their father and I separated, and he was not very good about visiting or calling them regularly. My pediatrician said I should explain to the children that "Daddy really loves you a lot, even though he doesn't call," so that they wouldn't feel rejected by him. But my psychiatrist said, "Your ex-husband is very self-centered, and he really doesn't love anyone except himself very much. Don't tell the kids that Daddy loves them a lot, because that is teaching them that loving doesn't require any show of concern for the loved ones."
>
> I was so confused, because both of them made some sense to me. So I was nervous all the time. I just didn't know how to handle it, and the kids had a really bad time because of my anxiety. The five-year-old decided she had to take care of me, and she kept asking me what she could do to cheer me up. The three-year-old became a real behavior problem, because of having picked up my anxiety, I think.

The belief that only the experts know how to raise a child damages mother-daughter relationships by feeding a daughter's belief in her mother's inadequacy. (It does the same for sons.) Women's fear of not being naturally perfect mothers keeps them from sharing with their daughters their uncertainties and confusion, as we saw earlier. As a result, many daughters look at their mothers' imperfections and see a woman who couldn't manage to follow the experts' advice, rather than understanding her confusion, her struggle, and her good intentions. Some adult daughters, who achieved less in school than they now think they could have done, have told me they hold their mothers responsible for failing "to make me toe the mark." "She should have used tough love," said one. Others have said that their mothers should have followed the experts' advice to place responsibility for schoolwork squarely on the adolescent's shoulders. Many women learned to appreciate their mothers more once they themselves had children; through their own experience they learned not just how difficult, but how impossible, it is to know what is right.

Mothers who feel that they aren't meeting good child-rearing standards often refrain from informing other people of their "failures." On account of this, rarely do mothers learn that they are all in the same boat, terrified of failing but certain that that's just what they are doing.

Daughters shouldn't have to wait until they give birth before they begin to understand their mothers' frustration in the face of the myth that only the experts know what to do. Realizing how powerful the myth is, how confusing the experts' advice can be, and how hard most of our mothers tried to wade through that morass can take us a long way toward understanding and appreciating our mothers.

Myth Seven: Mothers (and Daughters) Are Bottomless Pits of Neediness

> "What does she want from me?"
> —*Countless men, about their*
> *wives, through the ages*

Many stories and images promote the myth that women have unmeetable emotional needs and make ceaseless demands on other people. Mothers, the myth would have us believe, drain everyone around them of their love, autonomy, and self-respect. We know the tales of woman as witch, sorceress, Circe, Scylla and Charybdis, and Cleopatra; the fear of being faced with unmeetable demands is even entrenched in the Bible, such as in Ecclesiastes: "And I find more bitter than death the woman, whose heart ensnares and nets." Closer to our own day, Freud wrote that daughters feel intense hostility toward their mothers for not meeting (as no one could) their "insatiable" and "immoderate" needs.

Problems in relationships are routinely blamed on women's supposedly unmeetable needs for affection. In fact, women blame their own "neediness" for causing trouble. Rosalie had this to say about her relationship with her husband:

> Sam always wants me to be compassionate and supportive when he's upset, but when I need a little compassion and support, he throws up his hands and says, "What do you want from me?! Nothing is ever enough for you! Nobody could meet your needs!"

Since men are raised with the myth of women's neediness, and most are also raised to be inexpressive, many worry that they won't be able to respond in kind to a woman's nurturance (or that it's not masculine to do so). They worry, too, that if they can't respond adequately, she will reject or abandon them. Instead of acknowledging their fear of their own inadequacy, many men claim that women's needs are unmeetable, thus perpetuating the myth.

A husband who fears that he will lose his wife because of his emotional inadequacy often deals with this fear by demanding endless demonstrations of loyalty, commitment, and reassurance from his wife. Yet the woman who responds by giving a man her all is vulnerable to criticism. She is labeled the smothering, engulfing woman/mother who overwhelms men and children with love and nurturance long after they have had enough, the "seductress" who uses her warmth and sexuality to control and manipulate men and children. And since girls and women absorb men's attitudes, in part as a way of pleasing them, they see themselves as men do. This reinforces their belief that their own needs (and those of other girls and women) are enormous.

Women's needs may seem enormous for other reasons. In general, women are brought up to be more expressive than men; we show what we want as well as what we have to give. Men's needs tend to be better masked—and are usually sensed and tended to by a woman (mother, wife, daughter, girlfriend) even before the man has to acknowledge them. Marnie, a newly married woman, told me,

> The minute he walks in the door after work, my husband Bart expects me to know whether he needs to talk or to be left alone. But when I tell him I'm hurt because he doesn't take an interest in how I'm feeling after my day at the office, he says, "How am I supposed to know how you feel if you don't tell me?!" But when I do tell him I've had a rough day, he says I shouldn't burden him by "emoting all over the place."

Women have been encouraged to appear helpless, needy, and dependent so we will be attractive and unthreatening to men. For many men, this works—until the woman's neediness starts to infuriate them. As Suzette wrote in a letter to me, "Allen loves to feel strong and protective when I burst into tears. But I feel like he allows me about thirty seconds of sympathy, and then he expects me to stop crying. If I don't, he rants and raves about my being such a 'big baby.'"

Like the members of any undervalued or oppressed group, women sometimes do need extra support, because in addition to dealing with the ordinary problems of daily life, they have to cope with extra stresses and wounds. Our culture increases women's real needs for support and then uses those needs to "prove" that we are simply overemotional. This does not prove, however, that women inevitably have huge emotional needs.

A major reason for some women's intense need for affection is that they, like some men, were inadequately nurtured when they were children. Therapists have reported that such children grow up feeling that they can never be loved enough. This makes it particularly hard for women, who are supposed to provide nurturance for others despite feeling so needy themselves. In addition, unpleasant restrictions of various kinds have been placed on our mothers' lives, including—for most of them—the lack of real choice about whether or not to get married, have children, and stay at home to take care of them. Furthermore, the success of their marriage was considered to be mostly their responsibility rather than one shared equally with their husbands.

These factors in combination have left millions of women unhappy and unfulfilled. As Betty Friedan pointed out in *The Feminine Mystique,* each unhappy housewife in our mothers' generation thought her unhappiness proved that she was ungrateful, selfish, and unwomanly; each was isolated by that fear, because she wasn't about to tell anyone else about her "failings." These days, stay-at-home mothers are in pretty much that same position, and mothers who also have paid employment are likely to talk to their daughters about how overwhelmed they feel by their double workload.

Small wonder, then, that mothers often turn to their daughters for attention, support, companionship, and, indirectly, confirmation that they are good, lovable mothers. Daughters more than sons are likely to fulfill these roles because they are taught to be nurturing and sensitive to other people's needs. In spite of some changes in the gendered basis of much child-rearing, this pattern remains even in the new millennium. According to Larissa, whose daughter is now a grown woman:

> My daughter was always my best friend. She was such a good, sympathetic listener—even when she was little. We'd have long talks while she helped me wax the floor or put up preserves. I don't know what I would have done without her.

The daughter in such a situation may begin to hide her own needs for nurturance as she tries to meet her mother's needs; then those invisible needs go largely unmet, and she feels insufficiently nurtured. When the daughter grows up, she too may become a mother who turns to her daughter for solace.

Mothers and daughters often describe this development as "My mother is more like a friend to me than a mother." Such a relationship can provide a great deal of genuine closeness and sharing, but it becomes a problem if it involves a total reversal of roles so that the daughter always takes care of the mother. More dangerous than a moderate degree of role reversal is mental health professionals' claim that any daughter's nurturance of her mother is a sign of "fusion," of pathology, because this claim sullies the loving give-and-take that can characterize such relationships. (This point is the subject of Myth Eight.)

The mother-daughter role reversal occurs partly because the daughter takes care of her mother and partly because, in some ways, mothers tend to nurture daughters less than sons. Although Renate is now in her late twenties, her recollection of this aspect of her mother's treatment of her is still painful:

> When I was seven years old and my brother was nine, he got more attention from Mama than I did—even when I was sick! When he was sick, she'd stop everything, make him chicken soup, and sit on his bed, playing board games and cards with him. But when I was sick, I just got the soup. She'd say, "Renate's so good at entertaining herself when she's sick." I really had no choice, because she never took the trouble to entertain me.
>
> I know that Mama loved me, and I knew it then. What hurt wasn't thinking she didn't care about me but feeling like I needed from her some attention that she was proud of me for supposedly not needing—yet it was obviously a great pleasure for her to give that kind of attention to my brother.
>
> And then, whenever Mama was sick, my brother was nowhere to be found. I was expected to take care of Mama, but no one ever gave me credit for it. As she told Papa, "You don't need to take care of me. Renate's my daughter: she's supposed to be my right arm—and she sure is." She'd beam proudly when she said that, and I felt at once glad to be doing what she wanted, glad to be her "right arm," but wistful because I had to be so grown-up all the time. It never felt OK for me to need to be taken care of, and I was hurt because I thought she wasn't particularly interested in doing that for me.

Any time a daughter spends providing nurturance is time that she is not receiving it, and this can leave her feeling her own needs are unmeetable. Then she becomes a mother and is supposed to give her infant the nurturance that she feels she never had. It is like asking a starving woman to serve a feast.

In addition, the presence of her infant daughter consciously or unconsciously brings back the mother's memories of her feelings of being neglected, so that her loneliness reemerges just when she is trying to take responsibility for her newborn. The combination of feelings can make it difficult to relax and love a baby. If that baby is not nurtured enough, the cycle is perpetuated. Woman after woman grows up feeling as though she will never be loved enough.

If mother and daughter understand why each other's needs may seem unlimited, we won't be driven apart by this fear. But when mothers and daughters believe the myth of women's neediness, the myth creates a barrier between them; believing the myth, each is terrified of being sucked dry by the other's allegedly limitless needs. Each feels daunted by the prospect of being expected to provide sufficient nurturing to the other; and each is likely to misread some need in the other as boundless need. Diane and Marie, a mother and daughter I interviewed, described the way this dynamic appeared in their relationship:

DIANE: When Marie was fifteen and her first real boyfriend broke up with her, I thought she'd never stop crying. At first, I held her and patted her back, but after an hour she was still sobbing. I felt so helpless. She seemed to need so much more than I could give her. But, then, she'd always been like that, needing me so much, and I never felt up to the task. Sometimes I'd just run to my room and close the door. I couldn't stand to see her when she was so needy.

MARIE: I felt the same way about her. One night when I was about seven, I saw Mom leaning on Dad and crying. She was saying, "I'm just a miserable, unhappy person." I don't know why she was upset, and she wasn't asking me for help. But she was always saying how great a help I was to her, how loving and sensitive I was, and I felt like I should have been able to make her happy.

Both Diane and Marie fell into the common trap of believing that we have to do something when someone close to us is upset. Often, the best thing to do is simply to be present and listen, or wait empathically and lovingly. We feel helpless and useless if we believe we should be able to banish their pain. Marie had an added burden: no one, including her mother, had taught her that children are not supposed to be able to solve adults' problems.

Passing On the Emptiness

A case conference in which I participated involved four generations of women and shows how the emptiness is passed on and
how it is blamed on mothers but not on fathers. The reason for the
family's presence at the clinic was that the eight-year-old daughter
was depressed, and the head therapist wanted to understand the
family's history and dynamics before recommending treatment.

I'll call the grandmother Bree, the mother Resa, and the daughter Rosemary. According to the mother and grandmother, the great-
grandfather (Bree's father) was jovial, and the great-grandmother
was cold and hard. Bree married Cesar, a cordial but deeply depressed man. When they had children, Bree was determined that
they not feel rejected by her, as her mother had made her feel; but
she was unable to respond to their needs for warmth, since she
took her father as a role model and acted jovial and chipper—but
not warm. As her daughter Resa grew up, she planned never to
have children, because she sensed that, like her mother, she had
little love to offer.

Resa did have a daughter, however, and she found the child primarily an obstacle to the satisfaction of her own needs. She went
through the motions, doing a few of the "right things," like buying
Rosemary clothes; but the relationship between mother and
daughter was basically empty, punctuated by frequent angry outbursts on both sides.

In the conference, the chief psychiatrist laid all the blame for
Rosemary's depression on the unmet emotional needs of the generations of women, each of whom focused more on her own needs
than on those of her children. Neither the psychiatrist nor the
women in the family asked, "Where was Bree's father's warmth?
Did he even spend time with his family? Is he remembered as
jovial rather than jovial-but-remote because as a man he wasn't
expected to be any more? And aren't Cesar's passivity and depression as likely contributors to Resa's brittleness as Bree's frenetic,
chipper style?" After all, depression seriously limits the emotional
resources one can offer. Bree and Resa bear intense ill will toward
their own mothers, because of their "unmeetable needs," and both
idealize their fathers.

When Rosemary began spending more time with her father, a loving parent, her depression began to lift, and she became more outgoing. What we can learn is that either a mother's or a father's neediness can harm a child, and either parent's love can help. This is an important lesson when we consider that therapists usually involve a troubled child's mother in therapy but rarely try very hard to involve the father. This traditional approach exaggerates the impact of the mother's neediness and overlooks the potential for fathers to meet their children's needs.

Myth Eight: Mother–Daughter Closeness Is Unhealthy

Women love connection. But in a society that is phobic about intimacy and extols the virtues of independence, we mistakenly regard connection and closeness as "dependency," "fusion," and "merging." So most mothers worry that they are keeping their children too dependent on them. When her child cries as she is left for the first day of nursery school or camp, the mother fears that she has failed; she feels ashamed of her child's "dependence" on her and her "need to tie her child to her."

We live in a culture that values independence and rationality over closeness and emotionality. Furthermore, men are usually considered independent and rational, whereas women are considered dependent, eager for closeness, and emotional.

Given these assumptions, relationships between two women are often regarded as overly dependent, because both are presumed to be unhealthily interested in closeness. In mother-daughter relationships, the danger of being branded "dependent" is intensified still more. An infant or young daughter is inevitably dependent on her mother. Even though mothers and daughters usually become more independent as the daughter grows up, they believe the myth and fear that they will be criticized or ridiculed for being "too close." The mother of a first-year college student explained, "Laura and I have always been so close. Since she left for college last month, every time I walk by her room, I get all weepy. I know I shouldn't feel that way. I guess we've been too close." Unfortunately, no one assured this mother that her reaction was a normal, human response to separation from a loved one, not a sign of too much closeness.

Similarly, for the mother whose child cries on the first day of school, memories of her own sadness the first day of school flood back, and she believes she is repeating the mistakes her mother made with her: "If only my mother had made me more independent," she thinks, "I'd know how to do that for my child." She blames her mother and herself.

But this thinking is destructive, because far more of mothers' and children's behavior is within the normal range than we have dared to believe. Sadness about separation the first day of school or camp is usually a sign of a mother-child relationship that is loving and worth holding onto, the security that comes from feeling you can turn to your mother, and a healthy fear of the unknown. How different would we feel if we lived in a society that encouraged us, on seeing a weeping child the first day of school, to think, How sad for the child and the mother—but how lovely that they care enough about each other that it is hard to part! Do we really believe that sadness about mother-child separation is pathological, whereas sadness about the loss of a spouse is normal?

Despite the unreasonableness of "overly dependent," "fused," or "engulfing" as descriptions of most mother-daughter relationships, the belief that mothers and daughters cannot see themselves as separate from each other is pervasive. Many mothers and daughters accept this description of their relationship as accurate. We worry that any closeness between us proves that we are fused, but on the other hand, any distance between us or interruption of closeness is unfeminine, because women are supposed to be loving.

In our culture, growing boys are encouraged to become increasingly different from their mothers; growing up, for boys, means leaving the world represented by mother and the female culture in order to become a real man. A woman who remains close to her mother may be considered too dependent but is not accused of being unfeminine for that reason. So daughters get the message both that we are too dependent on our mothers and that we are supposed to stay close to them, though staying close is mislabeled "dependency." Mother and daughter cannot win. There is no room for our behavior to be considered healthy.

The myth becomes entrenched, then, that—unlike sons, who eventually separate from their mothers and enter the "real" world—daughters and mothers never achieve that separation. The experts assume such dependency to be unhealthy. They believe the daughter enjoys her dependency so much that she cannot grow up, and the mother wants to keep her daughter close to meet her enormous needs. Women patients of therapists with such attitudes are directly affected by this approach, but few women escape the pull of the myth, learning the concept from friends who are in therapy or picking it up in the popular media.

Is it true that mothers and daughters cannot separate from each other? In general, no. On the extremely rare occasion, someone will be unable to recognize that another person is separate from herself; that is indeed a serious problem and a severe psychological disturbance. It is not typical of most mother-daughter relationships. When professionals—or we ourselves—talk about the mother's inability to see her daughter as separate from herself, variously called "mother-daughter fusion," "merging," "enmeshment," "engulfment," or "symbiosis," we're usually referring to a mother's suppression of her own needs in order to tend to other people. But to do that, a woman has to know she is a separate person; otherwise, she mistakenly assumes that the other person's needs are identical to hers. Successful nurturing requires substantial psychological separation of self from other. It's sometimes called "maturity." A mother's suppression of her own feelings can cause problems, but it does not necessarily decrease her sensitivity to her children's needs when they differ from her own.

A New Vision

A major force in encouraging more accurate and positive labeling of women's behavior comes from women like the Wellesley College Stone Center therapists' group (including Judith Jordan, Jean Baker Miller, Irene Stiver, and Janet Surrey—and, until recently, Alexandra Kaplan) and social worker Rachel Josefowitz Siegel. They have noted that the classic, influential theories about child development identify independence and separateness as the goals of emotional maturity. Although some independence is necessary (such as learning to feed and dress oneself, learning to protect one's body from harm), another important track of development has nearly been ignored. The growing ability to form and maintain relationships with other people is necessary both to survive (e.g., learning how to signal an adult when you are hungry so that you will be fed) and to enjoy life fully. Psychologist Janet Surrey calls this "relational ability." Despite the importance of relational ability, any deviation from independence is usually regarded in our culture as an alarming aberration rather than a valuable step toward deepening one's interpersonal relationships.

The Wellesley group has found that "women do not want to separate from their mothers. Even when adolescent daughters and their mothers are in conflict, the daughters usually still report that their mother is their best friend. They want to keep that relationship authentic and add other strong and close relationships." Surrey calls this a "model of growth through addition and enlarging of relations."

Jordan and Surrey point out that closeness involves mutual empathy, and in Surrey's words, mothers and daughters take care of their relationship and find it rewarding: "the self gains vitality and enhancement." In a related point psychologist Kathy Weingarten points out that speaking openly to one's children about one's feelings and dilemmas—often criticized as being "too much" for children to take—does not always involve blurring a crucial boundary but rather is often a way of enhancing intimacy and mutual respect. Irene Stiver suggests that, although the traditional claim is that a young girl must turn away from her mother and attach more closely to her father, this switch—especially when it leads to outright rejection of the mother—is not necessarily healthy or growth-enhancing.

Women who attend seminars given by Siegel, the Wellesley group, and others like them report feeling empowered, warmed, and optimistic about their relationships with their mothers and with other women. Many of us are told that problems with our mothers arise because we are too connected, and so we should move away emotionally; this contradicts the way we have been raised—to establish and maintain connections. We don't always recognize the contradiction; fed by the male superiority myth, we may first react to being told we're too close to our mothers with embarrassed agreement. We may then try to win praise for dissociating ourselves from women and becoming more emotionally distant. Most mothers invest a great deal of effort in enriching connections with their daughters. When daughters mislabel those connections as problems, they tend to distance from their mothers.

Ironically, many therapists and friends who have told us we are too close to our mothers are the same ones who have encouraged our total devotion to the men in our lives. To make a man the center of one's life is not considered pathological, but to be close to one's mother is dangerous.

Homophobia Rears Its Head

Mother-daughter closeness can even be mislabeled unhealthy because of homophobia, a fear of homosexuality that is unfortunately still strong. Mothers often have physical contact with their children, and most find this contact pleasurable. For many North Americans, however, physical contact between any two people is riddled with conflict. Women who are already worried that their own needs are too great become preoccupied with such questions as, When does touching cross the line between affection and sex? Is there such a line? If I feel warmth or pleasure when I touch my baby, is that naughty, selfish, or sinful? Should I not touch her?

Some mothers fear that they themselves have lesbian tendencies, or that their daughters will become lesbians if they provide any physical pleasure for each other. For this reason, many mothers limit their physical and emotional contact with their daughters severely. One woman reported, "My mother announced to me, when I was just old enough to understand what she was saying, that she would no longer hold or kiss me, because it was time I learned not to expect warmth from the world." This woman said that her mother did not treat her sons in that way but did the same with her other two daughters.

One of my students described a poignant, early memory:

> I was five years old, and my family was at a picnic. . . . We had just finished eating and had lain down to nap. I moved to curl up next to my mother and to place my head on her chest. She pushed me off curtly, telling me that I was too old for that sort of thing anymore. I moved away, hurt and angry.

Her hurt and anger have only recently begun to subside. She realizes that her mother hadn't loved her any less but had been trying to do the right thing by physically distancing herself.

In some cases, someone other than the mother may set the limits. Some fathers may intrude because they are jealous of their wives' physical closeness to their daughters. Regardless of how much her mother then retreats, the daughter usually believes that her mother wants the distance. Not understanding society's prohibitions against homosexuality, daughter knows only that mother has rejected her. Children typically respond to rejection by wondering, What did I do to make her love me less? Since we don't like to be around people who make us feel unloved (although we may keep trying to win their affection), we back away from our mothers.

In contrast, mothers and sons are encouraged to maintain some sensual/sexual tension between them, because our society is heterosexually oriented. Furthermore, because men tend to regard women as inferior, many women long for a close relationship with a male in which she can have some vicarious power. A mother's relationship with her son makes this possible. Out of her need to be needed by him she may intensify her nurturing, boasting that her son never lifts a finger to help in the house. According to the French writer Colette, her mother, Sido, said this about her daughter and son: "Yes, yes, of course you love me, but you're a girl, a female creature of my own species, my rival. But in his heart I never had any rival."

The myth that mother-daughter closeness is unhealthy is enormously destructive because it pathologizes what is probably women's greatest source of strength—the capacity to form loving, mutually supportive relationships.

Myth Nine: Women's Power Is Dangerous

Women's power is generally assumed to be dangerous, but men's is not. This is ironic. While most of women's power is used for other people's benefit—to nurture, protect, and teach—a great deal of men's power is channeled for their own benefit into power lunches, corporate politics, war games, and violence against women. Because women have so much control over us when we are very young, and because mother-blaming is encouraged, many people think that women can control our lives in damaging, destructive ways. Furthermore, any expression of power by members of a low-status group tends to be regarded as too much power.

Some mothers have great power in the family—although if you ask them, few actually feel this power—but even in that sphere, that mothers are more powerful than fathers is a common misperception. According to psychiatrist Dr. Teresa Bernardez, "The reality that marriage is protective of the mental health of men but not of women, that women and girls are increasingly victims of physical and sexual abuse and often found among the poorest of groups, is in stark contrast with the mythical power assigned to women in the family."

Mothers are among the most powerless people in our whole society; they know that most of their mothering work is undervalued or unnoticed. Furthermore, once we understand how truly powerless our mothers feel, we see the power they have over us in a different light.

When women feel powerful as mothers, they are usually terrified that their power is destructive. And daughters often think of mothers' power in negative terms: "She has the power to make me feel totally worthless, just by looking at me the wrong way." We don't think of the positive side of our mothers' power over us— their support, nurturance, and even empowerment of us—partly because mothers have so little power in the world outside the home and partly because motherwork gets so little respect.

Women in therapy frequently believe their mother's power is dangerous. Fifty-three-year-old Margo wrote to me,

> Every time I've made a major decision, I've dreaded telling Mother about it. It makes no sense, because she's always been supportive— and I haven't dreaded telling Dad, although he's sometimes been very skeptical about my judgment. I don't exactly know what has frightened me about Mother. It wasn't just the fear of disappointment if she didn't approve of me. It went beyond that. I really felt, somehow, that she had the power to destroy me.

We fear our mothers' power partly because we remember the great power she had over us when we were young. That fear may also be fed by our images of mothers as the bearers of life and our association of the power to give life with the power to take it away. When our mother said we children had done something wrong, we were pretty helpless: we could not argue, we could not remind ourselves that she was simply invoking a specific set of moral standards with which others might disagree. Her words were law. She had so much information that we didn't have but longed to know; she presented most of the world to us when we were very young. Most of what she told us was true ("That is a doggie"), important ("Don't cross on the red light"), or interesting ("No two snowflakes are exactly alike"). To some extent, she still has the power of knowledge, because she's been through things that we haven't— empty nest, a fifty-year marriage, aging, and so on.

Adult daughters often react to their mothers as though they (the daughters) were still powerless: "She makes me feel like an adolescent again when I visit her!" We must remind ourselves at crucial times that we are no longer as powerless as children—we can feed and clothe ourselves, look elsewhere for love, support, and approval if they aren't currently forthcoming from Mother.

One way to achieve a realistic perspective on our mother's power is to understand that her anger and tension are not always our fault. As long as we believe ourselves the major source of her anger or tension, she retains the power to make us feel deeply evil. Years ago, when I was waiting to hear whether I had gotten a particular job, I felt I was screaming at Jeremy and Emily all the time. I tried desperately to counteract this by saying, "Oh, kids, it's not you. I'm just so worried about this job." When our mother yells at us, we find it hard to believe the yelling is not really aimed at us in particular, not a sign of our failings; it's even harder when we are children.

When a mother seems to wield undue power over her daughter, the real reason is often hidden. It may be misdirected rage; many women suppress such anger to appear feminine or to avoid male violence or because they're not sure their anger is justified ("Have I the right to be angry that he never takes the kids to the doctor?"). Sometimes a mother takes out on her daughter her frustration about the thousand limits being a woman imposes on her own life, but few mothers are aware of this until it's pointed out. In my workshops, I ask mothers how they feel about teaching their daughters "feminine" behavior. Out pour the stories of ambivalence and pain: "Every time I tell her not to let men know how high her salary is, I feel confused. I don't want her to scare men off, but she shouldn't have to hide her accomplishments." What may have seemed to this woman's daughter like her mother wielding undue power over her was really her mother trying desperately to transmit social expectations to her.

Strange though it may seem, mothers often fear their daughters' power, too. As the forty-one-year-old mother of a teenage girl told me, "I know she notices everything about me, all my faults. No one knows my weak points better than Bonnie, and no one can be more ruthless about pointing them out." Our culture casts both women and girls in the role of enforcing social rules (see chapter 4); this endows both mothers and daughters with the dangerous power to spot deviations and shame the deviator. Mothers and daughters fear each other's power because each generation has knowledge that the other one does not. A daughter can make her mother feel like a fool because of what she does not know—"You haven't heard the latest?!" The mother possesses knowledge and wisdom not yet acquired by her daughter, intensifying the daughter's resentment of her mother's power. Knowledge does confer some power on each.

When my daughter Emily was nine years old and my son Jeremy was eleven, I learned how little I noticed my power to make them feel good (although I worried constantly about my power to upset them). I was taking them to weekly tennis lessons. Knowing nothing about tennis, I asked their teacher how they were doing; he replied that they were doing well but that Emily's progress was limited by her age and size. He said, "As she grows she'll be able to do more and will be less frustrated."

On account of this information, my admiration for Emily grew. As I watched her try gamely to do what I now realized was extremely difficult for her, I felt very proud of what a good sport she was. When the class took a break, I said to her, "Emily, your teacher said that what you are doing is very hard for nine-year-olds. I really admire you, because you keep trying even though it is harder for you than for the other kids." I wasn't sure that she had listened to what I said. Many days later, Emily came up to me and asked, "Do you really admire me because I try hard at tennis?" and she looked delighted when I confirmed that I did.

That incident impressed upon me the power to do good that we have over our children. My remark had stayed with her for a long time. It had mattered. We mothers are often surprised by our power to affect our children in positive ways, partly because our good mothering work is often ignored—until we forget to do it.

Like most mothers, I had believed that women's power is dangerous; even after the incident with Emily, I couldn't just relax and enjoy the beneficial effect I had had on her. Recognizing my power scared me to death, since like most mothers I felt that in most of my child-rearing I was just scraping by, lucky to avoid messing Emily and Jeremy up completely. So it seemed to me very likely that my power would have some damaging consequences.

A woman is supposed to give nurturance (Myth Two), to live up to the role of giver and protector of life. But anyone who has a lot to give can inspire fear in those she nurtures; if she has the power to make them feel secure, then she can also pull the rug out from under them. If she withholds nurturance, their sense of security can collapse.

As we acknowledge that our mothers' power may be less dangerous and more growth-enhancing than we had believed, we can become better allies. Furthermore, changing our assessment of our mothers' power can improve our feelings about our own power. Twenty-five-year-old Lillian told me after a workshop on mothers and daughters, "Now that I've had a chance to focus on some of the specific times that my mother ingeniously used her power to protect us from our abusive father, I seem to feel better about my own use of power. It doesn't scare me so much to think of myself as a powerful woman."

Fearing women's power over us more than men's is unwarranted, especially because the frequency of violent acts men commit against women, combined with men's greater political and economic power, certainly justifies some fear of men's power. We assume our mothers' power is evil, but we're less likely to assume that about our fathers' power—unless, perhaps, he is physically or sexually abusive (although, as noted, even daughters of those fathers often manage to forgive their fathers and accuse their mothers instead).

The more self-confidence we have, and the more we feel loved and supported by other people, the less we fear anyone's power and the stronger we can be in urging them to use their power for good. As we improve our relationships with our mothers, our fear of their power, and of anyone else's, will diminish.

Myth Ten: Both Stay-at-Home Mothers and Mothers with Paid Jobs Are Bad Mothers

During the Eisenhower era, the dominant idealized image of Anglo mothers was the stay-at-home Mom, whereas today it is widely understood that most mothers also have paid jobs. Despite the ideal during the Eisenhower years, the reality was that the majority of Black and working-class mothers had paid jobs—and indeed, had no other choice. Today, despite the fact that most mothers do paid work, there remains a substantial proportion of mothers with children living at home who have no paid employment. But in neither era has either group been considered good mothers.

This myth reminds me of the story told to me years ago by Ursula Franklin, a pioneer in academia who became a full professor of metallurgy when there were scarcely any women in the field of engineering. At the first parents' night in her daughter Monica's new school, Professor Franklin asked the teacher to introduce her to "Monica's new friend Emma's mother, that paragon of virtue who stays home, bakes cookies, and takes her kids to the park." The teacher smiled. Emma's mother had told the teacher she wanted to meet Monica's mother, whom Emma described as a paragon of virtue "who gives Monica responsibilities and isn't always breathing down her neck, asking, 'Why are you home late from school?'"

Probably the major reason that some women choose to be stay-at-home mothers and that mothers with paid jobs feel worried and anxious is the notion that mothers need to be spending as much time as possible with their children. However, Ellen Galinsky reports in her new book, *Ask the Children,* that her research reveals that only 10 percent of children want more time with their mothers than they presently get, and children of stay-at-home mothers do *not* regard their mothers as more supportive than do children of mothers with paid work. But as long as mothers are the major targets of blame for whatever happens to their children, it seems unlikely that mothers' fears will be much reduced by these data, any more than the fear and guilt of mothers with paid jobs have been abolished by the many studies showing that having a "working mother" does not harm children. Why? Because studies of other people's children are hard to consider when one knows one will be blamed if anything goes wrong with one's own child. A mother's concern both for her child's welfare and her own wish not to be responsible for harming her child make it more difficult to take these important research results into account.

The Blaming of Stay-at-Home Mothers

Stay-at-home mothers who are independently wealthy (rare cases) or financially supported by a husband or other relative are often assumed to be variously overinvolved with their children, "pushy" mothers, lazy, poor role models for the Superwomen their daughters should aim to be, and boring to their husbands. The irony is that most of those images are antitheses of the reality of most stay-at-home mothers, given the pressure on them to provide intellectual stimulation, terrific nutrition (including homemade bread), moral education, the best possible birthday parties, participation in a wide enough variety of extracurricular activities and cultural exposures to get them into the best colleges, chauffeuring to and from all of the above, and a clean and tidy home—what Arlie Russell Hochschild calls "a seemingly limitless list of activities."

Stay-at-home mothers who are poor or on welfare—one-fifth of U.S. children live at or below the poverty line—are likely to be considered "rotten mothers" and lazy parasites undeserving of even a welfare check, although welfare checks *plus food stamps* fail to bring families up to the rock-bottom poverty level, a level at which no antiwelfare politician would want to live and which has been steadily declining for decades. Then there is the familiar claim that poor mothers intentionally have many children to increase their government support checks, a powerfully resilient claim despite the fact that the average mother receiving Aid for Families with Dependent Children has two children. As for the "lazy" image, recent statistics showed that three-fourths of welfare recipients had recent work histories. Furthermore, poor mothers who want to obtain an education to improve their own and their children's lives find themselves in a horrendous double bind: If they go on welfare to survive until they can graduate from high school or college, they and their children become the "undeserving poor," but if they do not go on welfare they cannot get that schooling. Finally, poor mothers in general and mothers from racialized groups in particular have been blamed for a host of social ills, including delinquency, drug abuse, and violence; but this blame has come from politicians (and their supporters) who have consistently voted down proposals that would improve the lives of these mothers and their children and include practical steps to solve their social problems.

African-American and other racialized women have had to cope with the added racist—and false—assumption that they account for the vast majority of welfare recipients. Furthermore, one reason many of these women are on welfare is that Black women are underpaid relative to white women, who are underpaid relative to white men. But this does not stop the blaming of individual mothers as though they, rather than the racist society, were at fault.

Apparently alarmed by Second Wave feminism, political conservatives and many major media figures began to promote the notion that feminists considered mothers worthless and the stay-at-home mother particularly shameful. Many feminists are frequently asked why feminists don't believe in motherhood. The truth is that the vast majority of feminists have always believed that motherhood is important but that becoming a mother should be a woman's choice made as freely as possible, as should whether or not to stay at home with her children. Finally, most feminists have believed that motherwork deserves great respect. As Alix Kates Shulman said in an interview, "I never felt any conflict between the [feminist] movement and motherhood. Feminism healed my conflicts. . . . In fact, it was as a mother that I most deeply engaged with feminists. I spoke up for mothers, defended mothers." How ironic it is that the authors of the book that includes the Shulman quotation wrongly accuse Second Wave feminism of being antimotherhood. Such mistaken assumptions have had the unfortunate effect of making stay-at-home mothers worry that (1) you cannot be a feminist and stay at home with your children, and (2) any feminist they meet—or indeed any-one influenced by a feminist—is likely to look down on them for their choice.

The Blaming of Mothers Who Work for Pay

Any mother who has a paid job will tell you that she constantly feels she is shortchanging both her family and her workplace. Mothers with paid jobs are routinely accused of being insufficient-ly devoted to their children—how can they be, when they are not full-time mothers, not available to be president of the PTA (al-though many paid workers also hold such volunteer positions)? And if—horrors!—a mother works for pay but has no financial need to do so, she is considered totally selfish. Factories and offices are filled with mothers who worry that they are damaging their children by placing them in day care, by being unable to accompany the class to the zoo, failing to be there with a willing ear when teenagers return from school and might want to talk. The fact that few fathers—even in the twenty-first century—chide themselves for their far lower (average) level of involvement in their children's lives does little to alleviate mothers' guilt. Nor is it much alleviated by ample research indicating, for instance, that:

- Day care is not damaging to children and can provide advan-tages, by encouraging social interaction.
- Preteen children of single mothers who have paid jobs regard their families as more cohesive and organized than preteen children of mothers with no jobs.
- Whether or not the mother is employed is not related to chil-dren's development in either the short or the long term; in either case, the quality and quantity of stimulation and of parent-child interactions are the same.

Many mothers are not aware of these research findings, but even those who are often feel terrified of not being perfect moth-ers. So much is at stake. What if their child is unlike most children in responding well to day care or in developing happily with a full-time mother or a mother who also works for pay? Her child's hap-piness is at stake, and what mother wants to risk raising a child who is an unhappy exception? As long as mothers are considered responsible for anything bad that comes to (or from) their children, this pressure cannot possibly abate.

Arlie Russell Hochschild points out, in her aptly titled book *The Time Bind: When Work Becomes Home and Home Becomes Work*, that women find home stressful because mothers still have most responsibility for household and child-related work, that they receive little appreciation or recognition for that work, and that their husbands do little to help out. By contrast, at work they feel more appreciated, have clearer definitions of what is expected of them, are more likely to receive praise (even extra pay) for work well done, and have friends there who provide emotional support and even fun. But mothers can't win; a mother who feels happier and more competent in the workplace will immediately feel ashamed and alarmed, wrongly assuming that this says something about her personal feelings about being a mother rather than about the institution of motherhood and the impossible pressures it involves.

There is plenty that virtually all mothers feel guilty about, whether or not they are working for pay.

Young adult daughters, especially those whose mothers came of age before or during the 1960s, are often surprisingly unaware of how few role models their mothers had for juggling the double load. Only in the past twenty years have more than a handful of women been admitted to engineering, law, and medical schools, not to mention even middle-management corporate jobs and other "nontraditional" fields. A board game from the 1960s called "What Shall I Be?" pictures women's career options as ballerina, stewardess, teacher, actress, nurse, and beauty queen. Young women who were raised in such different times may find it difficult even to conceive of how hard it is for their mothers to go from the context of their early lives to juggling family and paid work. African-American women, most of whom haven't had the option to stay home, have always had to do this juggling, usually while working in the lowest-paid jobs under horrendous conditions. Despite research showing they shouldered the double load effectively, respected by their children for doing so, they have had to struggle against the view by the dominant society that they were "too powerful."

People Are Talking: Seeking Solutions

The branding of stay-at-home mothers as bad mothers probably won't abate until motherwork receives more respect, an unlikely prospect in the near future. But individual women can vigilantly notice when such branding takes place and speak up about its unfairness. Women—and men—individually and in groups, privately and publicly, can support laws and policies to provide practical supports for full-time mothers. These subjects are rarely discussed, because motherwork is low-status work and rarely considered worthy of public discussion or government intervention (except to punish mothers who are considered neglectful or abusive).

In contrast, one of the most encouraging recent changes has been the increased openness with which mothers with paid work talk about their fears and the pressures they feel, a crucial first step toward finding solutions. Several book titles directly address the problem. In *Not Guilty! The Good News about Working Mothers*, Betty Holcomb bemoans the lack of attention paid to the real causes of these women's problems. These issues are also addressed in Joan Peters's *When Mothers Work: Loving Our Children without Sacrificing Ourselves* and Susan Chira's *A Mother's Place: Taking the Debate about Working Mothers beyond Guilt and Blame.*

Myth Ten persists because, in spite of the increased discussion of its dilemma, happy and practical solutions have not yet been found. A look at the most promising will shed light on the continuing nature and pervasiveness of mother-blame.

Beginning with feminism's Second Wave, many people put their hopes in equal sharing of child and household tasks between the sexes. We saw the much-heralded arrival of the New Man, who would do half of such work, making mothering manageable. Media coverage over the years has conveyed the notion that these men are legion, though hardly anyone has actually met one. Research by scholars like Joseph Pleck, a pioneer in tracking this issue, shows that fathers' "engagement time" with children is only two-fifths that of mothers. Although that is an increase from the one-third of more than a decade ago, we might note that work hours per year for the average worker—of either sex—have increased by a month in the past two decades. Thus, the average father does a slightly larger proportion of family work than before, but this has not noticeably decreased the burden on his wife, who is spending far more hours in the workplace while still coping with the ever-expanding list of what "good mothers" do. Furthermore, women's family tasks are disproportionately the daily kind, whereas men, who are more likely to do such things as changing the oil in the car, are less subjected to daily, home-related pressures. In child care, women spend proportionally more time doing maintenance, whereas men do the playing. Women spend more time multitasking family work and, in the views of both themselves and their husbands, have more responsibility for that work. Pleck notes that researchers have "yet to identify any child-care task for which fathers have primary responsibility." Finally, in two-career couples, men, unlike women, tend to keep weekends free for themselves, even if they do family work on weekdays.

A subcategory of Myth Ten is the notion that men would gladly do more family work, but their wives won't let them, because the wives either insist on doing it all themselves or are hypercritical if the men don't do everything exactly as they themselves would. This is a frequent theme in couples therapy, but it usually turns out that two factors are at play. One is that women feel ashamed not to be Superwomen who can do it all without a whimper or a hair out of place; they worry, What does it say about me as mother and wife if he helps? The other is that, no doubt due to the way men are socialized, a man who deeply and genuinely believes that family work is a shared responsibility is a rarity. Men usually acknowledge that they don't notice the daily work that needs to be done, that they are tired after work (as though their wives are not!), and that they are relieved to be left alone. Women who sense this often choose not to upset their husbands by even suggesting that they share the family workload; such a discussion too often leads to angry arguments. To keep the peace, many women work away on their own. As for the image of women as "controlling" because they insist that things be done "the right way," I cannot tell you how many husbands have acknowledged in couples therapy that they either honestly don't notice or don't care whether they have cleaned the baby's bottom completely; the really brave ones will admit that at some level they botch the job, hoping that they won't be asked to do it again. How poignant that women who cannot persuade their husbands to share the work at home feel as though *they* have failed, as though they haven't discovered yet how to be persuasive (while avoiding turning into a harridan).

While we wait (and work) for things to get better at home, it would be terrific to think that things are getting better on the job. We've heard about alleged transformations of the workplace to make it more "family-friendly," including implementation of family leave, flex-time, and flex-place (doing office work at home). But in fact men rarely take leave time for the birth or adoption of a new baby, and they rarely use flex-time or flex-place or put in requests to switch to part-time work while their children are young. There are understandable reasons for this. By and large, men are paid higher wages than women, so if either member of a heterosexual couple is going to leave work or switch to part-time, it makes economic sense that it be the woman, so these choices are often supported by her. (And researchers have found that part-timers, especially in high-pressure work like in lawyers' offices, are stigmatized.) This does not mean either parent would choose this if the economics were not so skewed, but it looks like society is in for a good long wait before we get to the point of truly equal pay.

Given how often women feel torn between being home and going to work, flex-place would seem especially attractive to mothers. However, workplace work done at home—like motherwork—is likely to be considered not "real work." Furthermore, even in a recent book of interviews with feminist mothers and their daughters, it was disturbing to read how many women who worked outside the home were damned for being absent, while mothers who did paid work at home were damned variously for being "there and not there," failing to set clear boundaries (they asked the children not to disturb them while they worked but then responded when the children spoke to them anyway during that time), or being "too available" by working at home rather than leaving for the workplace. In any case, until more resources like high-quality child care, before- and after-school programs, and eldercare are available, for women to work full-time, part-time, or on flex-time or even flex-place bases will continue to pose more practical problems than for men, who are not held as responsible for either child care or the care of old, ill, or disabled relatives.

Another recent plan for helping with the double workload was implemented for faculty on some U.S. campuses. Realizing that the period of their lives when women faculty need to be publishing at top speed in order to be awarded tenure is also women's prime childbearing and child-rearing time, a few universities implemented a "stop the tenure clock" policy. Traditionally, faculty are required to apply for tenure within a few years after they are hired. If they are not granted tenure fairly soon, they are not rehired. The new policy involved granting a faculty member an extra year before having to apply for or receive tenure right after their child (whether biological or adopted) is born. To ensure sex-fairness and perhaps even encourage men to do more child care, the policy was made available for parents of either sex. What happened? As with most programs primarily targeted (or considered targeted) at women, it quickly lost respectability. Women and especially men were thought to "use" having a child to buy extra time to do their research. In a sense, it was slightly bizarre to create a policy with an extra year for each child; everyone who raises a child knows it takes much more than a year before that workload decreases very much—and one even gets a good night's sleep. But although in reality it was not giving parents much of a break, the policy quickly lost respect.

People of either sex who try to use "family-friendly" policies are likely to be thought of as not taking their work seriously, wanting special favors, and wanting time to "goof off." Unless both top and middle management fully support such policies and take active steps to ensure that people who use them are not punished in concrete ways (demotions, lack of bonus pay or raises, and so on) or made to feel uncomfortable, the understandable fears of workers of both sexes will create huge barriers to using them. It is crucial as well to understand that the workers who have the lowest status and wages are the least likely to be offered "family-friendly" benefits and, even when they are offered, the least likely to be in a position to use them.

Does Society Really Care?

In a daring article nearly a decade ago, psychologist Louise Silverstein challenged us to focus debate and research on day care and maternal employment not on their possible negative consequences, but on the consequences of *not* providing high-quality, affordable day care. This would begin to address a major dilemma faced by mothers. But ten years later, this change in focus has barely begun. It is easy to see how a society that clings to mother-blaming might be reluctant to give up the former approach and afraid of what we might find out if we make the switch.

Our refusal as a society to address these issues hits the poor the hardest; 90 percent of American mothers have no choice about whether to do paid work. The paucity of good-quality, affordable day care, the continuing obstacles in most workplaces to being a mother and a paid worker, and the failure of men to share both family work and a belief in their responsibility for that work leave most mothers feeling isolated and overwhelmed.

In spite of this, the media imply that a mother with a paid job either succeeds or fails at combining the two solely because of her own, individual competence. That implication makes the woman who, for whatever reason, is a stay-at-home mother feel ashamed that *she* is not doing both.

Still worse, as Pamela Trotman Reid, Valora Washington, and Patricia Hill Collins point out, women have been set up against each other: the "white" mother with the double load is the Supermom, impossible for real women to match, whereas the African-American mother with the double load is likely to be stigmatized as a "too-powerful," emasculating, matriarchal woman. Washington notes further that while the vast majority of African-American mothers have historically had no choice about whether to work for pay, as the proportion of white women lacking this choice increases, the pejorative labels used for the "working mother" have begun to soften.

The daughters of mothers with paid jobs seem to be making progress in going beyond Myth Ten, though this progress is not uniform or smooth, as shown by the reactions of two daughters of one such mother, quoted in a recent book. When Trina Stevens's mother was at work, she said, "I missed my mother, but I wasn't lonely or scared. I understood why she had to work, and I didn't feel neglected. My father was gone and somebody had to provide for us." Her sister, Kianga Stroud, however, resented her mother for being away and felt neglected.

I was grateful and relieved that when my daughter Emily, while in grade school, was asked in a television interview whether it upset her that I left home each weekday to go to work, she looked surprised by the question and replied, "No, because I know she enjoys it, and she tells interesting stories when she gets home." But children who develop such attitudes still do so against a strong tide that pushes them toward blaming their mothers and their mothers' work for anything that goes wrong.

A Final Note about Myth Ten

It is no accident that most of the discussion of Myth Ten has been focused on mothers with paid jobs rather than stay-at-home mothers. This is partly because so little has been done to address the demeaning treatment of stay-at-home mothers that there is sadly little to discuss. However, it is crucial to remind ourselves that nearly everything said in the rest of this book about mother-blame applies with great force to stay-at-home moms.

Asking Questions about the Bad Mother Myths

As you think through what has happened in your mother-daughter relationship, and as you try to understand what is happening now, ask yourself these important questions:

- How can we lower the barriers between us while we still believe that men are better than women, that only the experts really know how to raise children, that mothers and daughters are bottomless pits of emotional need, that mother-daughter closeness is unhealthy, that mother's and daughter's power is dangerous, and that all mothers are bad?
- Can we stop automatically making negative assumptions about women? This form of prejudice is as troubling as any other.

Thinking carefully about the myths enables us to reinterpret our mothers' (or daughters') behavior in a better and more realistic light. For instance, when we think our mothers can't let us go, are trying to merge with us or keep us dependent on them (Myth Eight), we are tempted to blame them. If we realize instead that they are attempting to maintain a close relationship with us, then we realize our potential to be allies, understanding that we are shaped to label our interactions negatively and to demean both ourselves and each other. As allies rather than adversaries, we can better deal with frustrating or inhibiting aspects of the relationship, using the fine skills of communication and empathy that so many women have developed.

In some ways, the Bad Mother myths make it even harder than the Perfect Mother myths to see our mothers' humanity. But once we get some inkling of the pervasiveness and the power of the Bad Mother myths, we can begin to see how ludicrous they are. Turning back to the start of this chapter and reading these six myths aloud, all in a rush, is a good beginning; just doing that may show you clearly that very few human beings are so horrendous.

Then think about one myth at a time while assuming that most mothers are merely human. Take the male superiority myth: it can't really be true that most mothers are vastly inferior to fathers. As for the myth that only the experts know how to raise children, hasn't your mother done some good things, perhaps even against the advice of the experts? When we are tempted to believe that mothers and daughters are bottomless pits of emotional need, can't we recall unjustly equating our mothers' and our own normal, human needs with boundless neediness? When we think about times we have felt close to our mothers, hasn't some of that enhanced our growth rather than tying us tighter to their apron strings? And aren't there occasions when the constructive, loving aspects of mothers' (or daughters') power were clearer to us than the destructive ones?

I am not suggesting that we replace a pessimistic but realistic approach to mother-daughter relationships with a blindly optimistic one. I am suggesting that we look at what works to break down mother-daughter barriers so that both mothers and daughters feel better about themselves. The woman-blaming, woman-hating messages are tantalizing. They tempt women with the promise that if we dissociate ourselves from our mothers, we will be regarded as different from, and better than, they. By now we are depressingly familiar with the approach that divides women against each other. It is dangerous. It promotes both mother-blame and self-hate, in dramatic contrast to the empowering consequences of thinking about women in positive ways.

We cannot always distinguish fully when mother or daughter really has done something bad or wrong from when the myth alone has made us think so. The key is always to ask ourselves whether one or more myths *might* be distorting our view, for that enterprise of asking will at least bring us closer to the truth. Because having poor opinions of each other is so destructive to the mother-daughter relationship and to both mothers' and daughters' self-esteem, we should usually err on the side of giving each other the benefit of the doubt.

The Either-Or Tightrope

The coexistence of the myth that mothers are endlessly giving (Myth Two) and the myth that mothers are endlessly needy and demanding (Myth Seven) dramatically illustrates the narrow band of acceptable behavior for mothers; together, these myths make us misconstrue even modest needs in our mothers and daughters as unmeetable ones and misconstrue less than total support from them as emotional miserliness or even betrayal. Any giving that mothers fail to do becomes a sign that they are unnatural and unwomanly; conversely, even their normal desires become proof that their needs are unmeetable. Working in concert, the two myths pressure women to give unceasingly and to ask for nothing for themselves.

The narrowness of the band of acceptable behavior for mothers is part of the narrowness of that band for women in general. Women are caught between two sets of labels provided by society: the seductive-submissive-admiring-compliant label (what I'll call Type One) and the powerful-dominant-bitchy-cold-castrating label (Type Two). Who can imagine wanting to be classified either way? Mothers who try to live up to the Perfect Mother myths are likely to be given a Type One label; that is, if they try to be totally self-sacrificing and sweet, they will be considered overly emotional, overinvolved, and smothering. Mothers who don't behave in that way will probably be considered Type Two, rejecting mothers. It is hard to find behavior in mothers that is simply appreciated.

Mothers are tempted to behave in accordance with the Type One labels for several reasons. First, this behavior is considered "feminine." Second, in its milder forms it can be associated with being warm and loving. Third, Type One behavior is more likely to please the people with whom one lives and works than is Type Two behavior.

The crucial issue is not whether mothers spend more time behaving in Type One or Type Two ways; it is that most women—especially mothers—continually monitor their behavior, afraid they are either too warm or too cool, too intrusive or too laissez-faire, toward their children. Every mother I have interviewed describes what I call the Either-Or tightrope that she walks, between feeling she shows her daughter too much love and feeling she doesn't show her enough. If she is loving, is she being "too close" (Myth Eight)? If she is rather reserved, is she failing to be nurturant enough (Myth Two)? In spite of women's protests about these pressures, mothers' psychotherapists, families, and friends have not let up very much on the Either-Or pressure.

Never have I met a mother—no matter how admired by others—who has always felt confident that her mothering was just fine. And my own experience as a mother is the same. "Your child has asthma? Asthma is caused by mothers' overprotectiveness," says a psychologist colleague. "You let your twelve-year-old ride the subway alone? Don't you care about her?" says a well-meaning friend.

Thirty-year-old Susannah came to me for psychotherapy, certain she was a terrible mother because she alternated between "ignoring my kids and smothering them with affection." Like many of my women patients, her biggest problem was her harsh self-judgment: teaching her children to play on their own occasionally was not rejection, and missing them when they visited her ex-husband did not constitute overprotectiveness.

Daughters tend to grasp quickly how the Either-Or dilemma affects their interactions with their mothers: when anything a mother does can be classified in one of two negative ways, then any way she treats her daughter involves the same risk. Mothers walk a tightrope: if their daughters don't do the traditional, feminine, housekeeping tasks, they have failed to be demanding enough; but when their daughters want to help them with these chores, the mothers regard themselves as too demanding and selfish. Many daughters moan, "If I don't offer to wash the dishes after Thanksgiving dinner at Mom's house, she thinks I'm unfeminine and ungrateful. But when I do offer to help, she tells me not to bother, that she doesn't mind doing it, that it's really a one-woman job."

We have been shaped to think about mother-daughter relationships primarily in terms of the myths. Having journeyed through some of the major myths, you now have the beginnings of a new vocabulary, a repertoire of less mother-blaming interpretations of your mother's (or daughter's) behavior. You may not always choose to use your new vocabulary, but you now know that you have a choice.

6

Feeling Safe
Going Beyond the Myths

Now that you have read and thought about the effects that mother-blaming and its myths have had on your relationship with your mother, you may already feel less angry or anguished about her. But you may not yet feel such relief, because intellectual understanding of the myths isn't enough to transform intense, negative feelings that have built up over the decades that you two have spent together. Overcoming the effects of years of conflict, alienation, fear, or guilt can be damned hard, so you may still feel that the best solution is to live three thousand miles away from your mother. Grasping ideas is one thing; putting them into practice is another. As Karen, a young adult student, told me,

> I've learned so much about how I automatically blame Mom for things, and whenever I think about her I feel more compassion and less anger than I used to. But when I actually see her, she still gets to me. I still flare up instantaneously when she says certain things or looks at me in a certain way.

If, since starting to read this book, you've tried to behave differently with your mother or even to think about her differently, without success so far, do not despair. This chapter and the next two will help you begin to make your understanding of mother-blaming and the myths work for you.

First, we shall consider the stakes: how your life can be enriched by building bridges between yourself and your mother and what you stand to lose if you do not. Then, you'll learn ways

to feel safe and secure in rethinking your mother-daughter relationship and possibly in attempting changes directly with your
mother. Next, we'll consider general steps that everyone can take
toward overcoming mother-daughter barriers; these include ensuring that both daughter and mother feel supported and empowered as they start their work together, humanizing the daughter's
image of her mother, and forging an alliance with her. Finally, we
shall look at choosing and defining particular problems that need
work, and deciding how to do that work.

As you read through the remaining chapters, remember that
you can carry out most of the steps on your own, with a partner of
some kind, within a group, or directly with your mother if she is
living. You may need to modify some steps to fit your situation and
suit your style or needs. So I suggest that you read through this
chapter and the next two, noting which steps strike you as most
important or easiest to take, then deciding which order seems best
for you. Remember, too, that many techniques help you toward
more than one goal—for instance, interviewing your mother may
help support and empower either or both of you, it may humanize
your image of her, and it may help you to forge a working alliance.

No one can say it will be easy; but if you conscientiously follow
some of the steps I suggest, which other women have found helpful, the chances are good that you'll soon start to make headway.
My son Jeremy created this proverb: "On a staircase there is only
one real step. The rest are there only to help you along the way."
The one big step you're wanting to take is to improve your relationship with your mother, but you can't expect yourself to take it
in a single bound.

Similarly, if you talk directly to your mother about the problems between you, neither of you should expect always to know
just how to respond immediately, on the spot. Remember the
value of silence and time: allow both her and yourself periods of
silence during which to consider what you have heard, how you
feel, and what you want to do about it. Many unnecessary troubles
come from feeling we have to rush to respond to criticism or a
request from another person. Both daughters and mothers need to
ask for time to be silent, time to wait, time to think and feel things
through before responding. Asking for silence or time is a way to
show respect for each other, a way to say, "Making our relationship

better matters enough to me that I want to accord it time and energy." Since we live in a culture that values quick comebacks, we don't often think to ask for time, but learning to do so can be invaluable in working out problems in relationships.

For some daughters, reading and thinking may feel like enough preparation for talking to their mothers directly. But many daughters need to talk first to other women, partly to rehearse what they want to ask or tell their mothers, partly to learn that their feelings are not unique or weird, and partly to brainstorm. The brainstorming can include hearing how other women feel about their mothers, how those feelings have changed and what changed them, and how other women feel about being mothers.

Fundamentally, most of us want to be less angry, to feel closer and more relaxed in our relationships with our mothers. Life is easier when any relationship is like that. But we lose sight of that goal because we easily get caught up in laying blame or withdrawing altogether.

Most daughters will tell you, when they're frustrated, "You don't know *my* mother. She's unbelievably manipulative, overbearing, dependent, cold, critical," and so on. Most daughters will also tell you they've tried for decades to have Big Talks with her, to no avail. If you ask daughters to describe these Big Talks, usually they'll say they told Mother, "Stop hanging on to me," "Stop telling me how to run my life," "Stop being so critical of me," and so on. Rarely does a daughter (or a mother) come right out and say, "I want to mend fences, to bridge the chasm between us. I want us to be closer . . . under certain conditions, yes, but closer and more relaxed." Saying that is absolutely crucial, because it puts you and your mother on the same team.

Why is knowing you're on the same side so important? Because we become defensive or paranoid if we believe that the other person wants to hurt us or protect herself no matter the cost to us. Once a daughter is committed to improving her relationship with her mother, her mother is likely to sense that commitment even before the daughter talks about it. If mother and daughter both want to improve their relationship, their shared vision of a better future can take them a long way. The way to a better relationship isn't always smooth and permanent. There will be struggles and intermittent backsliding. Hanging on to the knowledge of your commitment and your goal will help you through those rough times and keep you from giving up and losing the progress you have made.

No matter how much insight you've gained, no matter how energized you feel for improving your mother-daughter relationship, some part of you probably still feels scared. And for some of you, fear, apprehension, and the wish to ignore the whole arena are still paramount.

Considering the Stakes

If part of you wants to avoid thinking about or working on your relationship with your mother, consider these important points:

- You have a lot to lose if you give up.
- You have a lot to gain if you don't give up.

If you give up, you will lose whatever fragments—large or small— of better times that you and your mother might have had. You may also lose the opportunity to understand and accept the good parts of you that are like your mother. Lie down in a quiet room, and imagine the consequences of giving up. Try to picture them as vividly as you can. Imagine the next holiday or the next family gathering—notice the knot that forms in your stomach as you recall the anger, sadness, or alienation that you feel in her presence. Remember the exasperation you have felt when you thought you could do nothing to lessen these feelings. Ask yourself whether you want to feel so bad and so powerless again.

You may want to consider the ultimate question: how you will feel when your mother dies. At that time, most daughters who have given up feel terribly guilty, and many feel frustrated and angry that they have no further opportunity to make the relationship better. This lost chance is especially poignant, because after a person dies, our warmest, most positive memories of them are the ones that tend to flood back. A woman in her midsixties described this process:

> My mother died after a three-year illness that gradually wore her down and changed her whole personality. She went from her warm, energetic self to being sharp, irritable, and passive. During those three years I was absorbed in adjusting to the changes in her.

But after she died, wonderful memories of the mother I knew for more than fifty-five years came back to me.

The most important message I have heard from women whose mothers have died is that the attempt to resolve remaining problems is essential. As Kenna said,

When my mother told me she had only six months to live, we used the time well. Our relationship had always been stormy, and we never saw eye-to-eye on many moral and political issues. But during her last months, our love and respect for each other remained clear and strong, even though we could not overcome all the problems between us. After she died, what mattered most was knowing that we had done our best to resolve our problems. We had really tried.

When you attempt to repair your relationship with your mother—or revise your vision of it—you'll be better able to retain its warm, funny, or loving aspects, and you'll feel better about yourself. Imminent death isn't always enough to enable mothers and daughters to break down all of the barriers between them. Some cold or rigid mothers become even more so as death approaches, but a daughter who has tried her best to break down the barriers is likely to be left with enriched memories of her mother and thereby increase her understanding of herself.

On a less dramatic scale, more than twenty-five years ago my mother and I were uncharacteristically reticent with each other, leading to unnecessary emotional distance between us around the time that Jeremy, my first child, was born. My parents, who lived a thousand miles away, came to visit a few weeks after the birth. Years later, I told my mother that I had been hurt because she hadn't offered to come immediately when Jeremy was born. She explained that she had feared that, if she offered to come right away, I would think she was intrusive and overprotective or lacked confidence in my mothering ability, so she had decided to wait until I asked her. I hadn't asked her to come right away, both because I was afraid of seeming too needy and because I thought that mothering came naturally, so I shouldn't need anyone at all.

If myths about women's neediness, women's power, and the

naturalness of mothering hadn't gotten in our way, and if we hadn't kept silent about that incident for so many years, we would have understood each other a lot better. Telling each other at the time about our concerns would have enabled us to base our decisions on real considerations rather than on fears about how our behavior might be misinterpreted or what it might "prove" about us.

If you don't give up on your mother-daughter relationship, you can gain the increased warmth and satisfaction that come from trying to improve relationships and the enhanced self-esteem that comes from finding qualities in your mother that you can respect and love. Since we so often think of ourselves as like our mothers, finding more to respect in them increases our self-respect. When we improve our relationships with our mothers, we feel like competent people who can have some effect on the world; if we can make real changes, no matter how tentative or small, in that relationship, we feel able to take on other challenges. We improve the way we get along with other women, including our daughters. If you're reluctant to work on your relationship with your mother, ask yourself what picture of mother-daughter relationships you are presenting to your daughter. Think about whether, if *she* were upset with *you*, you would want her to give up.

Lying down in a quiet room, imagine the positive results that might come from trying again. For example, call to mind in vivid detail the warmest, loveliest time you ever had with your mother—where you were, the sights, the sounds, the smells. If you were happy once, then perhaps you can be again. Molly, aged twenty, tried this exercise at a time when she and her mother had been "at each other's throats about my brother marrying outside our faith":

> Mother thought what my brother was doing was terrible; I didn't think it was so bad. For months, that issue overshadowed our whole relationship. Whenever Mother came to mind, all I felt was frustration and anger because her attitude was tearing the family apart. When I pictured our nicest time together, I remembered our planning a family reunion when I was twelve years old. We shopped for decorations together, did the cooking, and made a collage of family photographs. I felt warm and happy and close to her.

That memory reminded me that Mother was much more than "the-woman-who-is-causing-anguish-in-the-family."

Some daughters have fewer good memories to draw on. If you are one of them, recalling or finding out things about your mother other than her worst aspects can still be helpful. A student I'll call Nora described her difficult journey toward improved self-respect through understanding of her mother. She wrote in a paper, "I had been seeing my mother as 'crazy' and this was frightening. Would I be crazy, too?" Nora also blamed herself for the physical abuse she had suffered at her mother's hands, as well as the sexual abuse inflicted on her by a neighbor boy when she was four years old.

Nora's efforts to learn more about her mother's life and about what had led her to mistreat Nora paid off. By carefully exploring her own memories and listening to the stories of other abusive mothers, she learned that her mother was overwhelmed by having a large number of children, by her poverty, by her misery in an arranged marriage to a husband who beat her, and by her horror, confusion, and sense of powerlessness when she discovered that Nora had been sexually abused.

Nora's understanding didn't lead her to justify what her mother had done, but it did clarify her view of her mother as a woman who, under enormous pressures, coped in a way that inadvertently hurt Nora. More importantly, Nora realized that neither the sexual nor the physical abuse had been her own fault, nor had she deserved either one.

When someone who has endured the extremes that Nora suffered can feel better about herself by thoroughly exploring her mother's experience, there is certainly hope for those of us who have suffered less grievously at our mothers' hands. Remembering good times with your mother or learning more about her should help you to keep clearly in mind what you have to gain—or regain—as you prepare to work on your mother-daughter relationship. It's the reachable carrot at the end of the stick.

Feeling Safe

Once you have considered what you have to gain from revising your view of your mother or from approaching her again, and what you have to lose by not trying, you have to figure out what will make your approach feel as safe as possible. No matter how strong or optimistic we feel about the task ahead of us, we women too often try to ignore our apprehensiveness, especially about our mothers. The denial doesn't destroy our doubts and fears, however, and they are easier to overcome once we have faced them. You can increase your feeling of safety in three good ways:

1. **Humanize your image of your mother.** Reduce her from Perfect Angel or Wicked Witch, or both, to simply human. Dealing with a real person is always less scary than dealing with a larger-than-life character. Many techniques can help you humanize your mother: they may not all work for you; you will feel more comfortable doing some than others; and you may not need to do them all. Read through the section in chapter 7 on "Humanizing Your Image of Mother," and choose what you think will be most comfortable and effective for you.

2. **If you're balking at the prospect of trying again, try to figure out why that might be.** Are you so angry that you're afraid you'll lose control and do something completely horrible if you try to talk to your mother? If so, reread the section on anger in chapter 2, and try to figure out what feeling underlies your anger. You will probably be more comfortable talking to her about that underlying feeling than about your anger—and you'll likely be more productive, too. You may need to express your anger first in a safe place with a nonjudgmental, non-mother-blaming person, so that your first attempt to reach your mother is not overshadowed by your overwhelming anger.

   Perhaps you're blocked by the fear of further disappointment. You've approached her so many times, and nothing has worked. If so, reread several times the beginning of this chapter. Ask yourself whether you have honestly tried putting your mother and yourself on the same team before bringing up the problems that come between you. (This issue is treated in more detail in the next section of this chapter.)

You may feel too intimidated by your mother to approach her again. If so, try the technique used with great success by psychologist Dr. Albert Ellis. He suggests asking yourself, What's the worst thing that could possibly happen? followed by, If that does happen, it might be painful or humiliating or depressing—BUT IT'S NOT THE END OF THE WORLD! Our relationships with our mothers matter so much to us that we don't often stop to realize that, even if we approach them again and fail utterly, we probably shall survive.

Once you've identified your worst fears, you can take steps to minimize their bad effects. Are you afraid you'll be devastated if you make new efforts to get along with your mother and they don't succeed? Are you afraid she'll reject you or simply not love you any more than she seems to now? Do you fear that you'll burst into tears or explode with anger in front of her or that she'll make you feel guilty or ashamed of yourself? Most daughters have these common fears. What can you do?

You can try to work through them, to understand them fully; rereading chapter 2 and reading chapter 8 about specific feelings may assist you. Then you can face fully, ahead of time, how you will feel if nothing good happens when you try to deal with your mother differently. This reduces the element of surprise that makes us feel so vulnerable. You can remind yourself that you're no longer a child, so you don't need her approval or love as desperately as you used to. You may want them, but you don't need them as much. If she rejects you, now that you're an adult, you don't have to go to your room and sulk, feeling totally unloved; you can call a friend, reread old love letters, go to a movie, any of a million things adults can do to remind ourselves of our basic lovableness and acceptability.

Is your greatest fear that you'll cry when you try to talk to your mother? If so, remind yourself—repeatedly, if necessary—that you may feel foolish or vulnerable, but IT'S NOT THE END OF THE WORLD. Are you afraid she'll make you feel even more guilty and ashamed? Ask yourself if you can feel much guiltier than you already do. Are you afraid you'll have another fight with her? Ask yourself, What's one more fight? At worst, it will be another fight, and at best, with your new approach, it might bring some improvement. Remember, you'll be going to her better prepared than before both to understand the sources of your own feelings and to understand and interpret what she does in less combative, degrading, or self-demeaning ways.

Maybe you're blocked because your mother has been so impossible to deal with for so long that you simply cannot imagine her ever changing. Dealing with her may seem impossible because she seems flawless, or horrid, or some of each—superhumanly perfect or inhumanly evil. Your next step, then, should be to search for ways to see her as simply human, to find out in what ways mother is really a person. (See chapter 7 section on "Humanizing Your Image of Your Mother.")

If, after all your efforts, your relationship has not changed? At least you will not go through life tormenting yourself with the thought that you might have made a breakthrough if you had talked with her while applying your new thinking about mother-blaming and the myths.

3. **Decide to take small steps.** Don't aim to eliminate totally the tension between you two. Visualize yourself taking one tiny, slow step at a time toward her. Make a list of the tiniest possible steps you can think of—sending her a birthday card signed with your name but no added message; asking her a question about something in her life unrelated to you or your relationship to her; smiling at her, once; stopping for just a second to think before you reject her next invitation to dinner (even if you go ahead and reject it). In choosing which small, first step to take, consider what would be easy for you but mean a lot to her. If birthdays are important to her, try starting with a card on her birthday. If she seems terribly hesitant each time she greets you in person, try an immediate, unsolicited smile. And don't expect your small steps to have even small effects right away. Your

mother may need time to understand that your changed behavior is just what it seems—a reaching out to her, not a cover-up or a meaningless gesture.

Small steps at this stage increase your own comfort about dealing differently with your mother. No law says you have to make major changes all at once, and the more hopeless you feel now about the chances for change, the more important it is for you to experience small successes. No one—certainly not we or our mothers—can make major changes all of a sudden, and if you feel you have to take a huge leap right away, you're almost certain to fall on your face. Neither you nor she will be prepared.

Each of these ways to feel safe takes time and careful effort on your part. Humanizing your image of your mother can begin suddenly and dramatically the moment you decide to try to see her as human rather than as perfect or impossibly bad, but the humanizing process is continuous. Ideally, it never ends, because we will always be pressured to apply the Perfect Mother myths and the Bad Mother myths.

Similarly, confronting and trying to resolve interpersonal problems are rarely easy, and, in virtually everyone, doing so produces fear and apprehension. Trying to resolve a problem before we have identified what makes it hard to try is like attempting the high jump wearing work boots. As we deal with each mother-daughter problem, we need to stop and identify what is blocking us. This pause is not a luxury; it is an absolute necessity.

Understanding mother-blaming and the myths certainly gives us a framework that makes it easier to spot the real causes of mother-daughter problems. Because they are interpersonal problems and are often decades old, however, many of them will require a great deal of dismantling work. For that reason, the steps we take will often necessarily be small. But even when they are tiny, at least they are forward, not backward. As in football, every step toward one's own goal is far more heartening than a rush in the wrong direction.

A Relationship Built for Two

Obvious though it may seem, we often forget that relationships involve two people. Sometimes we spend so much time focusing on ourselves—our shortcomings, problems, and needs—that we overlook the ways our lives are affected and enhanced by others. Developing ideas, resolving problems, and enjoying life can be done, to some extent, on our own. But such efforts are very limiting when they take place completely in the absence of specific work to improve our connections to important people in our lives.

Often the message we hear from a therapist or anyone else is, If your mother won't respect your need for privacy, you'll have to stay away from her! rather than, I know your mother is driving you crazy; here are some suggestions for guarding your privacy without totally shutting her out. Then we become self-righteous and impulsive, rushing about demanding that others meet our needs. Many people in therapy hear a reasonable suggestion—"Identify what you really want in order to feel good"—and misinterpret it as "I have the right to demand what I want, and I should always get it!"

Trying to resolve issues with your mother is pointless if you think about only your own needs or anger. If you fit that picture, try some of the humanizing and alliance-building exercises from chapter 7. After all, if you describe your relationship with your mother as explosive or distant, she probably feels the same way and is no more eager than you for another explosion or empty encounter. Why should she make an effort to have a serious talk with you, if she thinks she has nothing to gain from it?

For example, you may note to yourself that your mother's overachieving style has undermined your self-confidence. But you can't realistically expect your relationship with her to improve if you begin with that kind of one-sided announcement. Why? Because most people don't respond well to anger, criticism, or accusations, especially in close relationships. Making your life or your relationship with her better is not all up to her, nor is it solely up to you to figure out the problems in your relationship. However, if your fundamental longing is not just for freedom from problems but rather for a better relationship with her, you have to offer her more than the information that she's driven you mad.

Remember, chances are she's spent years worrying about whether or not she was a good mother, whether she harmed you, whether you think she did terrible things to you, whether you—more keenly than anyone else—saw her failings as a mother. If you now add your accusations to her self-doubts and self-recriminations, you know what she'll do. You didn't need to read a book to find that out. Like any sane human being, she'll respond with some combination of anger, denial, self-blame, guilt, and depression. Those feelings do not increase her ability or inclination to work on a thorny relationship.

Even if part of you feels that she deserves to suffer, remember that you want to make progress in your relationship with her, and accusing or criticizing her gives her nothing to work on, nothing to do but feel horrible and powerless—and powerlessness paralyzes. She'll feel paralyzed by the apparent impossibility of making up for the damage she's done to you. The worst crime you can accuse most mothers of is that they made their children unhappy. To most mothers' way of thinking, nothing they can do could atone for that.

Just as you have begun to take small steps toward change, she too needs to feel she can take small steps that might make a difference. She needs to feel supported and empowered in order to face your shared barriers. We all need to feel supported and empowered in order to do that kind of work. Two of the most important sources of empowerment will be: (1) her belief that the two of you can truly form an alliance about at least some issues; and (2) her hope for a better relationship with you in the future.

Support and Empowerment

What are some steps we can take to feel supported and empowered enough to approach our mothers about specific problems? A combination of further education and rehearsal can be extremely helpful.

Further Self-education

Before you talk to your mother, you may want to explore your feelings and expectations carefully by talking with a partner, a friend, a sister, other relatives, a group of women, or a good feminist counselor. You will learn more about yourself, both by hearing their perspectives on your specific unresolved issues and by hearing the kinds of concerns they have about their mothers or daughters. You may join an ongoing group or consider forming one yourself. You may form one by word of mouth among friends or coworkers or by advertising in church, synagogue, or community group newsletters or women's newspapers and magazines.

Whether you work with one other person or a group, informal, unstructured discussion opportunities can be productive. However, you may want more structure, more sense of direction. If that's the case, you might each read this book or other books and articles about mothers and daughters (see my bibliography for suggestions) and use the chapter topics and steps in this chapter and the following ones as starting points for discussion.

For example, using chapters 4 and 5, discuss ways the mother-myths affect your own lives—the way you think about your mother and, if applicable, about yourself as a mother. Hannah realized that the time her father bought her a figurine of an angel when she was seven years old and sick in bed had stayed with her as a vivid memory of his warmth toward her; she had difficulty thinking of any single illustration of her mother's warmth that seemed as dramatic to her. She commented, "I guess that the difference is partly because my mother was usually warm and loving, and Dad was more reserved. But I think I also expected her always to be nurturing and loving, and I didn't expect so much from him." Thinking about her perceptions of her parents in relation to the endless nurturance myth changed Hannah's view of her mother by drawing her attention to the warmth her mother had shown her but that Hannah had hardly noticed.

As a next step in self-education, try to describe your mother. Focus on the problems that plague your mother-daughter relationship the most. You may wish to use the technique I used in my course: write down the first three words or phrases that come to mind when you hear the word *mother*. Then, write a lengthier description of your mother. And finally, complete the sentence "In regard to my mother, I wish. . . . " If you are working on this with another person or in a group, each of you can do these things, and then you can circulate the descriptions (anonymously in a group if you wish), so that you can see commonalities and differences in your relationships with your mothers. After each of you has read the descriptions, you can discuss the material as a way to help see mothers as human beings.

Chapter 7 has an entire section called "Humanizing Your Image of Your Mother," much of which involves self-education or work directly with your mother. Two such helpful exercises are mentioned here, because they are particularly useful when you are working with someone other than your mother, whether with one person or a whole group. First, each of you should reinterpret the negative descriptions of mothers as strengths or, at the very least, as faults not aimed at hurting the daughter. Second, watch for instances in which the daughter's descriptions of her mother's positive features might have grown out of the daughter's feeling that she has to be her mother's protector or press agent. Of course, all mothers have some faults, not just good features that have been mistakenly labeled, and what a daughter describes as her mother's good points may be truly good. But these exercises help us see mothers in some reasonable perspective, without the preconceptions imposed by our culture.

The group can establish some ground rules for itself. One rule should be to prohibit mother-blaming and use of the myths to "explain" why you are upset with your mother. You are then forced to search for new ways to think about your mothers' behavior and motives and about the ways you interact with them. For example, if a woman says that her mother upset her because she is so demanding, the group members mustn't let the daughter get away with that. "Danger! Bottomless Pit myth!" they should warn. Then the daughter has to identify a specific, concrete instance of her mother's behavior. Group members or the partner should join with the daughter to consider whether that instance is proof of the mother's unmeetable, unreasonable needs or whether it can be understood some other way. In some instances, the partner or group may agree that your mother is wrong to refuse to see a therapist or talk to her friends about your father's extramarital affair, for example, and to insist on talking only to her daughter. Few daughters would want such total responsibility for meeting their mother's needs. The partner or group in this case can help the daughter go beyond simple mother-blame. Instead of saying, "Yes, your mother really is impossible!" they can encourage observations such as, "Perhaps your mother believes that a good woman never says bad things about her husband outside the immediate family, no matter what he does to her. So maybe you can let her know that it's perfectly fine to tell others, that at least you won't think she's wrong if she does that."

Sharing Perspectives and Solutions

A second useful rule for self-education sessions is to take time near the end of each meeting to discuss specific steps that you have found productive in dealing with your mother. How did Mary tell her mother that she wanted to talk about her mother's criticism of Mary's lover? Exactly what words did Jane use to ask her mother if she really loved Jane's sister best? Encourage the group members to brainstorm, each woman suggesting words she might use. When we can't imagine how we could actually raise a sensitive subject, this kind of exercise unblocks our creative juices.

We are each other's best sources of ideas for techniques and for highly specific "how-to" ideas. In my courses and workshops, women who describe to the group what they consider an intractable problem find that other women can suggest ideas they hadn't thought of. Overwhelmed and frightened by the desire to scream, "Why can't you let me run my own life?" at our mothers, we can't imagine how else we could get the message across—and so we say nothing at all. But many's the time I've watched one woman listen to another's description of the way she handled a problem and exclaim, "That's it! That's how I could say it. I never thought of putting it that way."

We must remind each other not to be too grandiose: we're not looking for grand success stories about sudden resolutions of problems that have existed since childhood. We can educate—and, therefore, support and empower—each other best with statements like:

> I realized that the reason Mother has all twelve of us for Thanksgiving dinner is not a love of suffering and enjoyment of back pains from the work. I now see that she's afraid she'll be criticized as a bad mother if she doesn't invite us, and she loves to have us all with her. Once I understood that, I caught myself last Thanksgiving having a knee-jerk, guilt-and-rage reaction when I saw her

tired expression. I couldn't bring myself to be very supportive or warm toward her, but I did feel I understood the real Mom a little better, and I felt good about that.

Rehearsal and Role-Play

Work in a group or with a partner is also ideal for rehearsal and role-play. Have each woman in the group choose someone to play the role of her mother and describe her mother's worst characteristics for the actor to portray. Then, let them rehearse the daughter's approach to her mother. The other members should take careful notes to give the daughter feedback about both the constructive and the risky or destructive things she does.

A method of rehearsal that maximizes your chances of doing constructive work and minimizes destructive interactions is called "expressive training." The principles and step-by-step directions for expressive training are outlined in appendix A. I hope you will read them carefully before you try them out, but I shall illustrate them here. As pointed out in the section on "A Relationship Built for Two," if we approach our mothers—or anyone else—with threats, demands, or criticisms, we are probably doomed to failure. When we are hurt or angry, though, we are inclined to do just that. So we need to say how we feel in a way that enables mother to listen to us and shows her what she can do to improve things between us.

According to expressive training principles, if I say, "Mom, you're always interfering in my life," that's a criticism, and she will probably either tune out or counterattack, "That's because you have such lousy judgment! Look at that creep you married!" But if I keep my remarks to a simple statement of how I feel, rather than what she does, I make a good start: "Mom, I feel hurt when you tell me to get rid of my husband. I feel hurt because I'm having a rough time with him and would appreciate your support, and when you give me such strong advice, I feel like you don't think I have very good judgment." In those sentences, you have not only described your feeling but also told her what specific step she took that led to your feeling; you have done it without attacking her. If she's halfway open to hearing you, you may be surprised by how well she responds when she needn't defend herself against criticism or attacks. When you attack her, she has difficulty paying attention to your needs since she has to protect herself from you. In the absence of an attack, she may say, "Well, let me know when you do want some advice," or she may pick up on your comment that what you really would appreciate is a little support.

If you state your feeling and its cause clearly, but your mother doesn't respond well and instead goes off on an angry tangent, hauling out old grievances or intellectualizing like crazy, come back to your simple statement of feeling and cause. Repeat it once, and then say, "I just wanted you to know how I feel and why. I don't expect you to react right now to what I have said. But I would appreciate it if you could think about it a little, and maybe we can talk about it later on." This technique is so simple, but in our talk-mad society it's rarely used. Your mother may be relieved to hear you make a short statement without expecting an immediate reply or instantaneous action. One way we can show genuine respect for each other is to ask for and offer each other time to digest each other's heartfelt words.

Some mothers won't respond very well, even when you choose your words carefully. They may reply, "I treat you like you don't have good judgment, because you don't!" I won't pretend that all mothers act like a dream if you find the magic words. But, at the very least, you'll like yourself better if you state your feeling and the cause of your feeling simply, with dignity, and without making threats, demands, or criticisms. That is a valuable lesson. It keeps us from confusing our own shortcomings with hers. It allows us to separate our tendency to act provocatively or hurtfully from hers. Keep in mind that seeing her flaws if she responds disappointingly need not lead back into mother-blaming; ideally, it leads to further exploration of what made her the way she is, mythical baggage and all. But even when we can't reach that ideal, freeing ourselves from the ritual of attack and counterattack is useful and empowering.

Expressive training techniques are useful in rehearsal with someone other than your mother, but they are also invaluable for the times when you talk directly to her (and in your other relationships as well).

Consider letting your mother know that you want to be able to talk to her about the barriers between you, and suggest that she might want to form a mothers' group and do similar kinds of work to what your daughters' group is doing. You might have the two groups meet together after they have met separately for several months. Use your creativity to arrange interesting exercises for the combined group. For instance, give the members of each mother-daughter pair the chance to learn about each other's views of their problems. Make sure that each member of a mother-daughter pair has role-played her version of one of their problems in the separate groups. Then, in the combined group, have the women who pretended to be the mother and daughter role-play the scene together as the actual mother and daughter observe. Finally, encourage the real mother and daughter to play the scene and get feedback from the rest of the group.

Now you have a framework for thinking about many of the specific problems between you and your mother; you now understand mother-blaming and the myths. By considering what is at stake, how to feel safe, and how both you and your mother can feel supported and empowered, you have prepared yourself to put that framework to use.

7

Mending the Relationship

You may be planning to talk directly with your mother about the barriers between you and may already know how you plan to approach her. Or you don't yet—and may never—want to have such discussions with her; perhaps you wish you could, but she has refused to do so or is no longer living. You may fall somewhere between these two extremes. However you are feeling right now, in preparing to work on particular mother-daughter problems, you should read carefully through this chapter and make sure to take the three essential steps that will be described here. You must:

1. Humanize your image of your mother; whether you discuss your problems with her or just try to think in new ways about them, you need to see the real woman behind the mother-myths.
2. Forge an alliance with your mother, either in fact or in your own mind.
3. Choose and define a problem on which to begin.

Humanizing Your Image of Your Mother

The more you love your children, the more shocked they are to discover that you possess a single strand of ambivalent—or negative—feeling. Insatiable for this love we expect to be absolute, we cannot forgive its mere humanness.
—*Marilyn French*, Her Mother's Daughter

Could a greater miracle take place than for us to look through each other's eyes for an instant?
—*Henry David Thoreau*, Walden

Humanizing your image of your mother includes becoming aware of the full spectrum of her characteristics and behavior.

Some daughters think of their mothers mainly in idealized terms, others mainly in blaming or demeaning ones, and still others in some of each. We tend to be less frightened of, and less angry at, ordinary people than we are toward those we regard as larger-than-life—whether in good ways or bad ways.

This section includes a variety of techniques for modifying your image of your mother to eliminate her mythical proportions. After you've read through them, try the ones that feel most comfortable for you. You may also think of others. Most daughters begin with the general techniques for demythologizing Mother. If you think of your mother primarily in idealized images, you will probably want to focus on the techniques for considering your mother's struggles (the real-life problems that have confronted her). If you think about your mother primarily in blaming or demeaning ways, the most important techniques for you will probably be those for considering your mother's worst aspects; as you attempt to understand their nature, you may find them less uniformly and thoroughly horrible than you thought. To end the humanizing work on an optimistic, growing note, all daughters can work on finding qualities to respect in Mother.

Demythologizing Mother

In scaling Mother down, or up, to human proportions, we have to tear away the mythical material that cloaks what she is really like. You might begin by looking directly at the way you (probably unintentionally) use the myths to categorize and label her behavior; in doing this, you may want to use the helpful psychological technique of exaggeration for the purpose of clarification. Make a list of as many things your mother does as possible, and then classify each bit of her behavior as either Angelic or Witchlike—referring back to chapters 4 and 5 as needed. You'll probably find that some of her behavior doesn't really belong in either category; trying to force everything she does into one category or the other will help you to see many of her simply human aspects.

One woman complained at the start of a mother-daughter workshop that she couldn't stand to visit her mother's apartment: "She always insists that I eat a huge meal." I pointed out that she had omitted that complaint on her "Angel or Witch" list. She replied, "I started to write it down, but then I thought that, really, it's neither

Angel- nor Witchlike behavior, really, is it?" I told her that, had I only heard her tone of voice and seen the look of complete exasperation on her face when she described her mother's pleas for her to eat, I would have been sure that her mother had tormented her about food. For that reason, I pressed her to include the conflict over food in the "Witch" column of her list. During the period for discussion of their lists, the other women in her small group heard her say,

> I realized, as a result of having to put all aspects of my mother's behavior on that list, that some of what she does really isn't terrible enough to justify my reaction. So if she wants so badly to feed me, and I can't simply say, "No, thank you," instead of deeply resenting her for pushing the food at me, I also need to look at why I feel so guilty and angry about the whole issue.

As long as Mother is assumed to be more or less than human, we can't expect ourselves to be only human. If Mother could be perfect, or we really believe she ought to be, then we'll ask nothing less of ourselves. And if we think her destructiveness is of superhuman proportions, our deepest fear is that so is ours. The Angel-Witch polarities keep us from asking our mothers all kinds of questions we would easily ask of anyone at a party.

You probably already know more about your mother than you think you do, and you can use this knowledge in humanizing your image of her. Based on what you know, make a systematic search for common ground. Ask yourself which of the following you share with her: values, fears, political attitudes, types of friends, religious beliefs, favorite foods, sources of joy and of frustration, mannerisms, gestures, physical features, sense of style, and so on. You may want to make a list of the ways the two of you are alike. You probably have some unreasonably high expectations and unreasonably low opinions of yourself, but at a gut level you know that in important ways you are "just a person," so finding commonalities between your mother and yourself should help you to humanize your image of her.

Seeing our mother as just a person is often lovely and moving. Fearing less intensely that she'll find us inadequate or infuriating, we can enjoy learning about her with interest, as we would about anyone else. Try to recall what you know about your mother's childhood, since children seem very human to most of us, and we are less likely either to worship or condemn them than adults. I remember my mother telling me just a few years ago that as a little girl, she had longed to have a puppy because she wanted to cuddle it. I had always known my mother feared cats, and I'd assumed that extended to all animals. When she told me of her childhood wish, all in a rush I had a glimpse of her as a cuddly, wistful little girl—neither a perfect, idealized mother nor one with the power to create all the world's evils.

She told me another story about her childhood that showed a quite different side of her. In first grade she shared a locker with a little girl who always got to school before she did. The other girl regularly left her lunch, containing a large dill pickle, in their locker, and when my mother opened the locker, the heavenly smell wafted out. Every morning for months, my mother ate that little girl's dill pickle. For a child who was otherwise very well behaved, this was an unusually mischievous thing to do! I now had another vivid image of my mother's humanity, involving neither idealization nor blame.

Writing Your Mother's Biography

By far the most valuable humanizing work you can do—whether or not your mother is still living—is to write or tape her biography. Thinking about your mother as a person begins with understanding that she did not magically appear in her full-blown, adult state, unrelated to her own childhood, the family who raised her, the wider environment in which she grew up, and the history of both her family and her culture. If your mother is living and willing to talk to you, I strongly urge you to interview her in person. Often your very request to hear her life story actually humanizes her—not just your image of her. This demonstration of their daughters' interest has made many mothers act less angry and distant. They feel less need to protect themselves from what they consider their daughter's superior attitude or lack of interest in them; and they are relieved of the need to seem perfect to get their daughters' respect.

If, for any reason, you don't interview your mother directly, get her life story from people who have known her well. If she has died, review the ways my students considered their deceased mothers' lives (see page 15).

If your mother is living, you could interview someone else's mother while having her interview yours, then trade notes. The changed perspective that can result from this exercise may astonish you. As Anna Quindlen observed,

> My friends speak about their mothers, about their manipulations and criticisms and pointed remarks, and when I meet these same women I can recognize very little of them in the child's description. They usually seem intelligent, thoughtful, kind. But I am not in a position to judge. To me they are simply people, not some lifelong foil, a yardstick by which to measure myself, to publicly find Mother wanting, to privately find the fault within.

Ask your mother (or the people you interview about her) to tell you everything about her life that she can remember, beginning with the circumstances of her own birth. If she'd rather start by talking about her parents, begin there. Sharing with her an interest in your common ancestors is a good way to begin to find common ground with her; she may then relax when she talks about her own life.

Before you begin, study appendix B; it includes the issues psychologist Karen Glasser Howe suggests that her college students cover in writing their mothers' biographies, as well as additional questions I have designed, some of which are focused on the mother-myths. Of course, feel free to modify them as you choose. Howe says that writing their mothers' biographies helps her students understand more about their mothers and feel more compassionate and closer to them.

Ask your mother about her experience with you from the very beginning. Spend substantial time on the period before you were born, because you're not likely to know much about that part of her life. If she was married or partnered, how did she feel their first official day together? How did she feel about changing her l ast name if she did? What were her expectations of the relationship? How was the first year? What surprised, disappointed, thrilled her? Did she feel self-confident about being a wife or part-ner, a cook, a housekeeper? If you are not adopted, did she plan to get pregnant? How did she feel when she found out she was preg-nant—what were the reasons she was happy, and what did she fear? How was the pregnancy? What were you like in utero—did you kick or were you quiet? What was your birth like? If you were adopted, how did she decide to adopt, how was it arranged, and what did she feel each step of the way?

Ask your mother how she felt the first time she saw you. (Let her know that if she felt nothing, that just puts her in the company of a lot of other mothers and doesn't prove she's unnatural.) Does she remember the first time she was alone with you, at home? How scared was she? What did she enjoy about you as a baby, and what drove her crazy about taking care of you? How did she feel about the restrictions that go with being a mother? Did she tell anyone she felt scared, and if so, how did they react? Did she think she was a bad or inadequate mother?

When your mother reaches the point at which she became a mother, let her know that you realize that no woman ever found mothering a breeze, and you want to hear what it was like for her. You aren't looking for Truth here but rather for her memories, her point of view.

Ask where she got advice on mothering and what it was. Did it work for her? (Or search her bookshelves for the child-rearing advice books that she used when you were little. Read them. You will get an idea of the "shoulds" she tried to put into practice.)

During the interview, pay close attention to her reactions. When she gets a twinkle in her eye, you'll want to ask more. But don't be chased away when she gets tense or looks sad or angry. She may be tense or sad because in the past no one wanted to hear about a particular experience, or no one has cared enough to lis-ten. Tension, anger, and sadness are signals that something is wait-ing to emerge, perhaps to be healed. Sometimes you must make a mental note of what was going on when the negative feeling appeared, wait a little while, and return to it later. Sometimes, if you wait quietly, she will go on.

I had read some excellent books about the difficulty of being a mother, and my own mother had always been open to talking about her experiences. But only after I systematically questioned her about her struggles did I glimpse whole, unsuspected vistas of her life—and, therefore, of both her humanness and our relationship.

On the positive side, I was surprised to learn how happy she was when I was a baby. Because I adored my babies but felt overwhelmed by responsibility and physical exhaustion, I assumed she had felt the same way. But she explained that during the era in which I was born, doctors instructed new mothers not to climb steps and to get plenty of rest. Today, women are pressured to be superwomen—to give birth, climb off the delivery table, and go cook supper while nursing their newborn. In contrast, my mother says that her need to rest was legitimized by her doctor, so she didn't feel guilty about having her mother and another woman help her out; this freed her to enjoy her baby.

On the negative side, I had never known that my mother had trouble breastfeeding me. When she told the pediatrician that I had colic, he told her that she was at fault, that she was making me nervous. That authoritative explanation made her nervous, and her milk dried up, apparently fulfilling the doctor's assessment of her inadequacy. For my mother, this trouble was created by a lethal combination: her insecurity, the myth that mothering should come naturally, and the myth that the experts know best about babies.

One woman whose mother was still alive but with whom direct contact caused her intense anguish developed her own technique for beginning to rethink their relationship. Arielle told me that she did not want to try interviewing her mother; during her childhood her mother had beaten her regularly, and this had made her feel worthless and deserving of mistreatment, especially because she, the oldest of many children, was the only one her mother beat. Simply being in her mother's presence so many years later revived those feelings of worthlessness. What she could do, she decided, was to write down everything she knew about her mother's life. She did that, and when she began arranging her notes according to the chronology of her mother's life, she had a sudden realization. She had always known that her mother's parents were strict and sexually puritanical and that they had warned her mother to "stay away from boys." Defying their warning, her mother became pregnant at the age of fifteen, and this was in an era and a rural area in which pregnant girls were forced to leave school. As Arielle recorded the date of her mother's dropping out of high school and then began to record the date of the next incident, which was her own birth, it struck her that her mother's pregnancy with her was the reason her mother had left school. This was particularly poignant because the most valuable contribution her mother had made to all of her children's lives was her tireless encouragement of them to get as much education as possible. Arielle realized that her existence was the reason her mother had given up her most precious dream, that of continuing her formal education. This new understanding did not tempt Arielle to justify her mother's physical abuse of her as a child, but it provided an explanation for the beatings other than "I deserved it," and this took some of the sting out of her feelings about her mother. There is no totally happy ending to this story, but Arielle did begin to find it somewhat less agonizing to be in her mother's presence.

Considering Your Mother's Struggles

When we see people from a distance, we seldom see their blemishes. An important way to overcome idealization of your mother is to consider closely her struggles, the real-life trials she has faced. For as long as I can remember, my father has had a sign in his office that reads: "Be kind, because everyone you meet is fighting a hard battle." Yet we are often blind to our mothers' brand of battles. A mother is expected to shoulder enormous responsibilities—the duty to evaluate our progress, the duty to point out where we need to change or improve, the socially sanctioned right to penalize us when she thinks we have gone too far astray, and the duty to know when to stop doing these things. So perhaps we shouldn't be surprised that, in focusing on what we expect her to do for us, we often overlook her struggles—or even the fact that she does struggle.

Furthermore, many mothers feel pressed to live up to the idealized images of motherhood, so they hide their difficulties from us. Many have been told that children shouldn't be "burdened" by information about their parents' imperfections or uncertainties. The result is that most of us don't hear much about the realities of our mothers' lives, and that information gap keeps us farther apart. The more we know about another person, the closer we usually feel to them—because we're more likely to discover what we share with them.

An experience I had some years ago uncovered the hidden battle of a woman who occupied a very powerful position. This is the most dramatic illustration I have experienced directly of the humanity behind what seemed to be an invulnerable woman. She was my boss, not my mother, but like a mother, she seemed larger-than-life. This woman had been promoted to a job no woman had held before; she supervised a large number of employees, each doing sensitive, complex work. One day, I heard that she was scheduled to have eye surgery. I wanted to get her a little gift. Since the only thing I knew about her personal life was that she loved music, I got a musical key chain. That seemed insufficient, so I hit on the idea of getting a small gift to appeal to each of her senses—other than vision—so she could enjoy them during her recovery. I bought a lime-scented soap, a velvet doodad to feel, and jellybeans for taste.

I heard secondhand that she was very touched by my gifts, because she thought I knew she was frightened of losing her eyesight and was trying to give her the message "Even if you lose your vision, you still have all your other senses to enjoy." I wished I had thought of that, but I hadn't known her well enough to be aware of her fear. I don't believe she had told anyone at work that she was afraid. We thought of her as powerful, so we never suspected her fears.

Since mothers often try to conceal their troubles and faults from their daughters, and since they have the power to make their daughters feel both wonderful and terrible, many daughters mistakenly assume that their mothers are invulnerable and all-powerful. As you begin to explore your mother's struggles, keep in mind that some of the difficulties mothers most frequently describe are uncertainty about how to care for children, isolation, physical exhaustion, sense of inadequacy, overwhelming sense of responsibility, and fear of failure. Other struggles with which many mothers have to cope include difficulties because of racial discrimination, poverty, disability or illness, unaccepted sexual orientation, having many children, a child's disability or illness or death, being a victim of abuse in childhood or currently, being underpaid or overworked or undervalued or sexually harassed on the job, divorce, abandonment, poor relationships with other family members, responsibility for other family members, and frustrated ambitions and dreams. Any mother has been plagued by at least some of these burdens.

So think about how the adversity your mother has faced might have affected her treatment of you. Do you remember times she seemed too tired to play with you or exceedingly irritable or very emotionally needy? Could those have been the times her burdens were heaviest? If you're not sure, ask her, or ask people who knew her then. For example, remember that, according to current estimates, at least one-third and probably closer to one-half of all mothers were the victims of some sort of abuse—sexual abuse as a child, sexual assault as an adult, or battering by a mate. Since the effects of abuse include poor self-esteem, insecurity, and fearfulness, a huge proportion of what daughters have regarded as their mothers' faults probably resulted partly from their having been victims of violence—but the daughters never knew.

Julia, a student in her fifties, told me she supposed she would write a paper about her mother's life in order to meet one of the requirements of my "Mothers" course, but she did not look forward to interviewing her elderly parent. She explained, "My mother never trusted me. All the time I was growing up, she watched me like a hawk. And I really resented that." After interviewing her mother for the biography, she came back to see me and told me,

> When I asked my mother, "When you were in junior high school, what did you want to be when you grew up?" I thought her mind was wandering, because she didn't seem to be answering the question. She said, "When I was thirteen, I was raped in an outhouse by the man I was later forced to marry: your father. And I never wanted anything like that to happen to you. So all the time you were growing up, I watched you like a hawk."

Those few words precipitated Julia's total reinterpretation of her mother having watched her so closely. She realized that this was not a sign of her mother's mistrust but rather of her love for Julia and her wish to protect her. Julia said that after telling that story, her mother looked at her, opened her eyes wide, and said, "So you see, dear, I really never had much chance to think about what I wanted to be."

As we learn about our mother's struggles, the bad things she's done to us usually seem less destructive, less malicious, and even less serious because we understand their sources—her worry about an impending divorce, or her concern about where our next meal was coming from, and so on. We can better appreciate the good things she's done when we know that she did them in spite of adversity, that she didn't sail serenely through motherhood, that child-rearing took effort and tears and strength and ingenuity. If we can find these buried qualities in her, we can discover them in ourselves as well.

These humanizing techniques will apply to very specific problems between you, some of which will be discussed in chapter 8. For example, learning about your mother's struggles or her viewpoint may shed important light on your belief that she wasn't as nurturing and supportive of you as she should have been. A close friend told me that she recently realized that, compared to her peers' descriptions of their relationships with their mothers, hers was pretty distant. "Oh, I know," her mother said.

> That's because your pediatrician told me that it was important for me to teach you to be independent, and I tried very hard to do that. Just lately, I've realized that, in trying to make you independent, I shut you out emotionally. I guess there are ways to be independent but still loving and connected, but I have only begun to learn for myself what those ways are. In my family, with ten of us kids, both of my parents were too busy to be very close to us emotionally. They just didn't have the time.

Considering Your Mother's Worst Aspects

Considering your mother's worst aspects, if properly done, can actually reduce your tendency to blame her or put her down. As we saw in chapters 2 and 3, blaming and demeaning someone are quick-and-dirty, but ultimately unproductive, ways to deal with someone's unappealing or hurtful behavior toward us. Understanding and growth can come from our attempts to stop taking the easy way out and really try, as the Native American motto goes, to walk in the other person's moccasins.

You can do this in various ways, all of which involve trying to project yourself into your mother's situation. If you are very angry at or alienated from her, you may not be eager to try these exercises, but the results are worth making the imaginative leap. At the very least, they acquaint you with another part of life, another space on the wheel of human experience. At best, they also bring genuine understanding of your mother's life. Simone is a writer, who at seventy-two tried walking in her mother's moccasins by writing a short story about their relationship:

> She had always been very hard on me, making me take responsibility for the worst and hardest chores on our farm. I grew up feeling like Cinderella in her pre-fairy-godmother period. I wrote a true-to-life story about my relationship with Mother, but the magazine that had commissioned the story said it was too downbeat and the mother was too one-dimensional and rotten.
>
> My first reaction was, "But that is what she was really like!" In order to get my payment for the story, I added some new material about the mother supposedly being frustrated and lonely doing hard farmwork. I thought that the added bits were complete fiction. But years later, I talked to a woman who had known my mother when she married my father; the woman told me that Mother had desperately wanted to be a concert pianist, but Dad forbade it. She was an accomplished musician when they met, but he wanted her to help with his farmwork. All she had ever told me was that she played piano for fun.

As stories like this illustrate, we often know more about our mothers than we think, once we correctly interpret years' worth of signs and innuendoes.

You can choose from among a number of techniques for exploring your mother's worst aspects. You might ask her outright why she treated you as she did during a particularly painful incident, how she felt and what she thought at the time. This may be too daunting a task at this stage, but sometimes illuminating information is missing simply because no one has asked about it. Or, like Simone, write (or imagine) a story about your mother's life.

Include everything you can think of about her, but especially try to make her a sympathetic character; this may be hard if you don't feel great about her right now, but you'll find the effort worthwhile. A woman named Phoebe said after a workshop on mothers and daughters,

> When I started writing about my mother, all I could think of were the ways she irritates me. But since the assignment was to try to make her a sympathetic character, I really dug into my memories—and the first thing I remembered that was good was the smell of her chicken soup. That brought back a whole flood of good feelings, including how soft her cheek felt when I was four years old and had a fever.

If just trying to make her a sympathetic character doesn't work for you, try this: think of the worst thing your mother has ever done to you. (You may wish to refer to the notes you made at the start of the book.) Then, imagine that you were the one who did it. Now, write a short story in which you explain why the character behaved as she did. If you prefer, just jot down a two-line explanation of the character's motives. Or, find other women who have done similar things to their daughters, and interview them to find out what led to their behavior. My student Nora began to understand what had led her mother to beat her only after she talked to other abusive mothers.

Finding Qualities to Respect in Mother

So far, the humanizing exercises have involved either learning more about your mother's life and struggles or trying to understand what led to her upsetting behavior. Now you can focus more specifically on her good points—not what seem to be her superhuman qualities but just her human good points, such as her sense of humor or her talent for word games.

First, see if you can think of reasons she deserves your respect; some of the material you learned in finding out about her struggles may be helpful here. An early-middle-aged woman I'll call Stacey learned at age seven that her mother had a severe emotional disturbance that sometimes made it impossible for the family to have company in their home. At the approach of the twenty-first century, Tipper Gore called mental illness "the last great stigma of the twentieth century," and in the 1950s, its social stigma was far greater than it is now. In spite of this Stacey's mother told her,

> Honey, I want you to know that the reason I sometimes do strange things is that I have what is called a "mental illness." I have tried very hard to fight this thing, but I really can't help it. I know that when I'm acting strangely, you can't have your friends over to the house, and I don't want them to think it's just because you don't like them. So I want you to feel free to tell the friends you really care about that my mental illness is the reason you don't bring them home with you to play.

As most children would do, Stacey took her mother's words as a matter of course. Not until she turned forty did Stacey appreciate the sacrifice her mother had made for her. Stacey grew up in a small town where her mother still lives and faces the consequences of Stacey's having told her friends about her mother's problems. The townspeople still think that mental illness equals insanity, and Stacey's mother has suffered a great deal because of the ignorant misconceptions about her that have spread through the town. Stacey told me,

> Not only do I wish that people would stop gossiping so viciously about my mother, but I wish that they would stop and think about what she did. She knew damned well that, when she gave me permission to tell, word would get around fast, and people would distort the truth. And that's what they've done in some unbelievably grotesque ways.
>
> Instead of people gossiping about Mother behind her back, by all rights they should give her a medal for heroism.

Daughters of any age whose mothers had paid jobs while raising them might think about how fragmenting and just plain exhausting is the daily juggling of mothering and workplace tasks. If reasons to respect your mother don't immediately come to mind, try other methods. Ask other people what they respect about her, or think about features you admire in other women, then consider whether they might apply to your mother. Use your imagination—pretend you have to write her response to a help-wanted ad explaining why she deserves to get the job, or write a presentation speech for an award to be given to her. The job or award can be of any kind; you might begin with something that seems trivial, like her fondness for hummingbirds. Go on from there to think what that tells you—she has tender feelings for small creatures or a reverence for nature, for instance. At least some of the humanizing techniques work for most daughters, but unfortunately, some mothers are at the really dreadful end of the spectrum. What can their daughters do?

Impossibly Difficult Mothers

> An eighty-year-old woman was told, "You can't be eighty years old!" and replied, "What do you mean? I have a fifty-three-year-old son!" She said this while sitting on the couch next to her fifty-four-year-old daughter.
>
> —*story told to me by a friend*

Your mother, like the one quoted above, may have done such hurtful things to you that her image can't be humanized very much. On the spectrum of mothers, these are the ones we're most tempted to go on blaming. But even if you are unfortunate enough to have a mother like this, your image-humanizing efforts are still important. Why? Because, as I wrote in chapter 2, blaming her takes some immediate heat off of you—"She's the problem, not I!"—but as long as you regard her primarily as your mother, and your Evil Mother, you are still poisonously bound to her. You'll continue feeling terrified of being like her, or believing that you are. As long as your view of her is mostly as "My mother, the mother," and you don't focus on anything about her *except* her role as your mother, your identity is tightly bound up with hers. Although humanizing your image of her may not make her any more lovable or palatable, try to understand how she got the way she is. Then you'll see the ways in which the forces that shaped you, including your own special, individual characteristics, differ from the forces that shaped her. You may discover that she was powerfully shaped, for example, by the male superiority myth; then, even if that same myth affected you a great deal, you can remind yourself that she has never gotten out from under its influence, whereas at age twenty-five, or forty-five, or sixty-five, you already know that the myth is false.

To understand whether your mother is truly impossible to work with, you have to try first to see her not as someone who suddenly existed as a full-fledged, monolithic mother the minute you were born, but as someone controlled by her culture. Ironically, many women who forgive Freud for the awful things he said about women, because he was a product of his time and culture, cannot do the same for their mothers.

Some of you may have a mother whom you consider, after careful thought, to be thoroughly unforgivable; there are, of course, some quite vicious mothers and some profoundly disturbed mothers. If nothing we have discussed seems to help, then so be it. But before giving up, let us consider an example of how we can think about a really destructive mother. As you read the story, put yourself in the young daughter's position, because if your mother was truly terrible, you probably doubted your own worth, as this child did. This is a continuation of the story of Resa and her daughter, Rosemary, who were described in Chapter 5. Rosemary had been brought to a clinic for treatment of her depression.

When Rosemary was eight years old, her divorced mother's relationship with a man called Mike was in trouble. Resa involved Rosemary in this, urging her to beg Mike to stay with them. During one argument between Resa and Mike, Rosemary crouched in the corner in the other room, hungry, shivering from the cold and from fear, trying to block out their screaming. She remembers her mother coming into the room after some time and saying "I can't do anything with him. You try!"

What do we make of Resa? Thinking back to the description of her parents and grandparents from chapter 5, we recall that Resa's mother and grandmother were rather frenetic, cold people—chipper, at best. Her father and grandfather were more pleasant and gentle but minimally involved in the family. Because of the male superiority and endless nurturance myths, Resa's mother and grandmother seem responsible for her difficulties, even though her father and grandfather probably contributed to her ungiving, self-centered character, too. And thanks to the male superiority myth, Resa believes that she has to have a man—hence, she told her husband to leave so that she could be "independent" only after she had latched desperately onto Mike.

You may want to blame Resa for her treatment of Rosemary—or, you may want to absolve her on the grounds that her parents and grandparents are at fault. Which view you take will depend in part on what you think about free will. Some will call Resa a blameless victim of circumstance, unavoidably shaped by her past, power-less to change. Some will say that, as an adult who chose to have a child, no matter what has been done to her, she has to take respon-sibility for not harming her child. Whichever view you take, Resa's treatment of Rosemary clearly grows out of her own needs, not out of her daughter's inadequacy: it's not her daughter's fault. If your mother seems irretrievably horrible, try to think of yourself as Rosemary, and realize that you may have hated or blamed your mother in an effort to prove that you did not deserve what she did to you. If you can understand this, then even if you don't end up loving or forgiving your mother, you will probably feel a lot better about yourself, and you won't base your improved self-esteem on the shaky foundation of tearing someone else down. If only your self-esteem changes, that's a lot.

Humanizing your image of your mother may begin with changes primarily in your thoughts—such as catching yourself using the mythical images and reminding yourself that your moth-er is neither Angel nor Witch—although changes in your feelings may well follow. Forging an alliance with your mother, whether directly or within yourself, in the form of changed attitudes toward her, is likely to be a more emotional process. The humanizing process changes the power balance between you: she comes to seem more nearly equal to you in power, being neither far more admirable nor far more despicable than you. Forging an alliance implies a somewhat equalized balance of power but has more to do with emotions, with a shared feeling of closeness or commonal-ity between you.

Forging an Alliance

Improving a mother-daughter relationship requires the efforts of both mother and daughter. Forging an alliance between the two of you is, therefore, extremely important. Many of the techniques discussed so far will help create this alliance, will help you to realize you are on the same team.

It's impossible to exaggerate the importance of this step; as therapist Nikki Gerrard has written, it does both people more good if we think of ourselves as building an alliance than if we think of one of us as "helping the other out" or single-handedly diagnosing and solving the problems we share.

The initial steps you can take to forge an alliance with your mother involve "getting started: looking at obstacles," "confronting your mother's power," and "clarifying your respective responsibilities."

Getting Started: Looking at Obstacles

If you wrote or taped your mother's biography, you have already begun creating an alliance with her. If you haven't yet done the biography, consider doing so now. A lot may change as she sees that you take her seriously enough to ask about her life, listen to her answers, and consider her an important source of information, a partner in your effort to make sense of your life and of the relationship that you two share. Many women who love reading novels and documentary histories about women never ask to hear their own mothers' stories. For alliance-building, *that* you ask matters more than what you ask.

If your mother doesn't raise the subject herself, ask her about her view of the relationship between the two of you, in the same way as you interviewed her about her life generally. Ask her to name a couple of things you have done that have brought her joy and a couple that have caused her grief. Remember that this is an interview, not yet a time to trade viewpoints or debate issues. The more you know about her view of the problem, the better you'll be able to assess the work you'll need to do together.

You may want to pretend—just in your own mind while you interview her—that you are not her daughter if you don't like something she says about you, because the usefulness of the interview for forging an alliance is to give you the chance to listen intently and build up a picture of how you and your relationship with her look from her point of view. Your mission is to gather information. Convince yourself that you are a stranger who's just met her at a cocktail party and is listening to her describe her daughter and herself. This kind of listening should give you a good idea of the aspects of your relationship that concern her the most, and she'll speak more freely if you can listen in a nonjudgmental and undefensive way. This is not the time to interrupt with, "But Ma, I don't do that!" or "You always liked my sister better!"

If you plan to have conversations with your mother about the barriers between you, review "A Relationship Built for Two" in chapter 6 to help orient you as you decide how to broach the subject. A good way to start is by telling her that you want your relationship to be closer or more relaxed, and that you would like her to set aside some time for the two of you to talk about how to make that happen. Suggest to her that you think of your relationship as a kind of kinetic sculpture that will always be changing because of things beyond your control—like aging, societal expectations, and so on—but that you two can shape, to some degree.

Give her time, if she needs it. Tell her you'll call in a few days to find out what she has decided. If she says she's not interested, you can urge her to tell you why she's reluctant, because once the reason is named, you may be able to deal with it fairly quickly. If she says she is afraid you'll tell her all the things she has done wrong as a mother, you can assure her that is exactly what you do not plan to do. Or, you might give her this book. Say that you have read it, and suggest that you talk after she has had a chance to read it. Even if she needs more time or if you never overcome her resistance, you will probably feel better for having asked why she's reluctant to talk. You may understand, for example, that what she feels is fear rather than lack of interest in you or such intense anger at you that she can't imagine talking to you about the relationship.

If your mother is adamant about not discussing the relationship with you, she may need more time, and she may raise the issue with you if she can choose a time when she feels ready. But even if she doesn't, you will find in this section some more indirect ways to forge an alliance with her. For example, whether or not you do her biography and whether or not she agrees to talk to you about your relationship, you can tell her about some of the material from chapters 3, 4, and 5 in this book. You might start with a small step, such as describing the polarized images of mothers, the ways mother-blaming results from both the Perfect Mother myths and the Bad Mother myths. She is likely to understand quickly, since she will have experienced them herself, and then you will have a shared framework. Reassure her explicitly that you don't want either to idealize or to demean her. It may be the first time since she became a mother that anyone has named the stereotypes, called them bad, and said, "Let's go beyond them."

You may want to describe some of the myths to her, especially those you think have affected her the most. In this way, you make it clear from the outset that your purpose in talking to her is to begin a journey of exploration with her; therefore, she'll feel less need to try to maintain herself on the mother-on-pedestal position or will be less afraid of being in the put-down, cast-aside one. You can have this conversation with your mother even if she doesn't want to discuss your relationship directly.

Consider spending some time talking to her about her current emotional state. Because mothers are supposed to take care of other people's needs, we may rarely think to ask them what they need; because they are supposed to help us deal with our fears and work toward our goals, we don't usually ask them about their fears and aims. For that reason, when we do ask them such questions, we show our mothers in a very moving way that we want to be allied with them. Freda Paltiel, Health and Welfare Canada's former senior advisor on the status of women, suggests that you ask your mother to describe her real self in terms of her "needs, risks, and tasks": What are her needs, both in her relationship with you and otherwise? What risks does she feel she is taking, both in working on her relationship with you and at this point in her life generally? Are there risks she wants to take? What tasks does she want to accomplish, both in her relationship with you and in general at this point in her life?

Confronting Your Mother's Power

Now you must confront head-on the issue of your mother's power. Although the humanizing exercises may have equalized the balance of power between you in your mind, your mother needs a chance to work on that issue by herself and possibly in conversation with you. As we saw in chapter 5, mothers do have certain kinds of power over their children, and in our culture everyone is urged to regard that power as dangerous. Precisely because it is regarded as dangerous, many daughters and sons are overly sensitive about it, mistakenly labeling their mother's displays of interest and concern or offers of advice and nurturance as her misuse of power. You must bring this issue out in the open. Talk explicitly about the unfairness of a mother's power being so quickly damned as destructive. Also, tell your mother what kinds of power she does have over you—the power to inspire you or to make you feel loved, as well as the power to make you feel inadequate or ashamed, and so on. Daughters are often surprised to find that their mothers don't realize how much power they still have over their adult offspring. In fact, as described in chapter 5, mothers usually feel quite powerless.

Until we realize that mother is not omnipotent and certainly does not feel she is, that her power is not as dangerous as we think, and that we are not powerless in relation to her, we cannot forge a true alliance. One way we deal with mother's power is to try to reduce her impact on us through mocking her, as Portnoy did. Novelist Rebecca Goldstein wrote, "I've transformed [my mother] into a parody . . . in the attempt to dilute some of her awesome strength."

While writing this book, I recognized that I was exaggerating, in my own mind, my mother's power and her destructive use of it. I had been feeling distant from her and wanted to call and say how much I loved her. It startled me to notice how hesitant I was to make that call. When I thought about why, I realized that I was very much afraid that she would make light of my expression of love, even though there was no reason to expect this. In fact, she has usually been very warm and expressive toward me. But what if she should be busy or preoccupied when I called? The prospect of being rejected by our mothers can be shattering—no matter how remote it seems or how old we are.

Be sure, too, to give your mother a chance to describe the power you have over her. A typical mother told me, "With one look or comment, my daughter can make me feel like an old fool or like I'm really OK." In responding to pressure to regard mothers' power as dangerous, daughters often fail to consider their own influence.

But in order to build a true alliance with them, daughters must know how they affect their mothers.

You and your mother need to base your alliance partly on your understanding of the limits of each other's power. Since both mothers and daughters are women in a misogynist culture, we have limited power to improve each other's lives. We don't like to acknowledge this, because we usually wish we could help each other a great deal more. Often we are reluctant to tell each other about our needs, because we don't want to reveal each other's powerlessness. So discuss with your mother what you each wish you had the power to do for the other, and acknowledge the frustration and powerlessness you both feel because, for instance, you can't make the rest of the family show more respect for her mothering work, and she can't protect you from sexual harassment or force your husband to treat you with respect. This is painful to consider, but the best emotional context in which to do so is the assumption that mothers and daughters want to overcome the barriers between them and that this is a worthy, healthy aim.

Clarify Your Respective Responsibilities

Now you and your mother should discuss what are and what are not your responsibilities. For instance, suggest that both of you do have the responsibility to:

- Respect each other's strengths.
- Respect each other's right to be imperfect without being considered a failure or betrayer.
- Understand that much of what you have done to enrage or hurt each other came not from ill will but from cultural attitudes reflected in mother-blaming and the myths.

Also establish that both of you recognize that, for example,

- A mother is not responsible for meeting all of a daughter's needs (Myth Two).
- A daughter is not responsible for establishing and maintaining a mother's good reputation through her impeccable behavior (Myth One).

Then look through chapters 4 and 5, and see whether either of you has been holding herself or the other person inappropriately responsible for the consequences of any of the other myths.

Since your goal is to be closer to or more relaxed with your mother, you will have to screen out mother-blaming messages. Even though you may now be careful about attributing all your problems to your mother, other people won't take such care. You'll need sensitive antennae to twitch a warning when the destructive messages come your way.

For example, as I prepared to write this chapter, a famous author appeared on television to publicize her latest book, in which she claims that successful Superwomen are insecure because of their mothers' needs for overachievement and their own "enmeshment, their inability to separate from their mothers." Such statements are often made with such authority that it is hard to see the mother-blaming errors in them. Once you understand that you must screen out such messages, you'll be halfway to establishing and maintaining a true alliance with your mother. With that alliance as a foundation, you are now ready to go beyond thinking about the myths in general and to work on the mother-daughter problems that specifically plague your relationship.

Choosing and Defining a Problem

Once you have humanized your image of your mother and forged an alliance with her—either directly or in your own heart—you may find that some of your problems will diminish. But some are likely to need more patient, prolonged work. You can do a great deal of the work described in this section on your own, by talking with someone other than your mother (a friend, a therapist) or by talking with her directly. In any case, the basic steps to follow are:

1. Identify one problem at a time.
2. Identify the feelings you have about the problem.
3. Identify the sources of the problem and of the feelings about it.

Remember that you are beginning a process of teaching yourself and your mother about each other. Either one of you can identify a problem, but be sure to consider both your and her feelings about it and both your and her perceptions of its causes. You may find it easier to begin by identifying a troublesome feeling that you have about your mother, trying to describe its causes, and then attempting to find out what your mother's feelings and beliefs about its causes are. (You will probably want to turn back to chapter 6 and review the helpful principles and techniques of expressive training.)

The problem you choose need not be your most serious problem; you may feel more comfortable beginning with a somewhat minor issue that you both can handle. You may wish to begin with something that came up as you worked on your mother's biography.

One mother-daughter pair discovered during the biography exercise that they had very different ideas about the meaning of "independence." The daughter defined it as "no more than a couple of visits a month," while the mother thought her daughter could remain independent and still see her every week. Both mother and daughter felt great relief when they both identified as the cause of the problem their specific concern about the frequency of contact. They discussed their different views of how frequent visits should be, a more constructive approach than accusations about the daughter not caring or the mother being too demanding. In a series of discussions, the daughter described her amorphous fears that her mother wanted constant involvement with her and "nothing would ever be enough"; the mother described her fear that her daughter really wanted nothing to do with her. Primarily, both felt fear—for the daughter, fear of engulfment, and for the mother, fear of rejection. The specific cause of their problem was that they hadn't bothered to tell each other their real wishes and fears. Each made mistaken assumptions about what the other wanted.

Eleanor, a seventy-eight-year-old widow, and her daughter, Makaisha, had an almost opposite experience. Eleanor fell and broke her hip, and she went to stay with Makaisha after her hospital stay. Leaving the hospital, they got into a terrible quarrel over an apparently trivial matter. When a visiting nurse came to check on Eleanor several days later, she burst into tears and said she wanted to live on her own but thought that would hurt

Makaisha's feelings. The nurse called in Makaisha and helped the women talk about how they each really felt.

They began politely, each saying truthfully that she loved the other and felt terrible about their quarrel. At that point, the nurse urged them to acknowledge any other feelings they had. Makaisha said, "I'm confused because I wanted Mother to feel at home here, but she seems so tense, and I don't know what to do." Eleanor replied, "I do feel tense here, but that's because I'm used to being on my own. When my insomnia bothers me, I worry that my bustling around with my walker will disturb or worry the other people in the house." Each woman had guessed how she was affecting the other, and neither had expressed her worst concern. The nurse told them they had made a good beginning, and she arranged for a social worker to come to the house the next week.

The social worker made a series of visits, during which she told the women that their concerns about each other's feelings were admirable, but their denial of their own feelings was creating tension between them. Over a period of weeks, Eleanor was finally able to express her longing to live on her own again and to admit she was reluctant to say so for fear of seeming ungrateful. Makaisha was able to say that she had thought a good daughter should be able to make her mother completely comfortable in her home. Once she knew what her mother really wanted, she stopped feeling her mother was "impossible," and the tension between them subsided.

When you and your mother choose a problem together, remember that there is a big difference between agreeing on a problem and agreeing on the source of the problem. For example, try to avoid saying, "The problem is that you can't let go of me." That is an accusation and a criticism (see chapter 6 section, "Expressive Training"), so she's unlikely to agree with you and will probably become defensive. Instead, define the problem according to expressive training principles. For instance, one daughter said, "I'd like us to talk about the fact that I feel guilty—and then angry about having to feel guilty—because you chide me if I go one day without phoning you."

In choosing problems to work on, you may want to review your list of the worst things your mother has ever done to you and see which ones plague you the most, or consult any notes you made while reading this book. If possible, ask your mother to make a list of the worst things you have ever done to her. You might also want to review the list of myths in chapters 4 and 5, considering which ones might be creating or exacerbating the problems between you. Then recast what happened, minus the myth(s). For instance, if she always told you the people you dated weren't good enough for you, ask yourself whether she might have been trying to be the all-knowing, completely protective mother (Myths Three and Two). Put yourselves in each other's shoes: if you had been the mother, what would you have done in this situation? Was there any way she could have done just the right thing? And what does she wish you had done when the problem first arose?

These conversations can be difficult, because women often find it harder to see beyond the myths in their own mothers' lives than in anyone else's. As mentioned, hundreds of women have each told me that her mother is the only masochist in the world. Through their awareness of the myths and mother-blaming, many such daughters have been able to understand their mothers' "Look what I sacrificed for you" not as proof that they revel in misery but as a perhaps justified, if misguided, plea for recognition and appreciation.

Another way to start work with your mother is to spend a little time with her and note when problems arise and how you feel. This is especially helpful if, when you think of your relationship with her, you feel so upset, numb, or alienated that you can't focus on specific problems.

Suppose, for example, you notice that both of you become tense when you discuss how often you talk to each other on the phone. As you see it, she can't let go of you and makes you feel guilty for not calling her enough. Try assuming instead that she wants to stay connected with you. Ask yourself what myths might have transformed that wish for connection into what seems to you like her inability to let go and her wish to make you feel guilty. That is the task that Tamika, a woman in her midthirties, set for herself:

I had a long talk about this with my best friend, and we realized that the myth that mother-daughter closeness is bad was making me suspect my mother of wanting "too much" closeness, and the

myth that women's power is dangerous made me accuse her of trying to make me feel guilty.

Tamika never talked this through with her mother. The insights
from talking to her friend about the myths made all the difference.
Next time she had a busy week at work and didn't phone, Tamika
got out of her old rut. When her mother called her, instead of saying, as usual, "Why do you have a fit when I go one week without
calling you?" she tried, "Hi, ma! You've been on my mind all week,
but they've been driving me crazy at work, and I didn't feel fit for
human conversation."

Nothing Tamika said to her mother was untrue. She didn't pretend to be thrilled by her mother's call, nor did she carry on a
lengthy conversation with her. She did avoid complaining or accusing her mother, and that had two important results:

1. Something passed between them besides complaints, accusations, and demands—when you create that space, connection and warmth sometimes seep in.
2. Tamika adopted a new attitude toward her mother, one that
   left open the possibility that her mother's motives might be
   better than Tamika had assumed.

In exploring or even attempting to identify your feelings, try to
remember or reconstruct the first time you felt this way about
your mother. For instance, if you are phobic about telling her anything about your love life, think back to the first time you felt
uncomfortable doing that. What had you said, and how did she
respond? You may find your upsetting feeling outdated if, for
instance, you told her you had kissed on your first date, and she
expressed shock and dismay. Now that you are forty-five years old,
she may be less shocked; if she isn't, you may be less devastated
by her reaction. But even if your feeling is not outdated, recalling
its origins can help you understand it.

If you haven't done so before, ask your mother how she would
describe the development of the problems between you. Did you
always clash, or did you get along well until a certain point? When
was there a change for the worse? Does she recall what caused the
change? Did mother-blaming and the myths play a role in the
change? Her answers may help you two identify the sources of the

barriers between you; at least they will give you a starting point for your work. Let's look at some examples.

One daughter whose mother refused to talk to her about their relationship asked her mother's sister when the mother-daughter problems had begun. The aunt replied:

> When you were eleven, your teacher told your parents he was concerned about you, because you weren't yet interested in boys. Your mother had been very popular in high school, and when this teacher said authoritatively that your lack of interest in having boyfriends was a problem, she was very worried. She didn't want you to miss out on the fun she had had, and she feared that her delight in your academic success had retarded your social development. That was when she started pushing you to go to boy-girl parties, against your wishes.

From her aunt's account, this daughter understood that her mother had been trying to be a good mother. That knowledge was helpful to her, although her attempts to talk to her mother about the problem never did succeed.

If your mother feels that your relationship took a dramatic turn for the worse when you hit adolescence, explore together what it was about your reaching adolescence that provoked conflict. Were you expressing hormonally based increases in aggressiveness that you hadn't learned how to handle? Was she frightened by the prospect of you as a sexual being—did she feel unable to teach you how to protect yourself from the vulnerability that accompanies sexuality? Did she fear that you would be sexually aggressive and that her friends would hear about it and think she was a terrible mother? Once you ask such questions you can easily see how your problems might have been aggravated by such myths as "The measure of a good mother is a 'perfect' daughter."

You may identify your marriage as a point where your mother-daughter relationship suddenly took a downturn. Both Lily and her mother, Vy, agreed that Lily's marriage to Bert had been the beginning of a painful series of conflicts between them. Vy said,

> Lily's marriage made me a mother-in-law. And when Bert put me down, Lily sometimes joined in. When I told her privately that that

hurt my feelings, Lily said I had taught her that a woman must always take her husband's side. She was right: I had taught her that. Why should she side with me? Who ever got respect by siding with a mother?

Vy had seen that her daughter acquired status by siding with a man instead of with her mother, but she hadn't yet realized that that was a result of both her and her daughter's belief in the myth that men are superior. Vy saw that later, as she and her daughter discussed how the myths had affected them, and much of her pain was relieved. Until then, she had known only that her daughter often mocked her and that she herself had somehow helped make that happen—but she thought that her own stupidity and her daughter's dislike of her were the roots of the problem.

For her part, Lily felt frustrated and angry: "I have to be loyal to my husband, but I have an obligation to my mother—and I care about both of them." Looking at the list of myths, Lily and Vy immediately recognized that the myth of male superiority had played a major role in the development of the tension between them.

A daughter's divorce is often a turning point for mothers and daughters. It can turn the relationship in either direction. It alters for the worse when a daughter, feeling vulnerable and believing in the endless nurturance myth, falls into the trap of expecting her mother to stand by her 100 percent and feels betrayed by anything less. Or the negative turn can come from the mother's side. Many an unhappily married mother is threatened by a daughter's divorce, because it shows her that she too has a choice: she doesn't have to put up with unhappiness. Having that choice both attracts and frightens her, and this confusion makes her angry. She may resent her daughter for provoking her ("unfeminine") anger and making her think about the frightening prospect of living unsupported by a man.

When a daughter divorces, her mother may pull away. Sherry was twenty-seven when she and her husband separated. Her mother reacted by stopping her weekly telephone calls:

I'd known for a long time that the relationship between my parents was emotionally very distant, but not until I told my mother about my divorce did I realize how bad things were between them. She got very shrill and started lecturing me that a woman's place is with her husband, no matter what. I knew she was trying to convince herself, and I was sad that she couldn't see that. The only way she could run from her wish to leave Dad was to stay away from me.

Some daughters have found that just waiting is helpful, until mother realizes that daughter isn't pushing her to leave her marriage. Other daughters have told their mothers explicitly, "I left Fred because leaving was right for me. But that doesn't mean that I think you should leave Dad. Only you can make that decision."

Most mothers will hesitate to encourage their daughter to leave a miserable marriage. But when the divorce is a fait accompli, a mother may feel freer to admit to herself and her daughter that marriage is not perfect; she no longer need try to persuade her daughter to stay in the conventional married role. One of my students describes her experience:

> After six years of marriage, I told my mother that I was leaving my husband. I said I was fed up with nurturing a man who was not capable of returning the nurturing. She understood. . . . The separation and divorce left me feeling vulnerable, but free [to stop pretending marriage is perfect], as it did my mother. Our relationship began to feel truly loving, and I felt her acceptance of me. I began to develop more self-esteem and greater satisfaction in my job.

As you work on particular problems, from time to time you may have to take measures to keep up your motivation. Remind yourself what you're working toward by recalling a time when you and your mother had a good relationship. Also remind yourself that you don't have to choose between telling your mother how you are feeling and trying to increase the closeness or reduce the tension between you. The two are not mutually exclusive. For example, you can tell her you don't like her criticism of you because it gets in the way of your enjoyment of your time together.

After choosing a problem to work on, trying to identify your and your mother's feelings about it, and discussing what you each regard as the sources of the problem, it will probably help to read how other mothers and daughters have worked on issues together. Once again, even if you are not working directly with your mother, you can benefit from the insights of other women. The following chapter consists of stories about mothers and daughters and how they have worked on their relationships.

8

What Mothers and Daughters Have Done

A reliable signal that our mother-daughter relationship needs mending is our emotional distress—or our mother's. We began this book with a look at the upsetting emotions that daughters feel, then examined the mother-blaming myths that cause or aggravate them; now we have come full circle—back to the emotions themselves. Now, with the help of the language of the myths, we can take a fresh, active look at what to do about those painful feelings.

Sometimes the anguish can be quickly alleviated through insight and sharing, but sometimes it requires sustained, long-term effort. Reading these stories of mothers and daughters should give you some idea of how you want to proceed; I hope you will feel how real are the possibilities for change. Not all of the stories are about easily solved problems, because mother-daughter problems can be so complex and delicate; but all of the examples do show how a mother, a daughter, or both have worked on some difficulty between them and achieved some improvement, even if they have not eliminated the difficulty altogether.

I can't discuss all of the key feelings and issues that can plague any stage of the mother-daughter relationship, from the daughter's birth through the mother's and the daughter's aging; however, I have chosen a variety of examples from different stages. Some of these stories will hit closer to home for you than others, but I encourage you to read them all; other women's ways of thinking or speaking or acting may be useful to you, even if their concerns differ from yours.

A Principle for All Feelings

Anguish in our mother-daughter relationships usually results from a rift between us, so we need to focus on repairing the rift rather than on laying blame. A daughter may react to some interruption in her connection to her mother by feeling ambivalence, betrayal, despair, anger, guilt, sadness, or numbness and alienation. Often, we aren't even aware that our unmet need for connection is the problem. Feminist therapist Nikki Gerrard described what happened one Sunday in her house:

> My six-year-old daughter was whining about being bored, and I got irritated and angry. I wanted to scream at her, spank her, and maybe send her to her room. I thought that her bad behavior was a sign that she couldn't play on her own, and I was feeling that I was a bad mother for not having taught her how to do that.
>
> Suddenly, something clicked. I realized that I was assuming that her independence—or lack of it—was the issue here, and I was so focused on that that I hadn't wondered what else might be going on. I thought about what makes me cranky and irritable, and I realized that often it's because I'm uncomfortable about a break or a distancing in a close relationship. So I took my daughter in my arms and said, "I love you." I told her that she was precious to me, and I stroked her hair. She sucked her thumb and lay there like a contented cat. After a while, she got up, went outdoors, and played. A rift in our relationship had been repaired, and now she felt fine.

This is a good and useful model for all of us. I have tried it many times myself, including with my daughter and my mother. Recently, my daughter was upset about the trouble she was having with a school project. I called from the kitchen into the family room, "Emily, why don't you look it up in the encyclopedia?" Silence. "Honey, do you understand the assignment? You could call one of the other kids in the class and ask them." Irritated outburst from Emily. Then I remembered Nikki's experience with her daughter. "Emily," I said, "I'm sorry you feel frustrated, and I wish I could help." She was relieved: her school assignment had upset her, she had taken out her irritation on me, and then she had felt bad about that. When I stopped trying to find exactly what to do for her (Myth Three) and just tried to be warm and supportive, she was reassured because her irritation hadn't damaged our connection for more than a few minutes.

The relief that comes from repairing damaged mother-daughter connections was experienced by Janice and her mother, Marjorie, whose relationship was plagued by the myth that the measure of a good mother is a perfect daughter. Janice thought her mother was trying to force her to follow social rules for selfish reasons; her mother's angry behavior had seemed to be her mother's heartless attempt to make her fit an acceptable mold.

When Janice's lover, Aaron, moved in with her and her two pre-teen children, Marjorie was terribly upset. She thought that Janice and Aaron were selfish for not waiting longer, to make sure their relationship would last, and that the children would be hurt if Aaron later moved out. Also, having been extremely sympathetic through Janice's previous relationships with men, Marjorie said that, frankly, she did not want to get her hopes up this time. She had been agonized when Janice's previous relationships dissolved, and she was upset at the prospect of listening once again to Janice's anguish about a broken relationship. Says Janice:

My first reaction was hurt. I felt rejected, then angry. I wondered— and asked Mom angrily—why she couldn't be happy that I was so happy. Why couldn't she see that Aaron was wonderful to the kids and that they adored him?

Janice wanted Marjorie to feel as she felt. She longed for her mother's approval and felt betrayed when it did not come. But in her wish for Marjorie's support, Janice was being insensitive to her mother's feelings. Marjorie's feelings were understandable and were not aimed to hurt Janice, as Janice finally realized:

When I calmed down and put myself in my mother's position, I fig-ured that I would probably have felt the same way. I get fed up with friends who repeatedly go through a period of elation at the begin-nings of relationships, followed by longer times when they need my support as the relationship turns sour.

The first step that made a difference was trying to see the situation from Marjorie's point of view. Janice then put that understanding into action: she called Marjorie and said, "Mom, I wish you could rejoice with me, but I understand why you can't, and I respect your feelings."

For a while, Janice thought the problem was solved. She felt mature about acknowledging the different feelings that she and her mother had. But then she realized that she also felt estranged from her. After spending some long nights fearing that her next step might fail miserably, Janice phoned her mother again:

> I told her that I was feeling distant from her and didn't like that, especially since we've usually been so close. I said that I was still happy with Aaron, and so were the children, but that I felt uncomfortable because she and Aaron, two very important people in my life, felt totally unconnected to each other. I told her I didn't expect her to jump on the next plane and move in with us for six months so she could get to know and love Aaron. I didn't ask Mom to change her feelings. I just said our estrangement pained me and I wanted to be close to her again.

Four months later Marjorie spent a weekend with Janice and Aaron. Although nothing is perfect, and she does not yet adore Aaron, she knows that Janice wants to stay close to her. Finding a way to avoid blaming Marjorie for their estrangement and finding a way to live with her own decisions even though they were not what her mother wanted freed Janice from her resentment of her mother. A great deal of energy was released from self-doubt (for not pleasing her mother) and from mother-blaming, allowing Janice to use that energy to maintain and strengthen the bond with her mother.

Marjorie now felt less pressed to approve and participate wholeheartedly in everything Janice did, but she also learned that her daughter's involvement with a new man did not mean that Janice had stopped caring about her relationship with her mother or respecting her mother's opinions.

These stories illustrate the need for us to keep in mind that much of the distress in our relationships with our mothers comes from our longing for more connection with them.

Ambivalence

We have looked in detail at the polarized mother-images' power to make us deeply ambivalent about our mothers. When strong ambivalence is a characteristic of your mother-daughter relationship, you'll probably find it useful to consider how the two sets of myths can feed that feeling. For example, the Perfect Mother myth of mother's endless nurturing attracts us to our mothers, even as the Bad Mother myth of female inferiority may make us want to dissociate ourselves from them.

A daughter's ambivalence about her mother often appears or becomes particularly pronounced in adolescence, when her wish to have nothing to do with her mother is intensified by her need to feel grown-up. Editor Janet Goldstein recalls her mother saying to her, when she was a teenager, "I can't even stand in line with you at the movies right. I either stand too close to you or not close enough!" When a daughter wants her mother near, they are both plagued by the worry that closeness is unhealthy, and when they are close, each fears being overwhelmed by the other's "enormous" needs.

Teenage girls usually want to stay distant from their mothers in order to hide their increased sexual and aggressive feelings; but the confusion those feelings arouse makes them long more than ever to feel protected and supported. A mother who knows what her daughter feels is a potential source of comfort. But if the daughter's fear of her mother's disapproval is too great, her mother's knowledge about her feelings can also be a source of fear and shame, which lead her to shut her mother out. The daughter may experience her mother as a human mirror who will not retreat respectfully into shadow.

As adults we often moan, "When I'm with my mother, I feel like I'm fourteen years old again." We believe that our mothers see through us, see what we want most to keep hidden. We may feel that they have never recognized our maturity and independence. Ideally, mothers and daughters can find ways to be close, loving adults who interact as equals. Tamika's story in chapter 7 about her phone calls from her mother is an example of this kind of successful resolution.

Ambivalence can emerge with surprising intensity, often after a period of equilibrium and general closeness. As your mother ages, you probably begin looking after her in certain ways, helping her out, checking on how she's feeling. Although you may just be continuing your mutually caring relationship, you may worry that you have participated in a "role reversal," that you now "mother" your mother. You and your mother may want to stay close, but you worry that such mother-daughter closeness is unhealthy. Rosa, a mother-daughter workshop participant, put it this way:

> After my mother's arthritis got so bad, I started doing some of her housework—especially the things she had to kneel down to do. I wanted to help her, but I worried that she'd feel uncomfortable having me take care of her instead of the opposite; and I felt strange, too. Sometimes the strangeness really got to me, and I'd take it out on her, getting really irritable.

Rosa's negative feelings came not just from the newness of the situation but also from her belief that a grown daughter and her mother should be independent of each other. As Rosa recognized her ambivalence (mixed reactions of caring and anger), she gradually understood the effects of the myth that mother-daughter closeness is unhealthy. Furthermore, she saw that her feeling that she ought to be endlessly nurturing, combined with her fear of giving too much, threatened to paralyze her emotionally.

Rosa also saw that two myths had allowed her to take care of her father without feeling ambivalent. Because of the male superiority myth, she felt privileged to help him, and because of the endless nurturance myth, she felt womanly for doing so. Rosa said, "I've never felt irritated about taking care of my father since his heart attack. I expect so much of her, but not of him."

Weeks after the workshop, Rosa called to tell me that she had talked to her mother both about how strange her caretaking role felt and how much she appreciated all the caretaking her mother had done for her over the years. Her recognition of the power of the myths had resolved much of her ambivalence, and she could show her mother some appreciation and respect.

By acknowledging her discomfort to her mother, rather than taking it out in anger at her, Rosa established a new phase in their relationship. Although the changes involved some reversal of power and responsibility between them, they came closer to being psychological equals. They did this by straightforwardly acknowledging their human reactions—Rosa's discomfort and resentment, and her mother's discomfort and sorrow about her loss of physical ability. Rosa's mother had felt less deserving of her daughter's respect than when she was better able to take care of herself, but Rosa reduced the pain and isolation they both felt when she acknowledged her own feelings in a respectful, dignified way.

Women whose mothers are too ill or disturbed to have the kind of conversation Rosa had with her mother have told me that just understanding the way the myths affected them has helped relieve their emotional distress. For instance, would you feel the same if such an incident were happening instead between you and your father, or between a father and a son? Fifty-year-old Kirthi vividly described the double standard for older people in this way:

> I see the same pattern in all my friends' families, as their parents get old. The father—even if he's been a bloody tyrant all his life— is respected as he ages. His maddening habits (both the lifelong ones and the new ones he acquires as he ages) are considered his idiosyncrasies. But the mother—no matter how much she slaved to keep the family together and to take care of everybody—is called a bitch and "an impossible person to deal with" when she is difficult.

You'll feel less ambivalent about taking care of your mother if you try to redress the balance, to fight against a complete power switch—or at least focus on respect for her. You can sometimes achieve this by asking her to do what she can do—tell you what you were like when you were little or what she wanted to be when she grew up or what she's done in her life that makes her proud or what she thinks about some political or ethical issue. This is a good way to combat the pressure from our youth-mad culture for us simply to withdraw from older people, to stop caring.

You can also acknowledge her status as a resource person because of her age. Mothers can help demystify the process of aging for us. Some years ago my mother told me that, because of her hearing loss, she feels isolated when unable to hear a conversation that is going on right in front of her. I hadn't realized how much of the world we can miss because of changes that go with aging. Any discomfort or irritation I might have felt when her hearing problems caused me inconvenience was partly mitigated by my greater understanding of her experience and respect for her honesty in talking about it.

Betrayal

Daughters commonly feel betrayed by their mothers because the myth of male superiority leads mothers to undervalue or even demean both their daughters and themselves. In her early twenties, Genna came to such a realization in the aftermath of a shopping expedition with her mother:

> For so many years, I'd loved the times that Mom and I went to the beauty shop or clothes shopping. Then, one day, I felt horribly let down because she made a cutting comment about a beautiful suit that I bought. She said, "You'll certainly make me look dowdy when you show up in that flashy suit." I couldn't believe it—my mother was jealous of me.

Genna felt disappointed and betrayed—and those feelings about her mother were too painful to ignore. In order to feel comfortable with her mother, she would somehow have to to come to terms with what had happened. She knew that if she simply told her mother how hurt she was, her mother would say she was ridiculous to respond that way to a compliment. Genna discussed the matter with an old friend, and together they identified Genna's feelings:

> My immediate reaction had been to feel guilty for outdoing her. Then, I felt angry at her for making me feel guilty. Next I got mad at myself, because part of me was glad to outdo her. Finally, I saw how much pressure she had put on both of us to get men's approval and how that drove us apart. That's when I realized that, in addition to the warmth and the sharing in those expeditions, there was a frenetic quality, because the whole point was to make ourselves attractive to men!
>
> My mother's concern with men's approval was something she had picked up from her mother. I knew, because I had often heard my grandmother talk about "looking nice for the menfolk." Memories started to come back to me—all those years I felt so proud of

being thinner than she was but at the same time felt I could never be as strong and competent as she. And I recalled many times that she had shown her jealousy of me for being young and thin. I felt cheated: why had we spent so much energy competing with each other for my Dad's and my brother's approval, and each of us feeling like we had lost?

At first, I blamed her: she had trained me to do this! But I had noticed in my friends' families how the mothers thought they were supposed to teach their daughters to play up to men, and I finally saw that my mother wasn't so different in that respect. I also saw that it was no more her fault than the fault of my friends' mothers that they were that way. I felt more like we'd been duped together. And my resentment of her slowly began to fade. It didn't disappear entirely, though, because I still wished she had been strong enough to keep from being duped.

In a variation on the male superiority theme, because mothers think they should raise conventional daughters and sons, their daughters often feel betrayed. As twenty-nine-year-old Becky recalled:

I never felt like my anger was legitimate, like it could lead to anything good. My brother's anger could, though: if I yelled and screamed, I got put down for it, but if he yelled and screamed, my parents buckled under and gave him whatever he wanted. As for sex, the message from my parents was simply "Don't!" but my brother was given condoms and proud, knowing looks by our dad. I knew my parents were worried about me getting pregnant, and that worry seemed to get in the way of their making me feel anything good about my sexuality. It became only a burden to me.

Many women discover that their mothers thought they should teach their daughters to look up to men more than women even though they disliked some aspects of the female role and did not really want to compete with their daughters for men's favor. Mothers have sometimes found ways to opt out of the competition and avoid the female tasks they hated the most.

When I was growing up, I heard my mother say repeatedly (and, to my surprise, shamelessly), "I couldn't sew on a button!" I became the "tailor," sewing on buttons and hemming skirts and slacks for the family. I believed that my father thought I was better than my mother in this way. I felt embarrassed for her and at once proud and guilty for having outdone her. Not until I turned forty did I understand what had really happened. I asked Mother, "You know how you used to say you couldn't sew on a button? I just realized—anyone can sew on a button—including you, right?"

"Sure," she said with a grin, "but I wasn't gonna get stuck doing all that!" She had had no interest in competing with me for the title of Sewing Queen, but I had been so caught up in the race for men's approval that I felt smug about beating Mother at a game she wasn't even playing.

Some traditional therapists believe that intense mother-daughter competition for males' attention is inevitable and healthy, as well as crucial in helping the daughter escape her "enmeshment" with her mother and enter the "real, public world" represented by her father. This belief is absurd. It is childish to believe that loving father more must mean loving mother less; that belief is fed by the myth that men are superior and so no one would *want* to stay close to mother.

Because women are devalued, both teenage boys and girls are driven to prove they're different and separate from their mothers; a daughter wants to show how different she is from her mother, but she also resents her mother (perhaps unconsciously) for bearing the message that both of them are less worthy than men.

You may want to think back over key moments in your childhood when you were disobedient and rebellious against your mother. Ask yourself whether you might have been resisting some of the traditionally feminine things that your mother felt she should teach you. Isabella, who now has two children, bristled every time her mother gave her recipes or cooking advice:

> I felt like she was telling me that, without her help, I'd be a lousy cook. One day, a woman at work was talking about how much she hates to cook, and it hit me: I hate to cook, too! All those times when I was a kid, my mother would call me into the kitchen, with a big grin on her face, and say, "Let's bake cookies!" I think she thought that's what mothers were supposed to do. I never wanted to bake, but I didn't want to hurt her feelings. I resented her for acting like it was so much fun.

Like many daughters, Isabella felt betrayed by her mother's participation in the myth of men's superiority; she thought her mother's cooking was a sign of submission to men's expectations that women would cook. The recognition of that myth as a source of the trouble is the first step toward overcoming our feeling that our mother has betrayed us.

Despair

In Chapter 2, I told the story of Chava, who despaired of pleasing her mother, Sue, in regard to Chava's trip with her boyfriend. If despair is the major troublesome feeling you have about your mother, you may want to review what Ellen and Sue did to overcome that despair.

In addition to being concerned about not pleasing Mother, daughters despair, often unconsciously, because they see their mothers as victims and feel powerless to help them. In approximately one-third of North American families, the father physically abuses the mother; in a larger number of families, he humiliates her. Here, the daughter's dilemma is even more painful. At age thirty, Alison looked back on her adolescence with a father who frequently insulted her mother:

> It tore me apart. I hated him for insulting her, and that made me want to side with her. But I fled from the humiliation-by-association. When Dad intimidated Mom, I hated her for not standing up for herself. To me, her weakness meant that all of us women had to suffer our shame in silence.

For many daughters, decades pass before they realize how the myths of male superiority and the dynamics of male domination may have operated in their family and why their mothers deferred to their fathers in important ways. In recent years, increased public discussion of sexism in the home has not abolished that sexism but has often led to its transmutation into subtler forms; as a result, it can be harder for young women to put their finger on the ways these myths and dynamics were played out.

You can start to understand by asking your mother what she thought would have happened if she had been less deferential to your father or striven for an equal sharing of family power with him. A woman who asked her mother that question reported,

"Mother said that she knew she had more sense about managing money than Dad, but she let him make the financial decisions because she didn't want to embarrass him."

Because children usually feel powerless to help their mothers, they may respond to their mothers' victimization or even their undervaluation by developing behavior problems or becoming detached. Many children, however, hold on to the feeling that they ought to be able to protect and save their mothers. Daughters are particularly likely to feel that way, because of their nurturant self-image. For these children, feelings of powerlessness can lead to despair, and these feelings can be carried through a lifetime. Often adult daughters do not realize that they are no longer powerless.

Marianne, a Black civil rights activist, realized how deeply distressed she was because of her inability when she was a child to stop her mother's suffering at the hands of a racist employer:

> Mama and I had always talked about some of the awful things that white people did to our people, and Mama's teaching was what made me become so active in the civil rights movement. But sometimes I hated being around her when she'd come home from work worn out from fighting off the sexual advances of her foreman, who would say things to her like, "You know you want me, Black bitch." I couldn't stand to think of her suffering and not be able to help, so I'd just shut my feelings off.

At age thirty-six, Marianne reached a crisis in her life. The more people she helped through her civil rights work, the more she despaired about her past failure to help her mother. When she assisted an older Black woman in winning a sexual harassment suit before a human rights commission, Marianne realized that sexual harassment was one of the problems her mother had had to deal with; she could no longer avoid seeing how, for years, she had distanced herself from her mother's pain because she couldn't help. Now, at last, she had the power and therefore felt no need to pull away from her mother's suffering.

Marianne called her mother and asked to come for a visit, during which she explained her insight. "Mama wasn't surprised," she said. "She'd known all along why I backed off. But I felt better for knowing what had come between us, and after that I didn't have to keep my distance so much."

At difficult times in our own lives, we may despair when we find Mother doesn't give us what we want and we don't know why. Because mothers so often hide their troubles, we are bewildered by their emotional distance. Those are usually the most important times to ask directly what is going on in her life. One of my students realized, soon after having a baby, that her mother wasn't meeting her needs because she had other problems on her mind. The student had been longing for her mother's approval of the way she took care of the baby, and she had been disappointed when her mother said nothing about it. She saw the reason when her mother and grandmother came together for a visit:

> Part of this visit is to make sure that Grandma has a chance to see her great-granddaughter. All along I have been hoping that my mom would say, "You are doing a fine job with Alexandra," while she herself has been searching for reassurance from me that she is being patient and nurturant with her mother.

This kind of understanding teaches us that mother "neglects" us not because we're bad, nor because she disapproves or doesn't care, but because she is a human being who is trying hard to cope within the narrow boundaries of the supernurturant female role. Despairing daughters must realize that those narrow boundaries and women's restricted power in the wider society limit both mothers' ability to meet their daughters' needs and daughters' ability to protect their mothers.

Anger

Anger is a big part of so many mother-daughter relationships partly because mother-blaming encourages it and partly because anger is a common reaction to any unpleasant feeling. When we feel ambivalence, betrayal, despair, guilt, or sadness toward our mothers, we are likely to get angry at them for "making" us feel those ways. As we learned in chapter 2, an important step in understanding and overcoming our anger is to identify the underlying feelings that are fueling the fire. What follows are some of the most common anger-provoking situations that daughters encounter with their mothers.

"I Can Never Please Her"

We've already looked at some examples of the daughter's need to please her mother in order to show that Mother has raised a good daughter (Myth One).

A painful situation is that of the daughter who is considered overweight and thus gets caught in the conflict between her mother's need to have a "presentable" daughter and her own struggles to become independent and develop a sense of identity. The mother of an "overweight" daughter feels inept because her daughter doesn't fit the current feminine ideal, so she thinks she ought to do something; she may also worry about her daughter's health. But her offers of advice only highlight the daughter's "failure" of self-control, increase her self-loathing, and establish the mother as a handy target for all of this frustration. Twenty-year-old Amanda was one of my clients and told the following story:

> Mother wanted me to lose weight for my own sake, sure—but also for her, and I couldn't stand being her route to her club ladies' praise: "How nice! Amanda has finally lost some weight!" I felt like a piece of meat.

Using some of the techniques in this book, Amanda finally sat down for a heart-to-heart talk with her mother:

> I knew that basically Mother cared about me a lot, and telling her to get off my back hadn't worked, so I took a different tack: I tried to find out about her point of view. I asked her to stop talking about what being overweight might do to me, and asked her what my extra poundage meant to her. At first, she thought it had nothing to do with her own feelings. But when I asked directly if she felt like a failure for not being able to produce a slim daughter, she burst into tears and said, "I don't know what I've done to drive you to eat so much. Do you eat because you're unhappy, or is it just that I never taught you enough self-control? And if you're too fat, you'll never get a husband, and I'll never have any grandchildren."

Once her mother's worries were out in the open, the two women could talk about how unfair it was for both of them to be judged—or to judge themselves—by the shape of Amanda's body. They became partners. Amanda reported:

Mother sometimes still says she wishes I would lose weight; but she doesn't hate me for being "proof" of her failure as a mother, and I don't feel like she's trying to control my eating habits simply for her selfish reasons.

I have heard similar stories of daughters who believe their mothers "hate" them for marrying out of their faith, for choosing not to have a child, or for having women partners. Daughters in such situations often deal with their mother's disapproval or discomfort by intellectualizing or by attacking her: "She's being irrational!" "She's homophobic!" "She cares more about what her super-religious brother thinks than about how I feel!"

A daughter's choice of partner or decision not to have children can threaten her mother, but eliminating mother's and daughter's misinterpretations of each other's feelings can reduce some of their pain.

A daughter who had been married for five years to a man of a different religion told me that her mother hated both her and her husband. I had talked to her mother and knew that she did not hate her daughter but considered herself a failure for not having raised a daughter who married within their faith; her mother said openly that this was a question of feelings—of failure and fear that she would somehow be punished. Her daughter raged about her mother's hypocrisy and irrationality.

"Your mother never claims that her reaction is logical," I told the daughter, "but what's most important is that you love each other and want to reduce the tension between you. The one thing you never do is to let each other know you care. Each of you clings to a five-year-old grudge, and although it's been an excruciating time for you both, perhaps you can now create a calmer kind of connection. Why don't you begin by assuming that she doesn't hate you or want you to feel guilty but does want to get along better with you? She believes that you hate her. I never saw such a family for avoiding showing that they care."

The other daughter in the family had said something similar to her mother, and the next time mother and daughter talked on the telephone, the tension was reduced. Each woman felt less rejected, and each was willing to believe that the other wanted to reestablish a connection. They have not lived happily ever after, but their recognition of each other's desire for acceptance and reconciliation has repaired some of the hurt.

In a parallel situation, Glynis's psychiatrist prescribed a powerful sedative for her when her daughter, Miara, told her she was lesbian. Glynis had heard experts "explain" on talk shows that lesbianism was a mental illness caused by a cold and rejecting mother, who forced the daughter to yearn for women's love. Glynis felt bewildered, overwhelmed, and then angry, because her worry as she was raising Miara was that she loved her daughter so dearly that it might be "too much, smothering." Now she wondered desperately if her fear of loving Miara too much had somehow made her, unawares, too reserved. She was in such a state, feeling guilty to have "messed up Miara" and not being sure how it had happened, that she failed to assure Miara that she still loved her and wanted her to be happy. Miara felt betrayed, and this made her angry. Being around her mother was painful, because Glynis was depressed and withdrawn on the sedatives, and Miara was in no state to risk further rejection by asking for her mother's acceptance. In this case, a young gay man who worked in Glynis's office confided to her about how he had longed for his parents' acceptance of his sexual orientation, and as he spoke, it struck Glynis that she had neglected to make it clear to Miara that she was not angry at her but worried and ashamed of herself. She realized that this was probably why Miara had recently sounded so cold whenever Glynis phoned her. That shift to her daughter's perspective allowed her to take the first reparative step. She told Miara that she thought she now understood why Miara was so angry, and that began their rapprochement.

"She Knows Things I Don't Want to Hear"

Part of a mother's role is to warn her daughter when there is danger ahead. Unfortunately, that makes her the bearer of bad news, news the daughter may not want to hear. When I was a very young woman, my mother told me that a man I was involved with had hugged her "too closely." I pooh-poohed her concern: "Oh, Mom, you don't understand. He's just a warm person—and he's European. That's how they act." He turned out to be a womanizer of the most deceitful sort—but I hadn't wanted to hear her warning because it punctured my little happiness balloon.

I had been angry, wrongly believing that my mother was abusing her power over me; what she said would have helped me if I had been able to listen rather than blame her for interfering. Daughters who are starting an intimate relationship want to believe they'll live happily ever after. They don't want to hear from mothers who can foresee the misery ahead of us if they have a partner who is a batterer or an alcohol or drug abuser or a compulsive gambler or womanizer. Daughters resist acknowledging that the realm of relationships is not as safe as they want it to be. We mourn this loss of our innocence, and anger about loss—even inevitable ones—is a normal part of any mourning process. So we turn on our mothers in anger when their counsel leads to that loss.

"She's Too Bad" and "She's Too Good"

Like most daughters, you have probably sometimes resented your mother for being a poor role model and sometimes resented her for being too "good," setting a standard you could never meet. Adult daughters resent mothers who were poor role models for tasks like child-rearing. The exasperated young mother screams at her children, recognizing her mother's words and inflections, and blames her mother for failing to teach her better ways to cope.

Any adult woman seeking the impossible goal of being both Perfect Mother *and* Perfect Employee may be furious at her mother, either for not having shown her the path by attempting the dual roles or for having made the attempt but not found the secret to doing both superbly and serenely. A young woman attending a mother-daughter workshop said:

> My mother was a Supermom, right down to baking cookies every Thursday. The way she did it, mothering was a full-time job. But now that I'm a mother and have a paid, full-time job, I can't for the life of me figure out how to be as good a mother as she.

When a daughter who is trying to create a good relationship or raise a family finds herself repeating her mother's mistakes, she may nourish a festering resentment. As a young woman told me, "When my brother and I used to fight, Mother would become hysterical and shriek that we were going to kill each other. I refuse to act that way when my kids fight, but I don't know what to do. I got no clues from her."

When the mother has kept her own aspirations within the narrow traditional limits for women, she mirrors the poverty of possibility in her daughter's future and may draw her daughter's rage for that. Said one daughter,

> Mom did everything for Dad and for us kids, but she never did anything for herself. I adored her, and that narrowed my vision of what I could be, because I was so intent on watching her as a great mother that I didn't learn much about the richness and variety of life choices from her.

Daughters may find it maddening when their mothers seem to handle easily the tasks their daughters find difficult. Rarely does a woman find marriage or childraising easy. If your mother tried to conceal from you her difficulties, dilemmas, or problems, she may even have become afraid to acknowledge them to herself. You may feel that she sailed through all her problems; you may have thought something was wrong with you when you could not sail smoothly through your thorny problems.

Who, in most cases, led the daughter to believe that marriage and motherhood would mean living happily ever after? In most cases, the mother did some of that teaching. You may resent your mother for having protected you from reality, leaving you unprepared to be a wife and mother, not showing you how to cope. You may feel even more isolated from your supposedly perfect mother than from other women, at a time when you most need to turn to her for advice, information, and compassion. Thirty-year-old Fengxi felt this way about her mother and finally told her:

> Mom was shocked to learn I was afraid to tell her about my insecurity about motherhood because I saw her as perfection. She'd tried not to "burden" me by telling the truth about some of the difficulties of being a mother. But once she really understood that her perfect image was making me upset, out came story after story of her own struggles. She was relieved to tell me.

If your mother gets tense when you tell her you are frustrated as a mother or as a mother and a paid worker, don't assume that her tension reflects disapproval of you. She may feel ashamed for not being able to teach you how to flourish in those roles or for not having helped you avoid the traps and limitations she knows intimately.

"She's So Critical of Me Sometimes"

We long always to be able to lean on our mothers. The endless nurturance myth is so powerful that we feel enraged when we don't get what we want from them. Less commonly acknowledged than the mother who can't let go of her daughter is the fury of the adult daughter who expects endless nurturance from her mother when the mother is looking for rest from the long decades of maternal responsibility.

In a brilliant paper, "We Are Not Your Mothers," social worker Rachel Josefowitz Siegel writes that people expect all older women to be motherly, so we even turn to older women who are not our mothers, expecting understanding and advice—and getting angry if it's not forthcoming. When our own mother fails us, we can't imagine that she might want a break from advising and supporting.

After I read Siegel's paper, I caught myself turning to my mother and other older women for support, without letting them know that I'd gladly return the favor. Once I realized this and started asking, "And now, how are you?" I heard about both sorrows and joys I hadn't suspected they felt. Asking our mothers that question, and truly wanting to hear their answer, decreases their resentment of us; we now offer something back to them.

Certain times in our lives place us at special risk for feeling undernurtured. When a mother offers advice about baby care, her daughter assumes that her mother thinks she's incompetent. If her mother can describe some of the uncertainties she felt at such a time, her daughter can see that her mother's offer of advice is not a sign that her mother thinks she's doing badly. When Erica's mother did not volunteer that information, Erica took matters into her own hands: "I couldn't stand it. She kept showing me how to change Bibi's diapers, burp her, hold her. Until Mom came to visit, I thought I was doing okay. When Erica got up the nerve to tell her mother how she was feeling, she learned that her mother had felt just as insecure with her first child.

We are especially vulnerable to feeling undernurtured when

an intimate relationship ends. A mother who seems cold or with-holding at such a time may have a host of reasons other than that she doesn't care. If she thought you and your partner were poorly matched, she may be biting her tongue to keep from saying, "I always thought you were wrong for each other." Or she may be afraid of seeming intrusive or may not know what to say or do—a typical feeling when trying to respond to someone else's loss. If the relationship that ended was anything other than a traditional, heterosexual, legal marriage, she may feel particularly unsure what to say. Knowing these possible explanations won't stop you from longing for her support but will help you understand her behavior.

Anger is such a powerful emotion that it's hard to settle down and figure out what lies beneath it. We're at a greater loss if the object of our anger can't explain her behavior. Consider the following story of how a woman's anger at her mother-in-law's hostility toward her was based on mistaken assumptions:

My mother-in-law never seemed to think that anything I did was good enough for her son, Harold. She raved about the presents that "Harold" gave her, although she knew that I had shopped for them. "I'm so unfortunate," she'd moan, "because daughters-in-law never treat you well," although I went out of my way to be warm and attentive to her. After twenty-five years, I gave up.

One Christmas Eve, the family asked her about her early childhood. Dorrie's father was a rich, charming, but good-for-nothing man. Dorrie's parents left her and their older son in Ireland when they immigrated to the United States. Dorrie spent most of the first five years of her life with her grandmother. "Did your parents write to you from America?" I asked. "No," she said, "because I couldn't read. And I forgot what my father looked like."

According to Dorrie, "When I was nearly five, my brother and I were put, unaccompanied, on a ship to America. When we landed at Ellis Island, I recognized my mother but not my father. As they rushed toward me, I asked my mother, 'Where is my father?' Father was rarely home and was very distant from us emotionally.

"My mother had a suitor who adored her, but she would not leave my father, because she was afraid that her suitor might abuse me; her stepfather had done that to her."

Trapped in a loveless marriage in a foreign country, burdened with financial worries and a husband who was not a good provider, Dorrie's mother had little energy and love to give Dorrie. Her father gave Dorrie nothing at all.

Hearing the tale did not make the daughter-in-law feel more accepted by Dorrie, but it showed her that Dorrie's treatment of her was largely a manifestation of her miserable childhood experiences, which left her feeling empty and hurt. This helped take the sting out of Dorrie's rejection of her.

Sometimes, what comes across to a daughter as her mother's angry criticism is not so much criticism as fear and worry based on the mother's different perspective because she grew up in a different historical era than her daughter. Ann, a white lawyer, was furious because her mother, Frances, predicted dire consequences for her if she married her fiancé. "She's racist! I can't believe my mother is racist! She's the one who encouraged me to go into civil rights law," Ann told me. "I guess she's antiracist in principle, it's that horrible old story of, 'But I wouldn't want my daughter to marry one!'"

When I asked exactly what her mother had said, Ann replied that Frances had said, "Society isn't ready for interracial couples. You cannot imagine how much suffering you are in for. Not to mention what a nightmare it would be for your children!" Ann thought that the "society" argument must be a cover for her mother's deep-seated antipathy toward racialized people, though Frances had never before made racist remarks. Perhaps she had never really known her mother's deepest feelings? I urged Ann to try to talk further with Frances, painful though the conversation might be.

They agreed to talk again, and in the course of that discussion, Frances said, "You just wait until you walk into a hotel with him and the desk clerk says *you* can have a room but he can't! How will you both feel? Something clicked for Ann, who had attended a university with an extremely diverse population and worked for a law firm and on a number of task forces that were similarly diverse and whose members interacted at work and socially with relative ease. She had never experienced anything like what her mother described, although she had heard stories of such incidents from the 1960s and even the 1970s. She was born in 1973. Although many of her clients were suing former employers for racial discrimination, in her years of going out with Ted, she had heard no blatantly racist comments about them as a couple. She had noticed the odd stares they sometimes got from strangers, but she found them easy to ignore, because she simply had no respect for anyone who would be bothered by an interracial couple.

Ann told her mother about this, and when her mother again brought up the hotel example, Ann laughed and said, "Mom, they can't do that anymore! This is the twenty-first century. It is against the law. I know it didn't use to be when you were growing up, but it is now." Ann understood better why her mother had been so upset: she was unable to get out of her own time in history. Things were not simple, of course. In response to Ann's comment, Frances pointed out, "Racial discrimination in employment is against the law, too, but you spend most of your time at work on exactly that, don't you? Since when do laws immediately transform the world?" Ann acknowledged that her mother was right but then said, "Mom, no couple and no children are problem-free. You were a single mother and close to poverty when you raised me. That was hard for you. And you raised me to be a feminist. I'm glad to be one, but you know that sometimes makes life difficult. So, Ted and I will start out knowing that racism is something that we, and our children, will need to struggle with. But we love each other, and we both believe the struggle is worth it."

Ann's need to believe that she and Ted could cope with racial hatred made it hard to hear the truth in her mother's concerns, and she experienced it as criticism of her choice. Frances was so worried about the future suffering of her daughter, of Ted (whom she liked and admired), and of their children that it was hard for her to assume that the world had changed enough that her loved ones would be spared pain. Her deep love for Ann made it difficult for her to think about the obstacles Ann and Ted might have to confront together. Their talk helped because it made it clear that their positions were not as polarized as each had believed.

Guilt

Daughters describe feeling guilty about not making up to their mothers for the isolation, devaluation, and even humiliation they may have endured because of being women and, especially, mothers. Our impotence impairs our sense of power to affect the world. Still worse, we feel guilty when we realize that we, too, have often joined in demeaning our mother.

A daughter often knows that her mother is unhappy but feels she cannot help, as in the example of Marianne, the civil rights worker, in the section "Despair." That other people or institutions have caused our mother's unhappiness doesn't keep us from feeling bad about our limited ability to help, especially if she seems to have sacrificed her life and happiness for us. Jody, now forty-one years old, writes,

> Five years ago, something I'd barely noticed suddenly jumped out at me. My otherwise lovely father had a habit of putting my mother down. I can't tell you how many times I'd heard him relate the story of my mother's mispronunciation—forty years ago!—of a novelist's name. As Mom and Dad got older, while she quietly but carefully lowered the amount of fat in his diet, he started telling "jokes" about how ugly old women are. It had taken me years to see the sexism in my own family and to think about how much it had hurt my mother when I joined in the laughter at her. I felt so guilty when I realized it.

Jody had a series of long talks with her father, and once he realized how his putdowns affected his wife, he toned them down.

It helped Jody to recognize that she had not initiated the mockery of her mother; both she and her father had been influenced by the myth of women's inferiority. Understanding that process did not mean overlooking or minimizing the ways that she and her father had participated in demeaning her mother, but it released some of the energy that had been tied up in Jody's guilt so that she could use it productively to change both her and her father's treatment of her mother. We are better able to help our mothers when we understand the causes of their problems and therefore can see what needs to be done.

The daughter who worries about her mother's happiness feels especially guilty about separating from her. As Ladonna, a college student, explained,

> I had been my mother's protector for so long that when the time came for me to go to college, I was afraid she wouldn't be able to

get along without me. She isn't very happy with my father, but she thinks she shouldn't talk about that to anyone outside the family. I'm afraid she will be alone, and I feel guilty about that.

We may be able to encourage our mothers to find other confidantes, or they may do that themselves. In any case, as both Jody and Ladonna found, feeling guilty helps no one.

Another source of the guilt that daughters feel toward mothers has arisen primarily in recent years. When we have a successful career and they do not, we feel discomfort. When Keshawna turned thirty and was promoted to manager at the large bank where she worked, she wrote to me,

> I feel so guilty. My mother works as a secretary just down the street. She stayed home and took care of my five brothers and sisters and me until a couple of years ago. She would have loved to have a better-paying job with more responsibility, but she never had the chances I had.

I suggested to Keshawna that she and her mother have a talk about what prevented her mother from getting a job earlier. Later, Keshawna wrote that from that talk she learned that her mother had wanted to work earlier:

> But my father said everyone would think he wasn't a good provider if he let her get a job. So, to keep him happy, she stayed at home. And here I'd been thinking that just the responsibility for taking care of us—our very existence—was to blame for my mother's lack of a chance to do what she wanted.

The phrase "I feel guilty" causes problems. Guilt has a stagnating effect; all we can do is stew in it. Guilt immobilizes us, and confessions of guilty feelings can be counterproductive, because saying "I feel guilty" makes us feel that we have done something to make amends. As long as we describe ourselves as terrible daughters and claim to feel guilty about it, we think we have shown what good people we are. The danger is in believing that acknowledging guilty feelings relieves us of the responsibility to right our wrongs or to figure out why we feel "guilty" when we haven't really done anything wrong. (For instance, we may feel guilty for being unable to protect Mother from demeaning treatment, as discussed earlier. If that is the cause of our "guilt," we need to be aware of it so that we can direct our anger against the true impediments to her happiness, rather than feeling that we ourselves are the cause.)

Nikki Gerrard suggests that the word *guilt* is often used when another word is more appropriate. Next time you start to say you feel guilty, ask yourself whether another word seems better. Often, the better word is *ashamed* or *sad.* Shame implies that you have failed to meet a standard, so once you know that you feel ashamed, you can take some action. You can ask, Whose standard is this that I feel I've failed to meet? And is it a reasonable standard? So instead of saying, "It's Sunday, and I forgot to call my mother. I feel so guilty," you can see whether "calling Mother every Sunday" is your own standard, hers, or someone else's.

Wanda asked her mother how she felt about her regular Sunday calls. To her surprise, she learned that her mother felt limited because she had to stay at home and wait for Wanda's call. Mother and daughter were able to get away from a rigid schedule that neither of them liked, while acknowledging that they both valued frequent contact. If, unlike Wanda's mother, your mother values the predictability of your Sunday calls, you can take other action. For instance, you may be able to explain to her that you sometimes don't call because you are exhausted from work or need some time alone, not because you're avoiding talking to her.

If *sad* seems a better word than *guilty* for what you feel about your mother, you probably feel somewhat estranged from her. In that case, too, you can take some action, this time in the form of strengthening the connection between you (see "A Principle for All Feelings," earlier in this chapter).

At a conference on motherhood, a woman named Carol told the following story the morning after she heard a presentation on mother-blaming. Carol was raised by her mother, who tried to keep her family out of poverty by running her own business during terrible economic times. Carol had always resented her mother for giving her gifts in the form of cash instead of her personal time. After the mother-blaming panel, Carol telephoned her now-eighty-four-year-old mother, who lived fifteen hundred miles away, and said, "I've been angry at you for fifty years because you always gave me money or presents instead of your time. I just realized that, because of your financial struggles, you must have thought that cash was the most valuable thing you could give me."

According to Carol, her mother listened, was silent for a moment, and then asked in a small voice, "Does that mean you are not mad at me anymore?" Carol assured her that she was not, that the purpose of the phone call was to tell her that she was not angry but was sad that her anger had come between them for so long. A barrier between them had been surmounted, and both mother and daughter felt better.

Fear

Two of the primary fears of adult daughters in relation to their mothers are the fear of displeasing her (or even losing her love) and the fear of becoming like her.

Our fear of displeasing our mother is intensified by the myth that women's power is dangerous: if we displease her, we feel, some horrible fate will befall us. For some daughters this fear is partly based in reality, because they have very critical, demanding mothers. But all daughters ultimately fear losing their mothers' love. The daughter in feminist writer Robin Morgan's novel *Dry Your Smile,* says, as her mother lies on her deathbed, "She does have power. She has the power not to love me." More than anyone else, our mother is supposed to love us—and love us no matter what—so we are terrified to think that maybe she doesn't. If she won't love us now, then who will after she dies? If she died without my being sure that she loved me, then I would feel unlovable.

Surprisingly often, a daughter benefits by telling her mother how frightened she is of failing to meet her standards or of disappointing her in some way. Dina, age thirty-three, explains why:

My Mom was amazed that I worried so much about her opinion of me. One by one, I listed all the things about me that I thought she disapproved of, and as I did that, she recognized that her standards really are very high. But it got her thinking, just to hear how long the list was. She told me that she guessed she'd been pretty rough on me, but that hadn't been her intention. As we talked, I learned that she set such high standards because she was trying to be a good mother by making me measure up to what girls are supposed to be. She had bought into the idea that she would have failed if I weren't very sweet, patient, giving, skinny, and high-achieving though modest and unaggressive.

The fear of becoming one's mother, or becoming like one's mother, has been called matrophobia by poet Adrienne Rich. We fear repeating Mother's mistakes. Because nobody knows better than we how abject and ashamed her disapproval makes us feel, we fear our own power to make others feel that way. Working through the mother-myths on her own the year she turned forty, Arlene saw that her fear of becoming like her mother was

a convenient focus for my fear of not being valued very much. That insight has made it a lot easier for me, because I realized that I wasn't afraid of my mother; I was afraid of being *treated* the way she was. I also feel less fatalistic now—where I used to feel I was destined to end up like Mother, I now know I can shape my life differently. I don't have to put up with disrespect. I no longer have to fear that whatever happened to her will inevitably happen to me.

Particularly pronounced in North America's youth-mad culture is daughters' fear of aging, as our mothers age before our eyes. Aviva, now in her early thirties, has been frightened by signs of age in her mother. Aviva notices the effects of gravity and time on her own body:

I can't spring out of bed as fast as I used to, and I sometimes forget familiar facts. When I look at my mother, my love for her is mixed with fear, because in her face, body, and functioning I see my own future and my own mortality. And we all know that in America, old women are the least respected people.

Aviva eventually realized that her fear was exaggerated by the male superiority myth; she counteracted this myth by a conscious decision to value her mother more than ever because of her experience and wisdom. This reduced her fear of her mother, because if her aging mother could have her respect, she feels, "by the time

I get old, maybe old women will get more respect. I'm taking one small step for me, hoping it will be one giant step for womankind."

Sadness

Two of the most poignant causes of sadness about our relationships with our mothers are our knowledge of what has been missing in their lives and our sense of the distance between them and ourselves.

In her study of women whose mothers had died, doctor of theology Martha Robbins reported that the women mourned more over their mothers' lives than over their deaths. One of my friends, now in her early fifties, said,

> I cannot tell you what pain I feel when I see how much my mother is under my father's thumb. She waits at home every day for the moment when he walks in the door after work. All her energy is focused on his dinner. What should she make? Will he even notice it? I could get angry and say she's neurotic or cowardly or stupid— and I do all those things sometimes; but mostly I just feel so darned sad for her.

For such sadness, we must try to come to terms with our own limitations. We can't change everything in Mom's life, even if we can urge her to get a job, to do volunteer work, to think of herself as a worthy person for reasons other than her great pot roast.

More significantly, we can try to change how she feels. My friend acknowledged to herself how boring her mother's life seemed to her, but then tried to see her mother's point of view. Raised in a society in which a good woman sits and waits for her man to come home for dinner, her mother's self-worth revolves very much around her pot roast. So, my friend began to ask her mother about pot roast recipes. She reports,

> I used to feel bored by conversations like that, because I thought cooking and housekeeping were unimportant, easy tasks. But now, every time she starts to talk about her recipes or her needlepoint, I remind myself that she's trying to convince herself, and me, that she does something worthwhile. That makes it less boring and very

moving, so now my increased appreciation for what she does comes through, and I can tell that she feels that.

My friend now feels less need to mourn her mother's life. She has also found a way to repair the mother-daughter rift caused by the myth of women's inferiority. If her mother went daily to an office, my friend wouldn't have to be so concerned about the limitations of her mother's life. But she might certainly feel sad that her mother has never felt she did a very good job either at the office or at home.

In the section "A Principle for All Feelings" earlier in this chapter, I emphasized the importance of repairing broken connections between mothers and daughters. Listen now to the story of Maria, who was saddened by what she misperceived as her mother's withdrawal of love:

> I told my mother in anger eighteen years ago, when I was fourteen, that I was having a sexual relationship with another girl. Until recently, I believed that it had taken my mother seven years to stop disapproving of me because of this. I just thought she was homophobic and condemned me for loving another girl.
>
> But recently, I thought back to the comments Mother made years ago—"I'm concerned about your committing yourself to something that could limit your potential later in life, for which people will reject you" and "I think you'll regret not having children" (having children was a rare option for lesbians at that time). I had blocked out what she really said back then, and all I could think of was that she hadn't just said, "That's terrific!" I began to wonder whether in fact she might not so much have disapproved as been genuinely worried about my happiness. After all, it has taken me seven years to find a partner who makes me happy, and my mother has relaxed now that she sees me in a good relationship.

Maria told her mother about her changed understanding of what had happened between them, and her mother confirmed that she had been primarily worried about Maria's happiness. She admitted, too, to some surprise and some guilt—she had worried, Have I messed up my daughter?—since many people considered lesbian relationships a sign of mental illness—but her major concern had been for Maria's happiness.

Numbness and Alienation

As described in chapter 2, when upsetting feelings—especially but not only hopelessness—overwhelm us, we often go numb or feel alienated from our mothers. The story of my friend in the previous section—who now appreciates her mother's pot roasts—demonstrates how our hopelessness about our mothers' lives can distance us from them; so, too, can our feeling that trying yet again for greater closeness is pointless. When we don't know what else to try, and the pain of broken connections is too great, what can we do but go numb? I hope that some of the steps and techniques in chapters 6 and 7 and this chapter have suggested ways that you can open new doors.

Here's an example of a daughter who went numb not so much from pain as from a surfeit of anger. Jocelyn and her mother, Beth, had had terrible arguments from the time Jocelyn began to approach puberty; at that time, although a psychiatrist had told them that they were competing for the attention of Jocelyn's father, he had not told them how to work out ways to enjoy their mother-daughter relationship. When I saw them years later at a lecture I gave on mothers and daughters, they described the father to me as a very cold man. With so little warmth and attention from him to go around, mother and daughter had competed with each other for scarce resources. But now that the daughter was an adult and could find warmth and attention outside her immediate family, the fierce mother-daughter competition felt less necessary.

After Jocelyn left home, Jocelyn and Beth had masked their rage at each other under what they thought was a lack of love for each other. Visits between them were so rare that both were afraid of spoiling them with outbursts of anger. So they held it all in, never getting at the roots of their anger, and letting the efforts to hold it in create a wall between them. Sparked by the lecture, Jocelyn and Beth worked on their relationship, and Beth wrote to me:

> I had always thought Jocelyn was an impossible person, and she thought the same about me. Once we realized that we had had to

compete for the minimal approval of the high-status person in the family—my husband—we saw that the evil was not all within us. We had both been afraid he would reject us and make us feel worthless. Recognition of those shared concerns has created a bond between us. Now when we are together, we hold nothing back. When we need to argue, we argue. But now we know there's a lot of love between us. It's great not to feel numb anymore in the presence of my daughter. At the ends of our visits, we can now say to each other that parting is always hard, that we usually feel there is much left undone and unsaid, but that we love each other.

In similar ways, as described in the section "Anger," identifying the feelings that underlie numbness and alienation—and the myths that feed those feelings—enables mothers and daughters to build bridges between them.

All of the stories in this chapter are about ways that mothers and daughters have tried to mend their relationships, with varying degrees of success. Mothers and daughters will differ in the techniques they use and the pacing of the repair work, but most mother-daughter relationships—like richly woven tapestries—are worth mending.

9

It Is Only a Door

Emotionally healthy women who have the best connections with their mothers also have the best connections with other women.
— *Dr. Janet Surrey,* "Mother-Blame and Mother-Hate"

[I]f we step outside socially imposed injunctions, then . . .
daughters and their mothers wield powers for one
another's help as well as harm. They may even make of
one another revolutionaries.
— *Nancy Mairs,* Plaintext

As women, our vision of ourselves, our feelings about ourselves,
our pride in ourselves, are inevitably affected by our vision of,
and feelings about, other women. We are all the more profoundly
affected by women close to us, women with shared experiences
or similar features or gestures—especially our mothers. Some
days I notice that the way I move my hands or the inflection in
my voice is my mother's. Because I love and respect her, the gesture and inflection somehow seem right and fitting; they have a
place, they belong in the world. Without needing to be like her in
all ways, I can enjoy aesthetically and emotionally the symme-
try, the resonance, that comes from this. In part, it's a way of con-
necting, of weaving a strong and richly textured cloth that
stretches between us and through time. The weaving began before us and will continue after us.

Sharing strengthens us. Like it or not, we are involved with the
woman who raised us, whether we want to be like her or want to
avoid being like her at all costs. All daughters (even avoiders) can
gain from discovering what features, what gestures, what styles,
what values, we can love or respect—rather than hate and reject—
in our mothers. As Alice Walker has written, "We are together, my

child and I. Mother and child, yes, but sisters really, against whatever denies us all that we are." Sharing is easier once we see our
shared humanity and our shared dilemmas beyond the myths.

Beyond the Myths

In a sense, much of this is about forgiveness—of our mother and
ourselves—because we have been misguided by the myths of mother-blame. It is about accepting the only-human nature of both
mothers and daughters in a world that simultaneously raises us to
the heights of unattainable ideals and consigns us to sometimes appalling depths of devaluation, demoralization, and powerlessness.

As I have said, going beyond the myths allows us to think of
our mother as someone other than "My mother, the mother—the
woman who is only my mother and has no significance apart from
that." When you can think beyond her as a mother, you'll find that
all kinds of questions come to your mind. Feminist author Judith
Arcana was astonished by what she learned from her mother's
answer to an unusual question:

> One day, when I visited her as she lay in bed looking particularly
> frail, smaller and lighter than she ought ... she told me about a
> friend of hers who'd taken a psychology class ... [and] found the
> class silly.... The instructor had asked each person in the class
> to name an animal they'd like to be, if they could choose.... I
> said, "Come on, Ma, think about it—what animal would you be, if
> you could?" She thought for a time and said, "I'd like to be that
> big yellow spotted cat, you know, the one that runs faster than all
> the others." I was so unprepared for this revelation that I could
> only cry, cry for the contrast between the bedridden woman and
> the golden yellow cat. My mother the martyr, a woman who put
> her husband and children before her from the day of her marriage,
> would be a cheetah, racing over the African savannah.

Think over your relationship with your mother since you
became an adult. Imagine how different that story might have
been if:

- You hadn't suspected that every indication of closeness
  between you was evidence that (1) your needs and hers

were too great (Myth Six); (2) your mother was trying to control you (Myth Eight); and (3) wanting the closeness itself was wrong (Myth Seven).

- You hadn't had to worry that, even when you were a grown-up, any false move might humiliate your mother (Myth One) and might invalidate, in her mind, the life she has led (Myth Five).

- Society hadn't made it hard for you to acknowledge your "unfeminine" sexual and aggressive feelings (Myth Three) so that you needed to blame your mother either for appearing to handle her feelings so easily and skillfully that you could never match her or for handling her own feelings so poorly that she taught you nothing helpful for handling your own.

- Society didn't judge you so much on the basis of your wife-and-mother roles (Myths One and Two), making you either blame your mother for setting impossibly high standards by her own Supermom example or blame her for being a lousy role model.

- You hadn't expected her to know automatically what your needs were, and to meet them (Myths Two and Four).

- You hadn't assumed that she could have been—and could still be—a good mother if she'd only listened to the experts instead of to her own instincts or doing what her mother did (Myth Six).

- You didn't feel torn between allegiance to your mother and allegiance to your father, and between allegiance to your mother and allegiance to your husband; and our culture didn't push us so hard always to choose the man (Myth Five).

- Your mother hadn't been so limited in her options (Myth Five) that you feel guilty about your own success.

- You weren't afraid that any show of strength or assertiveness by your mother was a sign of her destructive power (Myth Nine).

- You didn't feel that both you and she were bad for being either stay-at-home mothers or mothers with paid jobs (Myth Ten).

There's Value in Every Step

As you begin to work on your mother-daughter relationship and choose the techniques and timing that feel right for you, remember to regard each step you take as valuable in and of itself. Don't aim to settle everything in One Big Talk. Don't try to do too much at once; if you do, you'll be working under too much pressure, and your efforts may be counterproductive. Don't think ahead to how many steps remain to be taken. I used to wake up in the morning, look at the huge list of tasks I had to accomplish during the coming day, and feel exhausted before I got out of bed. Then I had what seemed at the time to be an amazing insight: I didn't have to perform all of those tasks simultaneously every minute of the day. When I pictured the day as a long line rather than as a single point, I realized that I only had to do one thing at each point, and no human being could do more. I also saw that, even if I didn't finish on that day everything from my list, I would still have done some things, and there was value in that.

Be sure you don't make the mistake of assuming that this is a recipe book of easy steps that work magic—and that something is wrong with you if you don't immediately succeed. This book is intended to suggest a way to begin to make changes in your mother-daughter relationship. As you think differently about your mother and are less burdened by mother-blaming myths, your attitude toward her will change for the better. Chances are she will sense that and respond.

So realize that each step will help you along toward your final goal, but each step will also bring its own benefits that will probably stay with you. For instance, humanizing your image of your mother will be a relief, even if you never approach her directly about the problems between you. A mother who lived in a series of foster homes as a child and raised four children alone might be so bitter or overwhelmed that her daughters cannot discuss directly with her the problems that come between them; but at least her daughters can understand more about how unrealistic they were to blame themselves for their mother's rages or depressions. Remember, too, that even defining your "ultimate goal" for a relationship is tricky; in any relationship, both people are always changing, so a step may not end where you thought it would.

Keep in mind the limitations of the approach I have described. In a single book it is not possible to describe every type of mother-daughter problem or anticipate every result if you try these techniques. Furthermore, the degree and speed of your success in using these techniques will not depend just on you but also on the history of your relationship with your mother, what your father or your mother's other partner is or was like, whether or not you have siblings—and if so, what they are like—how much support you can get from other people while working on these issues, the fragility or strength of your self-esteem, and the degree of stability in the rest of your and your mother's lives. Your "race," religion, social class, ethnic roots, sexual orientation, age, and state of health will probably have important effects, too (although thorough research on how those important sources of variation work remains to be done). For instance, in a symposium on biracial children, Barbara and Robin Miller pointed out that Blacks more than whites in North America regard wisdom as coming from the older generation, so Black daughters may be more inclined than white ones to feel genuinely respectful toward their mothers.

Remember, too, that if your mother has died or for some other reason you can't talk to her, you can modify most of the techniques I have suggested.

We often hear that people never really change; but that should not lead to dire predictions about changing your mother-daughter relationship. People's basic characters tend to stay the same, but some people make significant changes under the right circumstances. Alcoholics stop drinking altogether; some people make major career changes; some become more mellow and some more assertive over time. Psychologist Karen Howe reports that nearly every student who wrote her mother's biography said, "I feel like I have met my mother for the first time." That is a major change that can give rise to even more significant ones.

Furthermore, we don't usually need major character changes in mother-daughter relationships, because the characters are not the major sources of trouble. Instead, we must understand the need to go beyond the myths and learn a different set of questions and procedures for understanding our relationships.

The Fear and the Exhilaration of Opening Doors

Beware, because getting to know your mother or seeing her in a new way will change you—at the very least, you'll learn more about yourself. No one can predict how much or in what ways you will change; the changes may be sudden or gradual, immediate or delayed.

A student in my course on mothers experienced a sudden, dramatic change after reading the first book I had assigned—Adrienne Rich's *Of Woman Born*. The student wrote:

Since adolescence, matrophobia—the fear of becoming one's mother—has been a significant force impelling me toward change and growth. My mother's barrage of criticisms, her reserved self-expression, and her tears provoked by most confrontations were interpreted by me with ease: "God forbid I should be as mistrustful as my mother. Or as fragile and weak."

. . . I did not attribute my mother's depression and plaguing self-doubts to the daily war she waged. Instead, I judged her acts as compromises and struggled with a nagging fear of powerlessness in the face of ardent wishes and goals for my future. I was not thinking to acknowledge her role as victim but freely identifying her victimization of others.

For another woman, whom I had interviewed, the change was delayed. She telephoned me weeks later to say,

Last night I began asking myself why I only focus on the ways my mother has upset me. Then I remembered what you had said about how easy it is to blame our mothers, and I was flooded with memories about good, funny, or touching things my mother had done for me. Then I had a moment of precious insight. I remembered that they used to call my mother's mother the Iron Woman. My mother's mother was so cold to her that I guess it's a miracle that my mother was ever able to show me any warmth at all.

Yet as Adrienne Rich says in her poem "Prospective Immigrants Please Note," there are no guarantees about where change will lead, for "The door itself/makes no promises./It is only a door." But it is likely that when you walk through the door that leads away from mother-blame, you will experience a surge of energy as what was bound up in your own mother-blame is set free. If you feel better about your mother, and if your relationship with her improves, consider taking one more step, putting some of that increased energy to use in wiping out the myths. Some of you will talk to one or two other mothers or daughters at a time, telling them what you have learned and suggesting what they might do in their own relationships. Others will refuse to listen to jokes that demean mothers and women in general, will challenge the opinions of scientists and other "experts," or will constantly question casual comments based on assumptions about women's limitless ability to nurture, limitless neediness, or destructive use of power.

I hope that some of you will directly challenge and oppose the institutions that perpetuate the myths. The position of mothers, and all women, will be enhanced by every step you take toward ensuring equal pay and reproductive freedom for women, every improvement in day-care facilities and facilities for ill or older people, every blow you strike against sexual harassment or against the devaluation of old women and poor women, every struggle you join to protect the rights of disabled women, racialized women, immigrant women, lesbian and bisexual women, or women patients in the mental health system.

A Beginning

Let me end by telling you about a small step I took years ago toward my mother. One day my son, Jeremy, then seven years old, had had a difficult day at school. That evening, my mother telephoned long distance from her home and talked to Jeremy for a while. A few minutes later, Mother called back because she was not sure whether I knew about the upsetting incident that Jeremy had described to her. She wanted me to be alert to any particular needs he might have that night. She then asked to speak with Jeremy again, just so that they could have a pleasant chat and she could remind him that she cared about him during this stressful time.

People may roll their eyes and talk about overprotective, interfering grandmothers, or at best fleetingly register the fact that Grandma had done a nice thing for her grandson. I put myself in Jeremy's place and imagined how I would feel if my grandmother took the trouble to call me back just to talk, at a time when I felt I had had a rotten day.

I could say that my mother did a nice thing. Or I could say that my mother did something out of deep compassion and genuine caring about other people. To call what she did "naturally feminine and nurturant," just part of a mother's job, would not do her justice. Few people do such compassionate, considerate things anyway, and no one is served if, when mothers do them, we hardly take notice because it is what we believe they are supposed to do.

That evening I found myself filled with pride and warmth for my mother. I appreciated how much we women have to work with, even if our nurturance and compassion have sometimes been taken advantage of and used against us. Taking care not to let ourselves be abused or ignored because of how we are, we can feel proud of our warmth and strength, and proud of each other's. I told my mother how I felt, and she seemed surprised but warmed by my appreciation and respect for her.

When we respect our mothers more, we gain more self-respect, and when we see the injustices they have suffered, we increase our own humanity. Because we see the pain—or the potential for pain—in which we share, we also glimpse the ways we can use our common humanity and strength to empower each other. Poet Susan Griffin recalls: "I remember my fury at the constrictions placed upon me as a child. I remember the look of innocence on my daughter's face. . . . And that when I realized I'd given birth to a girl my heart opened to myself and all the suffering of women seemed unreasonable to me."

In the past, the pain of that opening and viewing has led many women to retreat to the traditional rules for raising and restricting daughters; that retreat was encouraged by a society that refused to acknowledge its unfair treatment of women. But mothers' and daughters' support of each other, women's support of other women, and women's and men's growing acknowledgment of this unfairness give support to all of us. With such support, we can face the longings in our own and our mothers' pasts and shape something better for our mothers, ourselves, other women, and the coming generations. As you begin, I wish you well.

Appendix A

Expressive Training

The most important principle of expressive training is that someone who wants to improve her relationship with you can do it better under the following conditions:

- She is not bombarded by threats, demands, or criticisms.
- She is not overwhelmed by long, intellectual discussions or explanations of problems between you.
- She knows what concrete steps she can take.

The techniques for expressive training are straightforward and specific. Don't expect yourself to be able to implement them perfectly right away, however, for some of them are deceptively simple and require a great deal of practice and thought. The techniques are:

1. Choose mother or daughter to be the "actor" for a scene.
2. Have the actor write at the top of a sheet of paper a very brief description of a typical problem—for example, "Mom gives my twins milk, even though I have told her that they are allergic to it."
3. Have the actor identify and write down one, two, or three feelings she has about that problem—for example, "anger" and "worry."
4. Have the actor write down a concrete cause for each feeling. Concrete causes exclude threats, demands, criticisms, and intellectualization. They must be events that everyone would agree have taken place. For instance, the actor cannot write, "Because my mother doesn't care about my kids' health" or "Because Mom thinks I'm an incompetent mother"; those are criticisms and leave too much room for interpretation. A concrete cause would be "Because she

gave them milk after I had shown her the doctor's report, which confirmed that they are allergic to milk."

Special Note about Anger: Since anger is a secondary emotion, a concrete cause of anger would be "When she gives them milk, I worry that they will get another ear infection, and because she's already given them the milk by the time I find out about it, I feel helpless, and feeling helpless makes me angry."

5. Have someone play the "receiver." If the actor is the daughter, the receiver will play her mother, and vice versa. Instruct the receiver to try to prevent the actor from focusing on and describing her feelings and their causes. The receiver can criticize, change the subject, weep, intellectualize, or do anything to try to divert the actor from simply stating her feelings and their causes.

6. Before the role-play begins, instruct the actor to name her feelings and explain their causes. She should write them down. When the role-play begins, she is to try to avoid doing anything other than state what she has written on her chart. This gives her practice in avoiding threats, demands, or criticisms or getting involved in intellectualization or changes of topic. Advise the actor that an excellent way for her to end a scene is to say, in the face of the receiver's onslaught, "I just wanted you to know that that is how I feel and that is why I feel that way. You don't need to respond right now." This approach is useful not only in role-play but also in real life, of course. Your real-life "receiver" will probably need time to think about what you have said, and out of respect for her—as well as in the hope of making real change—you need to grant her that time to absorb what you have said.

7. Before beginning the scene, the actor may wish to tell the receiver what kinds of responses she usually gets from her mother or daughter.

8. Ask the other group members to be "directors." Each director makes notes about what actually happens during the role-play and gives the actor feedback of the following kinds, once the scene has been played out:

Feelings—"You said before the role-play that you had two feelings. During the scene, you stated the first one very clearly, but you didn't mention the second."

Causes—"You explained clearly and concretely the cause of your first feeling, but you didn't describe the cause of your second one," or "You described the cause of your second feeling, but you didn't say what feeling it produced in you."

Off-track behavior—"Near the end of the scene, you made a threat when you told your mother you'd never bring the kids to see her again," or "You didn't stick to your feelings and their causes. You let her involve you in an intellectual discussion about the merits of different kinds of allergy tests."

Appendix B

Guidelines for Mother–Daughter Interviews

The Interview Questions*

1. When and where were you born?
2. What were your parents like? (such as ethnic, religious, economic background)
3. What were the important influences on you as a child?
4. What was your relationship like with your mother? your father?
5. What is/was your relationship like with my father?
6. Did you work outside the home?
7. What are your main interests?
8. Are there some things that you have always wanted to do but never had the opportunity?
9. Student: Add two questions here of your own.

Questions Answered by Students*

1. What are your earliest memories of your mother?
2. What is your relationship like with her—in the past and now?
3. What messages or advice did she give you about being a woman?
4. In what ways are you like or unlike your mother?

---

*Questions designed by Karen G. Howe, expanded from material in Sue Cox, ed., *Female Psychology: The Emerging Self,* 2nd ed. (New York: St. Martin's Press, 1981). See also Karen G. Howe, "Daughters Discover Their Mothers through Biographies and Genograms: Educational and Clinical Parallels," in Jane Price Knowles and Ellen Cole, eds., *Woman-Defined Motherhood* (New York: Harrington Park Press, 1990), 31–40.

5. What have you learned from doing this biography assignment? Are there areas of your mother's life experience that you have learned about for the first time? Do you have any new understandings about your mother now?

6. How do you feel about your mother now?

7. What was your mother's reaction to being interviewed?

8. Other comments.

Additional Questions for Mother's Biography Suggested by Paula J. Caplan

1. While you were raising your children, what did you think that being a good mother meant? What did you think a good mother should do?

2. What was hardest for you about being a mother? What was your worst fear?

3. Did the experts ever give you information that went against what you thought or felt was right? Did you ever get different information from different experts?

4. Did you think that mothering should come naturally to you? If so, how did that belief affect you?

5. As a new mother, how did you feel (both positive and negative factors)? (If she doesn't raise these issues, inquire about whether she had feelings of isolation, fatigue, loss of freedom, fear, need for help of various kinds, concerns about changes in her marriage, concerns about her identity or about the interruption of her ability to carry out her dreams or ambitions. Ask also about whether she felt love for, closeness to, delight in, or fascination with her children.)

6. Did you want your daughter (me) to be like you? Why or why not? If yes, in what ways? If not, in what ways did you most want her to be different from you?

7. How do you feel now when you look at your daughter and notice that in some way she is like you?

8. How do you feel now when you look at your daughter and notice that she is different from you in some way?

9. Is it hard for you to support your daughter when she needs support that you never got or when she has opportunities that you never had? How does that feel?

10. How do you feel when your daughter does something untraditional or unusual?
11. Did you ever feel that your daughter betrayed you or let you down?
12. When have you most felt estranged from your daughter (or even felt that you had lost her)? Did that change? If so, how and why?
13. What are the pros and cons of having your daughter ask you for your advice or want your approval?
14. (If she is or was married) Have your husband and daughter ever seemed to take sides against you? Have they ever made you feel left out or inadequate or inferior?
15. What values or lessons do you hope you have imparted to your daughter?

Notes

The numbers preceding notes refer to page numbers on which the quotes appear.

Preface

xi   "came as a stunning": Jane Price Knowles and Ellen Cole, eds., *Woman-Defined Motherhood* (New York: Harrington Park Press, 1990), xvi.

xi   Melissa Meth: Ibid., xviii.

xi   Etta Bender Breit: Ibid., xix.

xi   Phyllis Chesler spoke: "Mother-Hatred and Mother-Blaming: What Electra Did to Clytemnestra," in ibid., 71–81.

xi   Janet Surrey talked: "Mother-Blaming and Clinical Theory," in ibid., 83–87.

xii   "When an old woman": Rachel Josefowitz Siegel, "Old Women as Mother Figures," ibid., 90.

xviii the term *mental illness*: Paula J. Caplan, *They Say You're Crazy: How the World's Most Powerful Psychiatrists Decide Who's Normal* (Reading, Mass.: Addison Wesley, 1995).

xx   Many of the pioneers: Examples of this work include Jean Baker Miller and Irene Stiver, *Healing Connections: How Women Form Relationships in Therapy and in Life* (Boston: Beacon, 1998); Judith Jordan, Janet Surrey, and Alexandra Kaplan, "Women and Empathy," in *Women's Growth in Connection: Writings from the Stone Center,* ed. Judith Jordan et al. (New York: Guilford, 1991), 26–50; Judith Jordan and Janet Surrey, "The Self-in-Relation: Empathy in the Mother-Daughter Relationship," in *The Psychology of Today's Woman: New Psychoanalytic Visions,* ed. Toni Bernay and Dorothy W. Cantor (Cambridge, Mass.: Harvard University Press, 1989), 81–104; Irene Stiver, "Beyond the Oedipus Complex: Mothers and Daughters," in Jordan et al., *Women's Growth,* 97–121; Janet Surrey, "The Mother-Daughter Relationship: Themes in Psychotherapy," in *Daughtering and Mothering: Female Subjectivity Reanalysed,* ed. Janneke van Mens-Verhulst et al. (London: Routledge, 1993), 114–24; and Alexandra Kaplan, Nancy Gleason, and Rona Klein, "Women's Self Development in Late Adolescence," in Jordan et al., *Women's Growth,* 122–40.

xx   books based on presentations: Sharon Abbey and Andrea O'Reilly, eds. . *Redefining Motherhood: Changing Identities and Patterns.* (Toronto: Second Story Press, 1998); O'Reilly and Abbey, eds.), *Mothers and Daughters: Connection, Empowerment, and Transformation* (Lanham, Md.: Rowman and Littlefield, 1999); and O'Reilly, ed., *Mothers and Sons: Feminist Perspectives* (New York: Routledge, in press).

xx   *Canadian Woman Studies*: "Looking Back, Looking Forward: Mothers, Daughters, and Feminism," special issue, *Canadian Woman Studies/Les Cahiers de la femme* 18, nos. 2–3 (fall/summer 1998): 46-50.

xx   Mariana Cook: Cook (photographer) and Jamaica Kincaid (introduction), *Generations of Women in Their Own Words* (San Francisco: Chronicle Books, 1998).

xx   Phyllis Chesler: *Letters to a Young Feminist* (New York: Four Walls Eight Windows, 1998).

xx   Maureen Reddy: *Crossing the Color Line: Race, Parenting, and Culture* (New Brunswick, N.J.: Rutgers University Press, 1996).

xxi *Sunbelt Working*: Louise Lamphere, Patricia Zavella, and Felipe Gonzales with Peter Evans, *Sunbelt Working Mothers: Reconciling Family and Factory* (Ithaca, N.Y.: Cornell University Press, 1993).

xxi Shari Thurer: *The Myths of Motherhood: How Culture Reinvents the Good Mother* (Boston: Houghton Mifflin, 1994).

xxi Alix Kates Shulman: *A Good Enough Daughter* (New York: Schocken, 1999).

xxi *Mothering against the Odds*: Cynthia Garcia Coll, Janet Surrey, and Kathy Weingarten, eds., *Mothering Against the Odds: Diverse Voices of Contemporary Mothers* (New York: Guilford, 1998).

xxii Judi Rogers and Molleen Matsumura: *Mother-to-Be: A Guide to Pregnancy and Birth for Women with Disabilities* (New York: Demos, 1991).

xxii children of lesbians and of homeless: For instance, Charlotte Patterson and Raymond Chan, "Families Headed by Lesbian and Gay Parents," in Lamb, 1999, 191–219; Charlotte Patterson, "Children of Lesbian and Gay Parents," *Advances in Clinical Child Psychology* 19 (1997): 235–82; Susan Golombok, Fiona Tasker, Clare Murray, "Children Raised in Fatherless Families from Infancy: Family Relationships and the Socioemotional Development of Children of Lesbian and Single Heterosexual Mothers," *Journal of Child Psychology and Psychiatry and Allied Disciplines* 38, no. 7: 783–91; Susan Golombok and Fiona Tasker, "Children in Lesbian and Gay Families: Theories and Evidence," *Annual Review of Sex Research* 5 (1994): 73–100; Julie Gottman, "Children of Gay and Lesbian Parents," *Marriage and Family Review* 14, nos. 3–4 (1989): 177–96; M. Ann Easterbrooks and Christine Graham, "Security of Attachment and Parenting: Homeless and Low-Income Housed Mothers and Infants," *American Journal of Orthopsychiatry* 69, no. 3 (1999): 337–46; Sally Koblinsky, Kari Morgan, and Elaine Anderson, "African-American Homeless and Low-Income Housed Mothers: Comparison of Parenting Practices," *American Journal of Orthopsychiatry* 67, no. 1 (1997): 37–47; and Valerie Polakow, *Lives on the Edge: Single Mothers and Their Children in the Other America* (Chicago: University of Chicago Press, 1993).

xxii Mothers with disabilities: Barbara Holland Baskin and Elizabeth Riggs, "Mothers Who Are Disabled," in *The Different Faces of Motherhood,* ed. Beverly Birns and Dale Hay (New York: Plenum, 1988), 239–57.

xxiii women tell their own stories: Patricia Bell-Scott et al., eds., *Double Stitch: Black Women Write about Mothers and Daughters* (New York: Harper Perennial, 1993); Elaine Bell Kaplan, *Not Our Kind of Girl: Unraveling the Myths of Black Teenage Motherhood* (Berkeley: University of California Press, 1997); bell hooks, *Bone Black: Memories of Girlhood* (New York: Henry Holt, 1996); Kelly Williams, *Single Mamahood: Advice and Wisdom for the African-American Single Mother* (Secaucus, N.J.: Carol, 1998); Rachel Josefowitz Siegel, Ellen Cole, and Susan Steinberg-Oren, eds., *Acts of Love: Jewish Mothers Tell Their Stories* (New York: Haworth, in press); and McCubbin and Thompson, eds., *Immigrant Families*.

xxiii Anne Adelman: "Traumatic Memory and the Intergenerational Transmission of Holocaust Narrative," *Psychoanalytic Study of the Child* 50 (1995): 343–67.

xxiii Joonok Huh: "Constantly Negotiating: Between My Mother and My Daughter." In O'Reilly and Abbey, 1999.

xxiii research focused on revealing the strengths: See, for example, Karen Wyche, "Let Me Suffer So My Kids Won't: African American Mothers Living with HIV/AIDS," in Coll et al., 1998: 173–89; Claire Reinelt and Mindy Fried, "'I Am This Child's Mother': A Feminist Perspective on Mothering with a Disability," in *Perspectives on Disability,* ed. Mark Nagler et al. (Palo Alto, CA: Health Markets Research, 1993), 195–202; Maurice Feldman et al., "Teaching Child-Care Skills to Mothers with Developmental Disabilities," *Journal of Applied Behavior Analysis* 25, no. 1 (1992): 205–15; Marty Wyngaarden Krauss and Marsha Malick Seltzer, "Long-Term Caring: Family Experiences over the Life Course," in *Down Syndrome: Living and Learning in the Community,* ed. Lynn Nadel et al. (New York: Wiley-Liss, 1995), 92; and Sharon Landesman Ramey and Halldor-Kr. Juliusson, "Family Dynamics at Dinner: A Natural Context for Revealing Basic Family Processes," in *Families, Risk, and Competence,* ed. Michael Lewis and Candice Feiring (Mahwah, N.J.: Lawrence Erlbaum Associates, 1998), 31–52.

xxiii Beverly Greene: "What Has Gone Before," and "Sturdy Bridges."

xxiv Robert Strom: Strom et al., "Perceptions."

xxiv Patricia Hill Collins: Collins, "Meaning of Motherhood," and Wilson,"Child Development."

xxiv the vast majority of clinical studies: For instance, see Karin Bell, "On the Relationship between Daughters and Mothers with Regard to Bulimia Nervosa," in *Why Women? Gender Issues and Eating Disorders,* ed. Bridget Dolan et al., 21–32 (London: Athlone Press, 1994); Kathleen Brown et al. "Maternal Influences on Body Satisfaction in Black and White Girls Aged 9 and 10: The NHLBI Growth and Health Study (NGHS)," *Annals of Behavioral Medicine* 17, no. 3 (1995): 213–20; Rachel Calam et al., "Eating Attitudes in Young Teenage Girls: Parental Management of 'Fussy' Eating," *Eating Disorders: The Journal of Treatment and Prevention* 5, no. 1 (1997): 29–40; Kate Campbell and Sue Levesque, "Mandatory Thinness and Mother-Blame: The Newspaper Coverage of the Marlene Corrigan Trial," *Canadian Woman Studies/Les Cahiers de la femme* 18, no. 2 (fall/summer 1998): 69–73; Kristin Flynn and Marian Fitzgibbon, "Body Image Ideals of Low-Income African American Mothers and Their Preadolescent Daughters," *Journal of Youth and Adolescence* 25, no. 5 (1996): 615–30; Rosalyn Griffiths et al., "Anorexie à Deux: An Ominous Sign for Recovery," *European Eating Disorders Review* 3, no. 1 (1995): 2–14; S. L. Jones et al., "Self-Esteem Differences as a Function of Race and Weight Preoccupation," *Women's Health Issues* 9, no. 1 (1999): 50–55; Kathleen Pike and Judith Rodin, "Mothers, Daughters, and Disordered Eating," *Journal of Abnormal Psychology* 100, no. 2 (1991): 198–204; Samuel Ritvo, "Mothers, Daughters, and Eating Disorders," in *Fantasy, Myth, and Reality: Essays in Honor of Jacob A. Arlow, M.D.,* ed. Harold P. Blum et al. (Madison, Conn.: International Universities Press, 1988), 423–34.

xxiv authors who call these practices: Judith Ruskay Rabinor, "Mothers, Daughters, and Eating Disorders: Honoring the Mother-Daughter Relationship," in *Feminist Perspectives on Eating Disorders,* ed. Patricia Fallon et al. (New York: Guilford, 1994), 272–86; and Jennifer Sanftner et al., "Maternal Influences (or Lack Thereof) on Daughters' Eating Attitudes and Behaviors," *Eating Disorders: The Journal of Treatment and Prevention* 4, no. 2 (1996): 147–59.

xv "is often the most obvious": Rabinor, "Mothers, Daughters," 276.

xxv "borderline personality disorder": Anath Golomb et al., "Maternal Empathy, Family Chaos, and the Etiology of Borderline Personality Disorder," *Journal of the American Psychoanalytic Association* 42, no. 2 (1994): 525–48.

xxv nonsexual abuse and neglect: Elizabeth Hutchison, "Child Welfare as a Woman's Issue," *Families in Society* 73, no. 2 (1992): 67–78.

xxv about other problems: John Carton, Stephen Nowicki Jr., and Ginger Baiser, "An Observational Study of Antecedents of Locus of Control of Reinforcement," *International Journal of Behavioral Development* 19, no. 1 (1995): 161–75; and Barbara Zax and Stephen Poulter, "A Multigenerational Inquiry into the Relationship between Mothers and Daughters," in *The Handbook of Infant, Child, and Adolescent Psychotherapy,* ed. Bonnie Mark et al. *New Directions in Integrative Treatment,* vol. 2 (Northvale, N.J.: Jason Aronson, 1997), 461–84.

xxix "Since I failed": Pat Conroy, *The Prince of Tides* (Boston: Houghton Mifflin, 1986), 94.

Chapter 1

1 "How are we": Letty Cottin Pogrebin quoted in Ingeborg Day, "Daughters and Mothers," *Ms.,* June 1975, 79.

1 "the plot is not": Marcia Westkott, "Mothers and Daughters in the World of the Father," *Frontiers* 3 (1978), 16.

2 "Angel in the House": Gerda Lerner, *The Female Experience: An American Documentary* (Indianapolis: Bobbs-Merrill, 1977); Karen Payne, ed., *Between Ourselves: Letters between Mothers and Daughters, 1750–1982* (Boston: Houghton Mifflin, 1983).

4 my earlier writing: Caplan, *Between Women: Lowering the Barriers* (Toronto: Personal Library, 1981); Paula J. Caplan and Ian Hall-McCorquodale, "Mother-Blaming in Major Clinical Journals," *American Journal of Orthopsychiatry* 55 (1985): 345–53; Caplan and Hall-McCorquodale, "The Scapegoating of Mothers: A Call for Change," *American Journal of Orthopsychiatry* 55 (1985): 610–13.

5 "She's a masochist": Paula J. Caplan, *The Myth of Women's Masochism* (1985; reprint, New York: Signet, 1987; new edition, University of Toronto Press, 1993).

5 Only a few books: Adrienne Rich, *Of Woman Born: Motherhood as Experience and Institution* (New York: W. W. Norton, 1976); Judith Arcana, *Our Mothers' Daughters* (Berkeley, Calif.: Shameless Hussy Press, 1979); Phyllis Chesler, *Women and Madness* (New York: Avon Books, 1973); Chesler, *With Child: A Diary of Motherhood* (New York: Berkeley Books, 1981).

6 Some began well: Nancy Chodorow, *The Reproduction of Mothering: Psychoanalysis and the Sociology of Gender* (Berkeley: University of California Press, 1978).

6 Nancy Friday, *My Mother/My Self* (New York: Delacorte, 1977). For thoughtful evaluation of some of the mother-blaming literature, see Pauline Bart, "Review of Chodorow's *The Reproduction of Mothering,*" in *Mothering: Essays in Feminist Theory,* ed. Joyce Trebilcot (Totowa, N.J.: Rowman and Allanheld, 1983), 147–52; and Marcia Westkott, "Mothers and Daughters in the World of the Father," *Frontiers* 3 (1978): 16.

6   1990s book *When You and Your Mother*: Victoria Secunda, *When You and Your Mother Can't Be Friends* (New York: Delta, 1990).

7   Jean Baker Miller, *Toward a New Psychology of Women* (Boston: Beacon Press, 1976).

7   A number of writers: Faith Conlon, Rachel daSilva, and Barbara Wilson, eds., *The Things That Divide Us* (Seattle: Seal Press, 1985); Andrea Dworkin, *Woman Hating* (New York: E. P. Dutton, 1974); Lucy Rose Fischer, *Linked Lives: Adult Daughters and Their Mothers* (New York: Harper and Row, 1987); Karen Fite and Nikola Trumbo, "Betrayals among Women: Barriers to a Common Longing, *Lesbian Ethics* 1 (1984); Jane Flax, "The Conflict between Nurturance and Autonomy in Mother-Daughter Relationships and within Feminism," *Feminist Studies* 4 (1978): 171–89; Audre Lorde, *Sister Outsider* (Trumansburg, N.Y.: Crossing Press, 1984); Valerie Miner and Helen Longino, *Competition: A Feminist Taboo?* (New York: Feminist Press, 1987); Letty Cottin Pogrebin, *Among Friends* (New York: McGraw-Hill, 1987); Janice Raymond, *A Passion for Friends: Toward a Philosophy of Female Affection* (Boston: Beacon Press, 1987); Alice Walker, *In Search of Our Mothers' Gardens: Womanist Prose* (San Diego, Calif.: Harcourt Brace Jovanovich, 1983).

10 women are more willing: Judith Arcana, *Every Mother's Son: The Role of Mothers in the Making of Men* (Seattle: Seal Press, 1986), 257; and Janet Surrey, "The 'Self-in-Relation': A Theory of Women's Development," in Jordan et al. (1985), 51–66; and Miller, *Toward a New Psychology.*

10 the real story ... According to a Plains Indian legend (Helen Carmichael Porter, personal communication, June 14, 1988), to develop into fully realized people, we need to experience the entire spectrum of human feelings. This range is represented by positions on a wheel. And since all humans share the same potential for feelings, in terms of the legend, we need to occupy every position on that wheel. We can occupy some positions through direct experience and others through hearing stories. Empathic listening to someone else's description of a life very different from our own can teach us about feelings and events that were previously quite foreign to us. Thus, by learning our mother's story, we occupy her space on the wheel and learn how the world—and our relationship—looks from her vantage point. In telling our own stories, we may glimpse some order in what has seemed the chaos of our lives.

Chapter 2

20 "drew shockingly rejecting portraits": Zenith Henkin Gross, *And You Thought It Was All Over! Mothers and Their Adult Children* (New York: St. Martin's Press, 1985), 174.

21 In a study of woman-woman relationships: Lorette K. Woolsey and Laura-Lynne McBain, "Issues of Power and Powerlessness in All-Woman Groups," *Women's Studies International Forum* 10 (1987), 579–88.

23 Anger: Crucial works to read on women and anger include: Teresa Bernardez, "Gender-Based Countertransference of Female Therapists in the Psychotherapy of Women," in *Women, Power, and Therapy: Issues for Women,* ed. Marjorie Braude (New York: Haworth, 1987), 25–39; Bernardez, "Women and Anger: Cultural Prohibitions and the Feminine Idea," Work in Progress Paper No. 31, Wellesley College, The Stone Center, Wellesley, Mass., 1988; Harriet Goldhor Lerner, "Sugar and Spice: The Taboos against Female Anger," *Menninger Perspective,* winter 1977, 5–11; and Harriet Goldhor Lerner, *The Dance of Anger* (New York: Harper and Row, 1985).

23   "between women's inferior status": Judith Lewis Herman and Helen Block Lewis, "Anger in the Mother-Daughter Relationship," in *The Psychology of Today's Woman: New Psychoanalytic Visions,* ed. Toni Bernay and Dorothy Cantor (Cambridge, Mass.: Harvard University Press, 1989), 139–62.

31   families of immigrants: Birgit Leyendecker and Michael Lamb, "Latino Families," In *Parenting and Child Development in 'Nontraditional' Families,* ed. Michael Lamb (Mahwah, N.J.: Lawrence Erlbaum, 1999), 247–62; and Jill McLean Taylor, "Cultural Stories: Latina and Portugese Daughters and Mothers," in *Urban Girls: Resisting Stereotypes, Creating Identities.* ed. Bonnie Ross Leadbeater et al. (New York: New York University Press, 1996), 117–31.

34   "I believe that prior": Ruth Minden, "Glancing Backward, Looking Forward: Insights into Mothering," paper, Ontario Institute for Studies in Education, 1986, 3.

36   Carroll Smith-Rosenberg, "The Female World of Love and Ritual: Relations between Women in Nineteenth-Century America," *Signs: Journal of Women in Culture and Society* 1 (1985): 1–29, quotations from 13, 14, and 15. I am not a historian, and historical review is not a major purpose of this book. For fascinating historical perspectives, see, for example, the article by Smith-Rosenberg and the works by Elisabeth Badinter, Gerda Lerner, and Jessie Bernard listed in the bibliography.

Chapter 3

38   average child care worker: U.S. Department of Labor. *Occupational Outlook Handbook, 1998–99* (Washington, D.C.: U.S. Government Printing Office, 1999).

38   "tending chickens": Jessie Bernard, *The Future of Motherhood* (New York: Dial Press, 1974), x.

39   the double load: Esther Greenglass, "A Social-Psychological View of Marriage for Women," *International Journal of Women's Studies* 8 (1985): 24–31.

39   Paradoxically, motherhood . . . Jennifer Chambers, personal communication, January 20, 1988.

40   recent writings by therapists: See, for example, Barbara Zax and Stephen Poulter, "A Multigenerational Inquiry into the Relationship between Mothers and Daughters," in *The Handbook of Infant, Child, and Adolescent Psychotherapy, New Directions in Integrative Treatment,* vol. 2, ed. Bonnie Mark et al. (Northvale, N.J.: Jason Aronson, 1997), 461–84; and Naomi Rucker and Karen Lombardi, "The Familial Menage-à-Trois: Mother-Daughter Sexuality and Father-Daughter Incest," *Journal of Contemporary Psychotherapy* 20, no. 2 (1990): 99–107. Critiques of such attitudes include Kathy Weingarten, *The Mother's Voice: Strengthening Intimacy in Families* (New York: Harcourt Brace, 1994); Elizabeth Hutchison, "Child Welfare as a Woman's Issue," *Families in Society* 73, no. 2 (1992): 67–78; Patricia Flanagan, "Teen Mothers: Countering the Myths of Dysfunction and Developmental Disruption." Coll et al. (1998), 238–54; and Molly Ladd-Taylor and Lauri Umansky, ed., *'Bad' Mothers: The Politics of Blame in Twentieth-Century America* (New York: New York University Press, 1998).

40   "Megaloid momworship": Philip Wylie, *Generation of Vipers* (New York: Rinehart and Co., 1946), 185–86.

41   The term Wylie coined, *momism*: The definition of *momism* as referring to mothers' "excessive domination" of their families comes from *New Webster's Dictionary of the English Language,* Deluxe Encyclopedic Edition, 1981.

42 Our everyday language reflects: For excellent readings on these issues, see Ethel Strainchamps, "Our Sexist Language," in *Women in Sexist Society,* ed. Vivian Gornick and Barbara K. Moran (New York: Basic Books, 1971), 347–61; Letty Cottin Pogrebin, *Growing Up Free: Raising Your Kids in the 80s* (New York: McGraw-Hill, 1980); Casey Miller and Kate Swift, *Words and Women* (Garden City, N.Y.: Anchor Books, 1977); Dale Spender, *Man Made Language* (New York: Routledge Chapman Hall, 1985).

43 Caplan, *The Myth of Women's Masochism.*

44 "I was Anne's mother": Nancy Mairs, *Plaintext: Deciphering a Woman's Life* (New York: Harper and Row, 1987), 72.

44 it continues today: David Allison and Mark Roberts, *Disordered Mothers or Disordered Diagnosis? Munchausen by Proxy Syndrome* (Hillsdale, N.J.: Analytic Press, 1998); Louise Silverstein and Vicky Phares, "Expanding the Mother-Child Paradigm: An Examination of Dissertation Research, 1986–1994," *Psychology of Women Quarterly* 20 (1996): 39–53; Vicky Phares, "Perceptions of Mothers' and Fathers' Responsibility for Children's Behavior," *Sex Roles* 29, nos. 11–12 (1993): 839–51; Jane Price Knowles and Ellen Cole, eds., *Woman-Defined Motherhood* (New York: Harrington Park Press, 1990); and Aghop DerKarabetian and Michelle Preciado, "Mother-Blaming among College Students," *Perceptual and Motor Skills* 68, no. 2 (1989): 453–54.

45 Two articles reported our findings: Caplan and Hall-McCorquodale, "Mother-Blaming," 345–53, and Caplan and Hall-McCorquodale, "Scapegoating," 610–13.

45 "The psychiatric world": Jane Price Knowles, "Introduction," in Knowles and Cole, *Woman-Defined Motherhood.*

45 studied children over a sixteen-year period: R. C. Herrenkohl, B. P. Egolf, and E. C. Herrenkohl, "Preschool Antecedents of Adolescent Assaultive Behavior: A Longitudinal Study," *American Journal of Orthopsychiatry* 67 (1997): 422–32, described by Paula J. Caplan and Jeremy Caplan, *Thinking Critically about Research on Sex and Gender* (New York: Addison Wesley Longman, 1999).

46 enlightened authors showed: For instance, Allison and Roberts, *Disordered Mothers.*

46 writing about their problems: Marcel Kinsbourne and Paula J. Caplan, *Children's Learning and Attention Problems* (Boston: Little, Brown, 1979).

47 school system depend heavily: Alison I. Griffith and Dorothy E. Smith, "Contributing Cultural Knowledge: Mothering as Discourse," in *Women and Education,* ed. J. Gaskell and A. McLaren (Calgary: Detselig Press, 1987), 87–103; Griffith and Smith, "Coordinating the Uncoordinated: How Mothers Manage the School Day," *Perspectives in Social Problems,* vol. 2 (1990): 25–43; Smith and Griffith, "Mothering for Schooling," *Perspectives in Social Problems,* vol. 2 (1990): 3–24.

47 mothers spend far more time: Joseph Pleck, "Employment and Fatherhood: Issues and Innovative Policies," in *The Father's Role: Applied Perspectives,* ed. Michael E. Lamb (New York: John Wiley, 1986), 385–412.

47 fathers ... have left their families: Paula J. Caplan et al., "Toronto Multi-Agency Child Abuse Research Project: The Abused and the Abuser," *Child Abuse and Neglect: The International Journal* 8 (1984): 343–51.

48 press release: "Study of Family Interaction Leads to New Understanding of Abusive Parents," University of Toronto Research Highlights, Simcoe Hall, University of Toronto, Public and Community Relations, October 1987, 1.

48 Mental health professionals were quick: Helen Thomas, *Child Abuse, Neglect,*

and Deprivation: A Handbook for Ontario Nurses (Toronto: Registered Nurses Association of Ontario, 1983), 21. For a scathing critique of mother-blaming in incest cases, see Florence Rush, "The Myth of Sexual Delinquency," *Women: A Journal of Liberation* 3, no. 3 (1972): 38–39; Rush, "Woman in the Middle," in *Radical Feminism,* ed. Anne Koedt, Ellen Levine, and Anita Ropone (New York: Quadrangle Books, 1973); and Rush, "The Sexual Abuse of Children: A Feminist Point of View," In *Rape: The First Sourcebook for Women,* ed. Noreen Connell and Cassandra Wilson (New York: Signet, 1974), 64–75.

48   even when the mother is absent: Beverly Birns and Shannon Lee Meyer, "Mothers' Role in Incest: Dysfunctional Women or Dysfunctional Theories?" *Journal of Child Sexual Abuse* 2, no. 3 (1993): 127–35.

49   "Even those women": Mary DeYoung, "Immediate Maternal Reactions to the Disclosure or Discovery of Incest," *Journal of Family Violence* 9, no. 1 (1994): 21–33.

49   professionals . . . blame mothers: Chandra Sen and Judith Daniluk, "Themes in the Relationships of Mothers and Their Incestuously Abused Daughters: A Feminist Analysis," *Feminism and Psychology* 5, no. 1 (1995): 47–60.

49   pattern of blaming the mother: Rucker and Lombardi, "Familial Menage-à-Trois"; Irving Kaufman, "Father-Daughter Incest," in *Father and Child: Developmental and Clinical Perspectives,* ed. Stanley Cath and Alan Gurwitt (New York: Basil Blackwell, 1998), 491–507.

49   "women are commonly accorded": Carole Ann Hooper, "Child Sexual Abuse and the Regulation of Women: Variations on a Theme," in *Gender Violence: Interdisciplinary Perspectives,* ed. Laura O'Toole et al. (New York: New York University Press, 1997), 348; Ila Schonberg, "The Distortion of the Role of Mother in Child Sexual Abuse," *Journal of Child Sexual Abuse* 1, no. 3 (1992): 47–61, also makes this point.

49   Dr. Kathleen Coulbourn Faller: "Decision-Making in Cases of Intrafamilial Child Sexual Abuse," *American Journal of Orthopsychiatry* 58 (1988): 121–28.

50   they are like alcoholics: Carolyn Cole, personal communication, May 1986.

50   "never to mention it": Carolyn Cole, personal communication, September 25, 1987.

50   Psychotherapists have had tremendous influence: Paula J. Caplan, *They Say You're Crazy: How the World's Most Powerful Psychiatrists Decide Who's Normal* (Reading, Mass.: Addison Wesley, 1995).

51   Margaret Mahler's work: Margaret S. Mahler, Fred Pine, and Anni Bergman, *The Psychological Birth of the Human Infant: Symbiosis and Individuation* (New York: Basic Books, 1975).

52   The irony is: Caplan et al. "Toronto Multi-Agency Child Abuse."

52   Suzanne Somers: Somers, on *Donahue,* February 2, 1988.

53   children of male prisoners of war: J. Sigal, "Effects of Paternal Exposure to Prolonged Stress on the Mental Health of the Spouse and Children," *Canadian Psychiatric Association Journal* 21 (1976): 169–72.

53   Aphrodite Matsakis: *Viet Nam Wife; The Other Forgotten Warrior* (Kensington, Md.: Woodbine Press, 1988).

55   All too rarely are therapists' pronouncements questioned: Caplan, *They Say You're Crazy.*

55   serious errors of logic: Paula J. Caplan and Jeremy B. Caplan, *Thinking Critically about Research on Sex and Gender* (New York: Addison Wesley Longman, 1999).

55 Phyllis Chesler has documented: Chesler, *Mothers on Trial: The Battle for Children and Custody* (New York: McGraw-Hill, 1986).

55 "disabled, a political activist": Rickie Solinger, "Poisonous Choice," in *'Bad Mothers': The Politics of Blame in Twentieth-Century America,* ed. Molly Ladd-Taylor and Lauri Umansky (New York: New York University Press, 1998), 383.

55 "approximately twenty-five child custody disputes": Renee Romano, "'Immoral Conduct': White Women, Racial Transgressions, and Custody Disputes," in ibid., 230.

56 people raised by lesbians: The absence of problems in the offspring of lesbians has been documented by, among others: Susan Golombok, Fiona Tasker, and Clare Murray, "Children Raised in Fatherless Families from Infancy: Family Relationships and the Socioemotional Development of Children from Lesbian and Single Heterosexual Mothers," *Journal of Child Psychology and Psychiatry* 38, no. 7 (1997): 783–91; Charlotte Patterson, "Children of Lesbian and Gay Parents," *Advances in Clinical Child Psychology* 19 (1997): 235–82; Susan Golombok and Fiona Tasker, "Children in Lesbian and Gay Families: Theories and Evidence," *Annual Review of Sex Research* 5 (1994): 73–100; Patricia Falk, "Lesbian Mothers: Psychosocial Assumptions in Family Law," in *Psychological Perspectives on Lesbian and Gay Male Experiences. Between Men—Between Women: Lesbian and Gay Studies,* ed. Linda Garnets and Douglas Kimmel (New York: Columbia University Press, 1993), 420–36; Julie Gottman, "Children of Gay and Lesbian Parents," *Marriage and Family Review* 14, nos. 3–4 (1989): 177–96. For information about how the courts deal with lesbian mothers, see Christine Allison, "The Making of a 'Bad' Mother: A Lesbian Mother and Her Daughters," in Ladd-Taylor and Umansky, *'Bad' Mothers,* 252–56; Falk, "Lesbian Mothers"; and Nan Hunter and Nancy Polikoff, "Custody Rights of Lesbian Mothers: Legal Theory and Litigation Strategy," in *Homosexuality: Discrimination, Criminology, and the Law,* ed. Wayne Dynes and Stephen Donaldson, *Studies in Homosexuality,* vol. 6 (New York: Garland, 1992), 225–67.

56 "Judges order pregnant addicts": Katha Pollitt, "'Fetal Rights': A New Assault on Feminism," in Ladd-Taylor and Umansky, *'Bad' Mothers,* 288.

57 Disrespect for mothers' reports: See Daniel Sonkin, ed., *Domestic Violence on Trial* (New York: Springer, 1987).

57 and that they manipulate: Jennifer Freyd, *Betrayal Trauma: The Logic of Forgetting Childhood Abuse* (Cambridge, Mass.: Harvard University Press, 1996).

58 Dr. Jaffe explains: Paula J. Caplan and Mary Lou Fassel, "Women Get Blame in Incest Cases," *Globe and Mail* (Toronto), February 10, 1987.

60 "Any society that wants": Caplan and Caplan, *Thinking Critically,* 74.

60 "focus intensely": ibid., 72.

61 fear of the unknown: Caplan and Fassel, "Women Get Blame."

61 to prove their manliness: Nancy Chodorow, *The Reproduction of Mothering: Psychoanalysis and the Sociology of Gender* (Berkeley: University of California Press, 1978); and Dorothy Dinnerstein, *The Mermaid and the Minotaur* (New York: Harper and Row, 1977).

63 "I simply found": Zella Wolofsky, "Reconciliation of the Mother-Daughter Relationship: A Personal Odyssey," paper, Ontario Institute for Studies in Education, 1986, 11.

64 "Black daughters learn": Gloria I. Joseph and Jill Lewis, *Common Differences:*

Conflicts in Black and White Feminist Perspectives (New York: Anchor Books, 1981), 96.

Chapter 4

69 Mothers are familiar: See Weingarten, *The Mother's Voice: Strengthening Intimacy in Families* (New York: Harcourt Brace, 1994) for discussion of her attempts to be a perfect mother.

70 "Daughters feel anger": Susan Koppelman, ed., *Between Mothers and Daughters: Stories across a Generation* (New York: The Feminist Press, 1985), xxxiv.

77 "Woman needs to give": Irene Claremont de Castillejo, *Knowing Woman* (New York: Harper and Row, 1973), 149–54.

77 "reflexive maternal": Mairs, *Plaintext*, 74.

78 "Inspire her": Lydia Howard Sigourney, *Letters to Mothers* (New York: Harper and Brothers, 1845), 124.

78 attitude involves "acceptance": de Castillejo, *Knowing Woman*, 15.

78 Toni Grant: *Being a Woman: Fulfilling Your Femininity and Finding Love* (New York: Random House, 1988).

78 "Women have been taught": Harriet Goldhor Lerner, "Sugar and Spice: The Taboo against Female Anger," *Menninger Perspective,* winter 1977, 7.

78 "a monster, anomalous": Dorothy Dinnerstein, *The Mermaid and the Minotaur* (New York: Harper and Row, 1977), 112.

78 "Self-affirmation": Sheila Rowbotham, *Woman's Consciousness, Man's World* (Harmondsworth, England: Penguin, 1973), 76.

78 Research shows: Fischer, *Linked Lives,* 116; and Anita Fochs Heller, *Health at Home: Women as Health Guardians* (Ottawa: Canadian Advisory Council on the Status of Women, 1986).

78 So resilient: Nancy Reeves, *Womankind: Beyond the Stereotype* (Chicago: Aldine and Atherton, 1971), 197.

79 "If you're not": Mary O'Brien, "The Reproduction of Mothering," paper presented at "Don't Blame Mother" conference, Toronto, May 21, 1987.

82 a wealth of research: Julia Graber and Jeanne Brooks-Gunn, "'Sometimes I Think That You Don't Like Me': How Mothers and Daughters Negotiate the Transition into Adolescence," in *Conflict and Cohesion in Families: Causes and Consequences,* ed. Martha Cox et al., *Advances in Family Research Series* (Mahwah, N.J.: Lawrence Erlbaum Associates, 1999), 207–42; Suzanne Randolph, "African American Children in Single Mother Families," in *African American Single Mothers: Understanding Their Lives and Families,* ed. Bette Dickerson, *Sage Series on Race and Ethnic Relations,* vol. 10 (Thousand Oaks, Calif.: Sage, 1995), 117–45; Robin Fivush, "Gender and Emotion in Mother-Child Conversations about the Past," *Journal of Narrative and Life History* 1, no. 4 (1991): 325–41; and Brent McBride and Pernell Ferguson, "Parental Expectations for Young Children: Day Care versus Preschool," *Early Child Development and Care* 79 (1992): 47–53.

84 Badinter painstakingly documents: Elisabeth Badinter, *Mother Love: Myth and Reality* (New York: Macmillan, 1980).

84 compelling evidence: Beverly Birns, "The Mother-Infant Tie: Fifty Years of Theory, Science and Science Fiction," Work in Progress Paper No. 21, Wellesley College, The Stone Center, Wellesley, Mass., 1985.

85 "Women do not have a handy gland": Jain Sherrard, *Mother-Warrior-Pilgrim* (Kansas City, Mo.: Andrews and McMel, 1980), 24.

85   "Eventually after twenty-two hours": Isabel Shessel, "On Being a Mother: Thoughts and Reflections," paper, Ontario Institute for Studies in Education, 1986, 5.

85   Tabitha Walrond: Barbara Ransby, "Another Black Woman Brutalized by the Courts," *In These Times,* July 11, 1999.

88   anger is considered unfeminine: Bernardez, "Gender-Based Countertransference," 25–39; Bernardez, "Women and Anger"; and Harriet Goldhor Lerner, *The Dance of Anger* (New York: Harper and Row, 1985).

89   "Praise is more obtrusive": Friedrich Nietzsche, *The Portable Nietzsche,* trans. and ed. Walter Kaufman (New York: Viking, 1954).

92   in early adolescence: Anne C. Petersen, "Those Gangly Years," *Psychology Today,* September 1987: 28–34.

92   teenage daughters tend to confide: Fischer, *Linked Lives,* 116.

95   legitimate reasons to be upset: Bernardez, "Women and Anger"; Lerner, *Dance of Anger.*

Chapter 5

97   "brought the violence on themselves": Paula Caplan, *The Myth of Women's Masochism;* Nicole Walton-Allen, "Laypeople's Perceptions of Family Violence: An Examination of Stereotyped Learning," master's thesis, Ontario Institute for Studies in Education, 1984.

97   "horizontal hostility": Florynce Kennedy, *Color Me Flo: My Hard Life and Good Times* (Englewood Cliffs, N.J.: Prentice-Hall, 1976), 87.

98   Even today. . . : Weingarten, 1994.

98   "[sons'] behavior may deviate": Judith Arcana, *Every Mother's Son: The Role of Mothers in the Making of Men* (Seattle, Seal Press, 1986), 98.

100 "I despise": Sigmund Freud, "Femininity," in "New Introductory Lectures in Psychoanalysis," 1932, *The Standard Edition of the Complete Psychological Works of Sigmund Freud,* vol. 22, trans. James Strachey (London: Hogarth Press and the Institute of Psychoanalysis, 1964), 124.

101 preferential treatment of their brothers: Karen Horney, *New Ways in Psychoanalysis* (New York: W. W. Norton, 1939).

101 "When the daughter": Kim Chernin, *Reinventing Eve: Modern Woman in Search of Herself* (New York: Harper and Row, 1988), 123.

102 "this tiny bit of flesh": Simone de Beauvoir, *The Second Sex* (New York: Vintage, 1974), 307.

103 T. Berry Brazelton: Brazelton, *Infants and Mothers: Differences in Development* (New York: Delacorte, 1983); *Toddlers and Parents* (New York: Dell, 1986).

104 DSM: American Psychiatric Association: *Diagnostic and Statistical Manual of Mental Disorders-IV* (Washington, D.C.: APA, 1994).

104 *Love, Ellen*: Betty DeGeneres, *Love, Ellen: A Mother-Daughter Journey* (New York: William Morrow, 1999).

105 "multiple intelligences": Daniel Goleman, *Emotional Intelligence* (New York: Bantam, 1995); and Howard Gardner, *Frames of Mind: The Theory of Multiple Intelligences* (New York: Basic Books, 1993).

105 "Bad Mothers": Molly Ladd-Taylor and Lauri Umansky, *"Bad" Mothers: The Politics of Blame in Twentieth-Century America* (New York: New York University Press, 1998).

106 that children *are* harmed: Caplan, *Myth of Women's Masochism.*

108 "insatiable" and "immoderate" needs: Freud, "Femininity," 122–23.

110 Betty Friedan: *The Feminine Mystique* (New York: Dell, 1963).

110 Daughters more than sons: Julia Graber and Jeanne Brooks-Gunn, "'Some-times I Think That You Don't Like Me': How Mothers and Daughters Nego-tiate the Transition into Adolescence," in *Conflict and Cohesion in Families: Causes and Consequences,* ed. Martha Cox et al. (Mahwah, N.J.: Lawrence Erlbaum Associates, 1999); Sharon Landesman Ramey and Halldor-Kr. Juliusson, "Family Dynamics at Dinner: A Natural Context for Revealing Basic Family Processes," in *Families, Risk, and Competence,* ed. Michael Lewis and Candice Feiring, 31–52 (Mahwah, N.J.: Lawrence Erlbaum Associates, 1998); Campbell Leaper, Kristin Anderson, and Paul Sanders, "Moderators of Gender Effects on Parents' Talk to Their Children: A Meta-Analysis," *Developmental Psychology* 34, no. 1 (1998): 3–27; Kim Gale Dolgin, "Parents' Disclosure of Their Own Concerns to Their Adolescent Children," *Personal Relationships* 3, no. 2 (1996): 159–69; Paul Amato, Sandra Rezac, and Alan Booth, "Helping between Parents and Young Adult Offspring: The Role of Parental Marital Quality, Divorce, and Remarriage," *Journal of Marriage and the Family* 57, no. 2 (1995): 363–74; Susan Adams et al., "Gender Differences in Parent-Child Conversations about Past Emotions: A Longitudinal Investigation," *Sex Roles* 3, nos. 5–6 (1995): 309–23; Marjorie Starrels, "Gender Differences in Parent-Child Relations," *Journal of Family Issues* 15, no. 1 (1994): 148–65; John Peters, "Gender Socialization of Adolescents in the Home: Research and Discussion," *Adolescence* 29 (1994): 913–24; Ravi Bhushan, "Found Voices: Women, Disability, and Cultural Transformation," *Women and Therapy* 14, nos. 3–4 (1993): 195–209; Janet Kuebli and Robin Fivush, "Gender Differences in Parent-Child Conversations about Past Emotions," *Sex Roles* 27, nos. 11–12 (1992): 683–98; Carol Wright and Joseph Maxwell, "Social Support during Adjustment to Later-Life Divorce: How Adult Children Help Parents," *Journal of Divorce and Remarriage* 15, nos. 3–4 (1991): 21–48; Barbara Newman, "The Changing Nature of the Parent-Adolescent Relationship from Early to Late Adolescence," *Adolescence* 24 (1989): 915–24; Robin Fivush, "Exploring Sex Differences in the Emotional Content of Mother-Child Conversations about the Past," *Sex Roles* 20, nos. 11–12 (1989): 675–89; Judith Wallerstein and Shauna Corbin, "Daughters of Divorce: Report from a Ten-Year Follow-Up," *American Journal of Orthopsychiatry* 59, no. 4 (1989): 593–604; and John Hagan, John Simpson, and A.R. Gillis, "Feminist Scholarship, Relational and Instrumental Control, and a Power-Control Theory of Gender and Delinquency," *British Journal of Sociology* 39, no. 3 (1988): 301–36.

115 the belief that mothers and daughters cannot see themselves as separate: For instance, see Signe Hammer, *Daughters and Mothers: Mothers and Daughters* (New York: Signet, 1976), 14–15; Mahler, Pine, and Bergman, *The Psycho-logical Birth*; Margaret Mahler, "On Childhood Psychoses and Schizophrenia: Autistic and Symbiotic Infantile Psychosis," in *The Psychoanalytic Study of the Child,* ed. R. Eissler et al. (New York: International Universities Press, 1952); Eichenbaum and Orbach, *Understanding Women.*

116 "mother-daughter fusion": A great deal of literature about psychotherapy is lib-erally sprinkled with these buzz words, including Mahler, Pine, and Bergman, *The Psychological Birth*; Mahler, "On Childhood Psychoses"; Eichenbaum and Orbach, *Understanding Women*; and most of the current writings about family therapy.

116 separation of self from other: Caplan, *Between Women,* 184–85.

116 Wellesley College therapists' groups: See all books and papers by Wellesley authors Judith Jordan, Alexandra Kaplan, Jean Baker Miller, Irene Stiver, and Janet Surrey—plus those by Rachel Josefowitz Siegel—in the bibliography.

117 "relational ability": Surrey, "The 'Self-in-Relation,'" in Jordan et al., 1991.

117 "women do not want to separate": Christina Robb, "A Theory of Empathy: The Quiet Revolution in Psychiatry," *Boston Globe Magazine,* October 16, 1988, 56.

117 Even when adolescent: Alexandra Kaplan, Nancy Gleason, and Rona Klein, "Women's Self Development in Late Adolescence," in Jordan et al., (1991), 122–40.

117 closeness involves mutual empathy: Jordan, "The Meaning of Mutuality," in Jordan et al., 1991.

117 take care of their relationship: Surrey, "The 'Self-in-Relation,'" in ibid.

117 "the self gains": Surrey, "Relationship and Empowerment," in ibid., 62.

117 Kathy Weingarten points out: Weingarten, "Sidelined No More," Coll et al., 1998.

117 Irene Stiver suggests: Stiver, "Beyond the Oedipus Complex," in Jordan et al., 1998.

118 "I was five years old": Wolofsky, "Reconciliation of the Mother-Daughter Relationship, 1.

119 "Yes, yes, of course": Colette, *In My Mother's House and Sido,* trans. Una Vincenzo Troubridge and Enid McLeod (London: Secker and Warburg, 1969), 125.

119 women have so much control: Dinnerstein, *Mermaid and the Minotaur.*

120 "the reality that marriage": quoted by Lucy Freeman, "Family Theme Highlights Spirited Annual Meeting," *Ortho Newsletter,* summer 1987, 26.

124 Ellen Galinsky reports: *Ellen Galinsky, Ask the Children* (New York: William Morrow, 1999).

125 "seemingly limitless list": Arlie Russell Hochschild, *The Time Bind: When Work Becomes Home and Home Becomes Work* (New York: Metropolitan, 1997).

125 one-fifth of U.S. children: Jeanne Brooks-Gunn, Pia Rebello Britto, and Christy Brady, "Struggling to Make Ends Meet," in *Parenting and Child Development in "Nontraditional" Families,* ed. Michael Lamb (Mahwah, N.J.: Lawrence Erlbaum Associates, 1999), 279–304.

125 "rotten mothers": Ruth Sidel, "Hearts of Iron," *Readings: A Journal of Reviews and Commentary in Mental Health Issues* 14, no. 9 (June 1999): 14–18.

125 average mother receiving Aid for Families: ibid.

126 "undeserving poor": Elizabeth Sparks, "Against All Odds: Resistance and Resilience in African American Welfare Mothers," in Coll et al. (1998), 215–37.

126 "I never felt any conflict": Quoted in Christina Looper Baker and Christina Baker Kline, eds., *The Conversation Begins: Mothers and Daughters Talk about Living Feminism* (New York: Bantam, 1996), 91.

126 authors wrongly accuse: ibid., xv.

127 ample research: See, for instance, Steven M. Alessandrini, "Effects of Maternal Work Status in Single-Parent Families on Children's Perceptions of Self and Family and School Achievement," *Journal of Experimental Child Psychology* 54, no. 3 (1992): 417–33.

127 Whether or not the mother is employed: Adele Eskeles Gottfried et al., "Maternal and Dual-Earner Employment: Family Environment, Adaptations, and the Developmental Impingement Perspective," in Lamb, *Parenting,* 15–37.

128 Arlie Russell Hochschild. . .Hochschild, *Time Bind*.

128 A board game from the 1960s: David Owen, "The Sultan of Stuff," *New Yorker,* July 19, 1999, 52–63.

128 African-American women: Greene, "What Has Gone Before" and "Sturdy Bridges"; Strom et al., "Perceptions of Parenting Success"; Cook and Fine, "Motherwit"; Carton et al., "An Observational Study"; and Reid, "Socialization."

129 Several book titles: Betty Holcomb, *Not Guilty! The Good News about Working Mothers* (New York: Scribner, 1998); Joan Peters, *When Mothers Work: Loving Our Children without Sacrificing Ourselves* (Reading, Mass.: Addison Wesley, 1997); and Susan Chira, *A Mother's Place: Taking the Debate about Working Mothers beyond Guilt and Blame* (New York: HarperCollins, 1998).

129 Joseph Pleck: Pleck, "Paternal Involvement: Levels, Sources, and Consequences," in *The Role of the Father in Child Development,* ed. Michael Lamb, 66–103 (New York: Wiley, 1997); Hochschild, *The Time Bind*; and Cynthia Fuchs Epstein et al., *The Part-Time Paradox* (New York: Routledge, 1999).

130 women's family tasks: Hochschild, op. cit.

130 "yet to identify": op. cit.

130 men tend to keep their weekends: Gottfried et al., 1999.

131 men rarely take leave time: Hochschild, op. cit.

131 it makes economic sense: Epstein et al., 1999

131 a recent book of interviews: Baker and Kline, 1996

132 Realizing that: Paula J. Caplan, *Lifting a Ton of Feathers: A Woman's Guide to Surviving in the Academic World* (Toronto: University of Toronto Press, 1993).

133 Louise Silverstein: "Transforming the Debate about Childcare and Maternal Employment," *American Psychologist* 46 (1991): 1025–32.

133 women have been set up: Pamela Trotman Reid, "Socialization of Black Female Children," in *Women: A Developmental Perspective,* ed. Phyllis Berman and Estelle Ramey (Bethesda, Md.: National Institutes of Health, 1983); Valora Washington, "The Black Mother in the United States: History, Theory, Research, and Issues," in *The Different Faces of Motherhood. Perspectives in Development,* ed. Beverly Birns and Dale Hay, 185–213 (New York: Plenum, 1988); and Patricia Hill Collins, "The Meaning of Motherhood in Black Culture and Black Mother/Daughter Relationships," in *Toward a New Psychology of Gender,* 325–40 (New York: Routledge, 1997). Hochschild, *The Time Bind,* also makes this point.

134 "I missed my mother": Baker and Kline, *The Conversation Begins.*

Chapter 6

147 Dr. Albert Ellis: Albert Ellis and Windy Dryden, eds., *The Practice of Rational-Emotive Therapy* (New York: Springer, 1987); Albert Ellis and Russell Grieger, eds., *Handbook of Rational–Emotive Therapy,* vol. 1 (New York: Springer, 1977); and Albert Ellis and Russell Grieger, eds., *Handbook of Rational–Emotive Therapy,* vol. 2 (New York: Springer, 1986).

155 "expressive training": The principles and techniques of expressive training as described here and in appendix A are in the form taught to me by psychologist Dr. Paul Kirwin at the Veterans Administration Hospital in Durham, North Carolina, in 1970, and were further developed and expanded by Dr. Kirwin in his work with psychologist Dr. Jacqueline Damgaard. See Paul Kirwin, "Affect Expression Training in Psychiatric Patients: The Verbalization

of Feeling-Cause Relationships," manuscript, Durham, N.C., Veterans Administration Hospital, 1970; Jacqueline Damgaard, "Structured versus Unstructured Procedures for Training Groups in the Expression of Feeling-Cause Relationships," Ph.D. diss., Duke University, 1973.

Chapter 7

158 "the more you love"" Marilyn French, *Her Mother's Daughter* (New York: Ballantine, 1988), 72.

158 "Could a greater": Henry David Thoreau, *Walden* and *Civil Disobedience* (combined edition) (Harmondsworth, Middlesex, England: Penguin Books, Ltd., 1985), 53.

162 "My friends speak": Anna Quindlen, *Living Out Loud: Home Thoughts from the Front Lines of Life* (New York: Random House, 1988), 104.

162 Karen Glasser Howe: Karen G. Howe, "Telling Our Mother's Story," in *Representations: Social Constructions of Gender*, ed. Rhoda K. Unger (Amityville, N.Y.: Baywood, 1989), 49; and Howe, "Daughters Discover Their Mothers through Biographies and Genograms: Educational and Clinical Parallels," in Knowles and Cole, *Woman-Defined Motherhood*, 31–40.

167 For example: Lenore Walker, personal communication, August 29, 1999; and David Finkelhor, "Current Information on the Scope and Nature of Child Sexual Abuse," *The Future of Children* 4, no. 2 (1994): 31, 46–48.

170 "the last great stigma": Tipper Gore, quoted in Lisa Rabasca, "White House Conference an Important 'First Step,'" *American Psychological Association Monitor*, July/August 1999, 11.

175 Nikki Gerrard: Nikki Gerrard, "Feminist Therapy and Oppression within Mental Health Systems: Contradictions, Struggles, Alliances, and Change," paper presented to National Women's Studies Association convention, Minneapolis, June 1988.

177 "needs, risks, and tasks": Freda Paltiel, personal communication, September 18, 1988.

178 "I've transformed [my mother] into a parody": Rebecca Goldstein, *The Mind-Body Problem* (New York: Laurel, 1983), 189.

187 "After six years of marriage": Wolofsky, "Reconciliation of the Mother-Daughter Relationship," 13.

Chapter 8

190 "My six-year-old daughter": Nikki Gerrard, "Women and the Psychological Development of Self: A Theoretical and Subjective Journey through Object Relations and Self-in-Relation Theories," paper presented to Institute of Section on Women and Psychology, Canadian Psychological Association, Montreal, June 1988.

207 maternal responsibility: Fischer, *Linked Lives*.

207 In a brilliant paper: Rachel Josefowitz Siegel, "We Are Not Your Mothers," paper presented at Association for Women in Psychiatry Convention, Denver, 1987.

213 the word *guilt*: Nikki Gerrard, "A Critical Analysis of Guilt in Relation to Women with a Focus on Mothers and Daughters," paper presented to Feminist Therapists Association First Annual Meeting, Toronto, May 1987.

214 "She does have power": Robin Morgan, *Dry Your Smile* (Garden City, N.Y.: Doubleday, 1987), 279.

215 matrophobia: Rich, *Of Woman Born*.

216 women mourned more: Martha A. Robbins, "Mourning the Myth of Motherhood: Our Mothers' Legacies," in Knowles and Cole, 1990.

Chapter 9

220 Emotionally healthy: Janet Surrey, "Mother-Blaming and Clinical Theory," in Knowles and Cole, 1990.

220 step outside: Mairs, *Plaintext*, 69.

220 "We are together": Walker, *In Search of Our Mothers' Gardens: Womanist Prose*.

221 "One day": Arcana, *Our Mothers' Daughters*, 33–34.

224 Barbara and Robin Miller pointed out: Barbara Miller and Robin Miller, "Confronting Racial Dichotomization: Mothering the Black-White Child," paper presented at "Woman-Defined Motherhood: A Conference for Therapists," Goddard College, Plainfield, Vermont, September 17, 1988).

224 Karen Howe reports: Karen G. Howe, "Telling Our Mother's Story," in *Representations: Social Constructions of Gender*, ed. Rhoda Unger (New York: Baywood, 1989), 44–59.

225 "the door itself": Rich, "Prospective Immigrants Please Note," in *Snapshots of a Daughter-In-Law: Poems 1954–1962*, 59 (New York: W. W. Norton, 1967).

227 "I remember my fury": Susan Griffin, "Forum: On Wanting to Be the Mother I Wanted," *Ms.*, January 1977, 100.

Bibliography

Abbey, Sharon, and Andrea O'Reilly, eds. *Redefining Motherhood: Changing Identities and Patterns.* Toronto: Second Story Press, 1998.

Adams, Susan; Janet Kuebli, Patricia Boyle, and Robin Fivush. "Gender Differences in Parent-Child Conversations about Past Emotions: A Longitudinal Investigation." *Sex Roles* 33, nos. 5–6 (1995): 309–23.

Adelman, Anne. "Traumatic Memory and the Intergenerational Transmission of Holocaust Narrative." *Psychoanalytic Study of the Child* 50 (1995): 343–67.

Albelda, R., N. Folbre, and the Center for Popular Economics. *The War on the Poor: A Defense Manual.* New York: New Press, 1996.

Alessandri, Steven M. "Effects of Maternal Work Status in Single-Parent Families on Children's Perceptions of Self and Family and School Achievement." *Journal of Experimental Child Psychology* 54, no. 3 (1992): 417–33.

Allen, Katherine, and Alexis Walker. "A Feminist Analysis of Interviews with Elderly Mothers and Their Daughters." In *Qualitative Methods in Family Research,* edited by Jane Frances Gilgun, Kerry Daly, et al. Newbury Park, Calif.: Sage, 1992.

Allison, Christine J. "The Making of a 'Bad' Mother: A Lesbian Mother and Her Daughters." In Ladd-Taylor and Umansky, 1998.

Allison, David, and Mark Roberts. *Disordered Mothers or Disordered Diagnosis? Munchausen by Proxy Syndrome.* Hillsdale, N.J.: Analytic Press, 1998.

Alta. *Momma: A Start on All the Untold Stories.* Albion, Calif.: Times Change Press, 1974.

Amato, Paul, Sandra Rezac, and Alan Booth. "Helping between Parents and Young Adult Offspring: The Role of Parental Marital Quality, Divorce, and Remarriage." *Journal of Marriage and the Family* 57, no. 2 (1995): 363–74.

Ambert, Anne-Marie. *The Effect of Children on Parents.* New York: Haworth Press, 1992.

Andersen, Margaret. *Mother Was Not a Person.* Montreal: Black Rose Books, 1972.

Appell, Annette. "On Fixing 'Bad' Mothers and Saving Their Children." In Ladd-Taylor and Umansky, 1998.

Arcana, Judith. *Every Mother's Son: The Role of Mothers in the Making of Men.* Seattle: Seal Press, 1986.

———. *Our Mothers' Daughters.* Berkeley: Shameless Hussy Press, 1979.

Arditti, Joyce A., and Debra Madden-Derdich. "No Regrets: Custodial Mothers' Accounts of the Difficulties and Benefits of Divorce." *Contemporary Family Therapy: An International Journal* 17, no. 2 (1995): 229–48.

Arnup, Katherine. "'Does the Word Lesbian Mean Anything to You?' Lesbians Raising Daughters." In Abbey and O'Reilly, 1998.

Aronson, Jane. "Women's Sense of Responsibility for the Care of Old People: 'But Who Else Is Going to Do It?'" *Gender and Society* 6, no. 1 (1992): 8–29.

Ascher, Carol, Louise de Salvo, and Sara Ruddick. *Between Women.* Boston: Beacon Press, 1984.

Atwood, Margaret. "Significant Moments in the Life of My Mother." In *Close Company: Stories of Mothers and Daughters,* edited by Christine Park and Caroline Heaton. London: Virago, 1987.

Badinter, Elisabeth. *Mother Love: Myth and Reality.* New York: Macmillan, 1980.

Baker, Christina Looper, and Christina Kline Baker, eds. *The Conversation Begins: Mothers and Daughters Talk about Living Feminism.* New York: Bantam, 1996.

Baron, Kathryn. "The 'Gaybie' Boom." *Los Angeles Times,* March 1, 1995.

Bart, Pauline. "Review of Chodorow's 'The Reproduction of Mothering.'" In Trebilcot, 1983.

Baruch, Grace, Rosalind Barnett, and Caryl Rivers. *Lifeprints: New Patterns of Love and Work for Today's Women.* New York: McGraw-Hill, 1983.

Baskin, Barbara Holland, and Elizabeth P. Riggs. "Mothers Who Are Disabled." In *The Different Faces of Motherhood,* edited by Beverly Birns and Dale F. Hay. New York: Plenum, 1988.

Bass, Ellen, and Laura Davis. *The Courage to Heal: A Guide for Woman Survivors of Child Sexual Abuse.* New York: Harper and Row, 1988 (especially section on "Working through Mother Blame").

Bassoff, Evelyn. *Mothers and Daughters: Loving and Letting Go.* New York: New American Library, 1988.

Baum, Charlotte, Paula Hyman, and Sonya Michel. *The Jewish Woman in America.* New York: New American Library, 1976.

Baunach, Phyllis Jo. *Mothers in Prison.* New Brunswick, N.J.: Transaction, 1985.

Beauvoir, Simone de. *The Second Sex.* New York: Virago, 1974.

Bell, Karin. "On the Relationship between Daughters and Mothers with Regard to Bulimia Nervosa." In *Why Women? Gender Issues and Eating Disorders,* edited by Bridget Dolan, et al., London: Athlone Press, 1994.

Bell-Scott, Patricia. "A Critical Overview of Sex Roles Research of Black Families." *Women Studies Abstracts* 5 (Spring 1976): 1–9.

Bell-Scott, Patricia, et al., eds. *Double Stitch: Black Women Write about Mothers and Daughters.* New York: Harper Perennial, 1993.

Benkov, Laura. "Yes, I Am a Swan: Reflections on Families Headed by Lesbians and Gay Men." In Coll et al., 1998.

Bernard, Claudia. "Black Mothers' Emotional and Behavioral Responses to the Sexual Abuse of Their Children." In *Out of Darkness: Contemporary Perspectives on Family Violence,* edited by Glenda Kaufman Kantor et al. Thousand Oaks, Calif.: Sage, 1997.

Bernard, Jessie. *The Future of Motherhood.* New York: Dial Press, 1974.

Bernard, Wanda Thomas, and Candace Bernard. "Passing the Torch: A Mother and Daughter Reflect on Their Experience across Generations." *Canadian Woman Studies/Les Cahiers de la femme* 18, no. 2–3 (1998): 46–50.

Bernardez, Teresa. "Gender-Based Countertransference of Female Therapists in the Psychotherapy of Women." In Braude, 1987.

———. "Women and Anger: Cultural Prohibitions and the Feminine Ideal." Work in Progress Paper No. 31, Wellesley College, The Stone Center, Wellesley, Mass., 1988.

Bernikow, Louise. *Among Women.* New York: Harper and Row, 1981.

Bhushan, Ravi. "Found Voices: Women, Disability and Cultural Transformation." *Women and Therapy* 14, nos. 3–4 (1993): 195–209.

Bidaut-Russell, Michelle, Elizabeth Smith, and Susan Bradford. "Gender Differences in Lifetime Psychiatric Disorders between Sons and Daughters of Alcoholic Mothers." *Alcoholism: Clinical and Experimental Research* 18, no. 2 (1994): 244–47.

Bilinkoff, Joan. "Empowering Battered Women as Mothers." In *Ending the Cycle of Violence: Community Responses to Children of Battered Women,* edited by Einat Peled and Peter Jaffe, 97–105. Thousand Oaks, Calif.: Sage, 1995.

Birns, Beverly. "The Mother-Infant Tie: Fifty Years of Theory, Science and Science Fiction." Work in Progress Paper No. 21, Wellesley College, The Stone Center, Wellesley, Mass., 1985.

Birns, Beverly, and Shannon Lee Meyer. "Mothers' Role in Incest: Dysfunctional Women or Dysfunctional Theories?" *Journal of Child Sexual Abuse* 2, no. 3 (1993): 127–35.

Blackford, Karen. "Erasing Mothers with Disabilities through Canadian Family-Related Policy." *Disability, Handicap and Society* 8, no. 3 (1993): 281–94.

———. "Mother to Daughter: The Shaping of a Girl's Values in the Context of a Parent with a Chronic Illness." In Abbey and O'Reilly, 1998.

Blaxter, Mildred, and Elizabeth Paterson. *Mothers and Daughters: A Three-Dimensional Study of Health Attitudes and Behavior.* Brookfield, Vt.: Gower, 1982.

Blieszner, Rosemary, Paula Usita, and Jay Mancini. "Diversity and Dynamics in Late-Life Mother-Daughter Relationships." In *Relationships between Women in Later Life,* edited by Karen Robert. New York: Harrington Park Press, 1996.

Bowe, Claudia. "The Urgent Crisis in Day Care." *Cosmopolitan,* November 1986, 298–302, 360–61.

Boyce, Glenna, Brent Miller, Karl White, and Michael Godfrey. "Single Parenting in Families of Children with Disabilities." *Marriage and Family Review* 20, nos. 3–4 (1995): 389–409.

Boylan, Clare. *Last Resorts.* London: Hamish Hamilton, 1984.

Brans, Jo. *Mother, I Have Something to Tell You.* Research by Margaret Taylor Smith. Garden City, N.Y.: Doubleday, 1987.

Braude, Marjorie, ed. *Women, Power, and Therapy: Issues for Women.* New York: Haworth Press, 1987.

Brazelton, T. Berry. *Infants and Mothers: Differences in Development.* New York: Delacorte, 1983.

———. *Toddlers and Parents.* New York: Dell, 1986.

Brett, Mary Ann. "Let's Hear from Disabled Mothers." *Toronto Star,* September 14, 1987, C9.

Briles, Judith. *Woman to Woman: From Sabotage to Support.* Far Hills, N.J.: New Horizon Press, 1987.

Brody, Elaine. "Women-in-the-Middle: The Mental Health Effects of Parent Care." Women's Mental Health Occasional Paper Series, National Institute of Mental Health, 1987.

Brody, Gene, Douglas Flor, and Eileen Neubaum. "Coparenting Processes and Child Competence among Rural African-American Families." In *Families, Risk, and Competence,* edited by Michael Lewis and Candice Feiring. Mahwah, N.J.: Lawrence Erlbaum Associates, 1998.

Broner, E.M. *Ghost Stories.* New York: Global City Press, 1995.

Brooks-Gunn, Jeanne, Pia Rebello Britto, and Christy Brady. "Struggling to Make Ends Meet." In Lamb, 1999.

Brown, Kathleen M., George B. Schreiber, Robert P. McMahon, Patricia Crawford, et al. "Maternal Influences on Body Satisfaction in Black and White Girls Aged 9 and 10: The NHLBI Growth and Health Study (NGHS)." *Annals of Behavioral Medicine* 17, no. 3 (1995): 213–20.

Burck, Frances Wells. *Mothers Talking: Sharing the Secret.* New York: St. Martin's Press, 1986.

Burstein, Janet. "Restorying Jewish Mothers." In O'Reilly and Abbey, 1999.

Butler, Sandra. *Conspiracy of Silence: The Trauma of Incest.* San Francisco: Volcano Press, 1985.

Caine, Lynn. *What Did I Do Wrong?* Toronto: Paper Jacks, 1986.

Calam, Rachel, Glenn Waller, Antony Cox, and Peter Slade. "Eating Attitudes in Young Teenage Girls: Parental Management of 'Fussy' Eating." *Eating Disorders: the Journal of Treatment and Prevention* 5, no. 1 (1997): 29–40.

Campbell, Kate, and Sue Levesque. "Mandatory Thinness and Mother-Blame: The Newspaper Coverage of the Marlene Corrigan Trial." *Canadian Woman Studies/Les Cahiers de la femme* 18, nos. 2–3 (fall/summer 1998): 69–73.

Canadian Woman Studies/Les Cahiers de la femme 18, nos. 2–3 (fall/summer 1998), "Special Issue: Looking Back, Looking Forward: Mothers, Daughters, and Feminism."

Caplan, Paula. *Between Women: Lowering the Barriers.* Toronto: Personal Library, 1981.

———. *"Don't Blame Mother:* Then and Now." In O'Reilly and Abbey, 1999.

———. *Lifting a Ton of Feathers: A Woman's Guide to Surviving in the Academic World.* Toronto: University of Toronto Press, 1993.

———. "Making Mother-Blaming Visible: The Emperor's New Clothes." In Knowles and Ellen Cole, 1990.

———. *The Myth of Women's Masochism.* 1985; reprint, New York: Signet, 1987; new edition, Toronto: University of Toronto Press, 1993.

———. *They Say You're Crazy: How the World's Most Powerful Psychiatrists Decide Who's Normal.* Reading, Mass.: Addison Wesley, 1995.

Caplan, Paula J., and Jeremy B. Caplan. *Thinking Critically about Research on Sex and Gender.* New York: Addison Wesley Longman, 1999.

Caplan, Paula J., and Mary Lou Fassel. "Women Get Blame in Incest Cases." *Globe and Mail* (Toronto), February 10, 1987.

Caplan, Paula J., and Ian Hall-McCorquodale. "Mother-Blaming in Major Clinical Journals." *American Journal of Orthopsychiatry* 55 (1985): 345–53.

———. "The Scapegoating of Mothers: A Call for Change." *American Journal of Orthopsychiatry* 55 (1985): 610–13.

Caplan, Paula J., Jessie Watters, Georgina White, Ruth Parry, and Robert Bates. "Toronto Multi-Agency Child Abuse Research Project: The Abused and the Abuser." *Child Abuse and Neglect: The International Journal* 8 (1984): 343–51.

Carton, John S., Stephen Nowicki Jr., and Ginger M. Baiser. "An Observational Study of Antecedents of Locus of Control of Reinforcement." *International Journal of Behavioral Development* 19, no. 1 (1996): 161–75.

Cauce, Ana Maria, Yumi Hiraga, Diane Graves, Nancy Gonzales, et al. "African American Mothers and Their Adolescent Daughters: Closeness, Conflict, and Control." In *Urban Girls: Resisting Stereotypes, Creating Identities,* edited by Bonnie J. Ross Leadbeater et al. New York: New York University Press, 1996.

Center on Hunger, Poverty, and Nutrition Policy. Statement on Key Welfare Reform Issues: The Empirical Evidence. Medford, Mass.: Tufts University Press, 1995.

"Chains of Violence." *Harvard Magazine,* September/October 1999, 19.

Chapian, Marie. *Mothers and Daughters.* Minneapolis: Bethany House, 1988.

Chawla, Saroj, and Anne-Marie Ambert. "Two Case Studies of Interracial Mothers and Daughters." In *The Effect of Children on Parents,* edited by Anne-Marie Ambert, 208–23. New York: Haworth Press, 1992.

Cherlin, Andrew. "By the Numbers." *New York Times Magazine,* April 5, 1998, 39–41.

Chernin, Kim. *In My Mother's House: A Daughter's Story.* New York: Harper and Row, 1983.

———. *Reinventing Eve: Modern Woman in Search of Herself.* New York: Harper and Row, 1988.

Chesler, Phyllis. *Letters to a Young Feminist.* New York: Four Walls Eight Windows, 1998.

———. "Mother-Hatred and Mother-Blaming: What Electra Did to Clytemnestra." In Knowles and Cole, 1990.

———. *Mothers on Trial: The Battle for Children and Custody.* New York: McGraw-Hill, 1986.

———. *Sacred Bond: The Legacy of Baby M.* New York: Times Books, 1988.

———. *With Child: A Diary of Motherhood.* New York: Berkeley Books, 1981.

———. *Women and Madness.* New York: Avon Books, 1973.

———. Personal communication, August 11, 1999.

Chess, Stella. "The 'Blame the Mother' Ideology." *International Journal of Mental Health* 11 (1982): 95–107.

Chess, Stella, and Jane Whitbread. *Daughters: From Infancy to Independence.* Garden City, N.Y.: Doubleday, 1978.

Chira, Susan. *A Mother's Place: Taking the Debate about Working Mothers Beyond Guilt and Blame.* New York: HarperCollins, 1998.

Chodorow, Nancy. *The Reproduction of Mothering: Psychoanalysis and the Sociology of Gender.* Berkeley: University of California Press, 1978.

Chodorow, Nancy, and Susan Contratto. "The Fantasy of the Perfect Mother." In Thorne and Yalom, 1982.

Christensen, Kimberly, Mary Ann Parris Stephens, and Aloen Townsend. "Mastery in Women's Multiple Roles and Well-Being: Adult Daughters Providing Care to Impaired Parents." *Health Psychology* 17, no. 2 (1998): 163–71.

Cicirelli, Victor. "Attachment and Obligation as Daughters' Motives for Caregiving Behavior and Subsequent Effect on Subjective Burden." *Psychology and Aging* 8, no. 2 (1993): 144–55.

Claremont de Castillejo, Irene. *Knowing Woman.* New York: Harper and Row, 1973.

Clifton, Lucille. *An Ordinary Woman.* New York: Random House, 1974.

Cohler, Bertram, and Henry Grunebaum. *Mothers, Grandmothers, and Daughters: Personality and Childcare in Three-Generation Families.* New York: John Wiley and Sons, 1981.

Cole, Carolyn. Personal communication, May 1986.

Cole, Carolyn. Personal communication, September 25, 1987.

Cole, Carolyn, and Elaine E. Barney, "Safeguards and the Therapeutic Window: A Group Treatment Strategy for Adult Incest Suvivors." *American Journal of Orthopsychiatry* 57 (1987): 601–609.

Colette. *In My Mother's House and Sido.* Translated by Una Vincenzo Troubridge and Enid McLeod. London: Secker and Warburg, 1969.

Coll, Cynthia Garcia, Janet L. Surrey, and Kathy Weingarten, eds. *Mothering against the Odds: Diverse Foices of Contemporary Mothers.* New York: Guilford, 1998.

Coll, Cynthia Garcia, Janet L. Surrey, and Phyllis Buccio-Notaro. "Incarcerated Mothers: Crimes and Punishments." In Coll et al., 1998.

Collins, Patricia Hill. "The Meaning of Motherhood in Black Culture and Black Mother/Daughter Relationships." In *Toward a New Psychology of Gender*, edited by Mary M. Gergen and Sara H. Davis, 325–40. New York: Routledge, 1997.

———. "The Meaning of Motherhood in Black Culture and Black Mother/Daughter Relationships." *Sage* 4, no. 2 (1987): 3–10.

Compas, Bruce, and Rebecca Williams. "Stress, Coping, and Adjustment in Mothers and Young Adolescents in Single- and Two-Parent Families." *American Journal of Community Psychology* 18, no. 4 (1990): 525–45.

Conlon, Faith, Rachel daSilva, and Barbara Wilson, eds. *The Things That Divide Us*. Seattle: Seal Press, 1985.

Conroy, Pat. *The Prince of Tides*. Boston: Houghton Mifflin, 1986.

Cook, Donelda, and Michelle Fine. "'Motherwit': Childrearing Lessons from African-American Mothers of Low Income." In *Children and Families "At Promise": Deconstructing the Discourse of Risk. SUNY Series, The Social Context of Education*, edited by Beth Blue Swadener and Sally Lubeck. Albany, N.Y.: State University of New York Press, 1995.

Cook, Mariana (photographer), and Jamaica Kincaid (introduction). *Generations of Women in Their Own Words*. San Francisco: Chronicle Books, 1998.

Coons, Phyllis, "New Alliances." *Radcliffe Quarterly*, December 1984, 31–32.

Corcoran, Jacqueline. "In Defense of Mothers of Sexual Abuse Victims." *Families in Society* 79, no. 4 (1998): 358–69.

Cowan, Philip, Carolyn Pape Cowan, and Patricia Kerig. "Mothers, Fathers, Sons, and Daughters: Gender Differences in Family Formation and Parenting Style." In *Family, Self, and Society: Toward a New Agenda for Family Research*, edited by Philip Cowan et al. Hillsdale, N.J.: Lawrence Erlbaum Associates, 1993.

Crean, Susan. *In the Name of the Fathers: The Story behind Child Custody*. Toronto: Amanita, 1988.

Crist, Patricia. "Contingent Interaction during Work and Play Tasks for Mothers with Multiple Sclerosis and Their Daughters." *American Journal of Occupational Therapy* 47, no. 2 (1993): 121–31.

Cunningham, Terry. "An Exploratory View: Attitudes of Black Teenage Females toward Familial Relationships." Atlanta: Atlanta University School of Social Work, 1980.

Dally, Ann. *Inventing Motherhood: The Consequences of an Ideal*. New York: Schocken Books, 1982.

Damgaard, Jacqueline. "Structured versus Unstructured Procedures for Training Groups in the Expression of Feeling-Cause Relationships." Ph.D. diss., Duke University, 1973.

Davidson, Cathy N. "Mothers and Daughters in the Fiction of the New Republic." In Davidson and Broner, 1980.

Davidson, Cathy N., and E. M. Broner, eds. *The Lost Tradition: Mothers and Daughters in Literature*. New York: Frederick Ungar, 1980.

Day, Ingeborg. "Daughters and Mothers." *Ms.*, June 1975, 49–53, 78–83.

Debold, Elizabeth, Marie Wilson, and Idelisse Malave. *Mother-Daughter Revolution*. Reading, Mass.: Addison Wesley, 1993.

DeGeneres, Betty. *Love, Ellen: A Mother-Daughter Journey*. New York: William Morrow, 1999.

DerKarabetian, Aghop, and Michelle Preciado. "Mother-Blaming among College Students." *Perceptual and Motor Skills* 68, no. 2 (1989): 453–54.

DeYoung, Mary. "Immediate Maternal Reactions to the Disclosure or Discovery of Incest." *Journal of Family Violence* 9, no. 1 (1994): 21–33.

Dickerson, Bette J., ed. *African American Single Mothers: Understanding Their Lives and Families.* Sage Series on Race and Ethnic Relations, vol. 10. Thousand Oaks, Calif.: Sage, 1995.

DiLapi, Elena M. "Lesbian Mothers and the Motherhood Hierarchy." *Journal of Homosexuality* 18, nos. 1–2 (1989): 101–21.

Dinnerstein, Dorothy. *The Mermaid and the Minotaur.* New York: Harper and Row, 1977.

Dodson, Lisa. *Don't Call Us Out of Name: The Untold Lives of Women and Girls in Poor America.* Boston: Beacon, 1998.

Dohrn, Bernardine. "Bad Mothers, Good Mothers, and the State: Children on the Margins." *University of Chicago Law School Roundtable* 2 (1995): 12.

Dolgin, Kim Gale. "Parents' Disclosure of Their Own Concerns to Their Adolescent Children." *Personal Relationships* 3, no. 2 (1996): 159–69.

Donahue Television Show on Alcoholism. February 2, 1988.

Doucet, Andrea, and Gillian Dunne. "Heterosexual and Lesbian Mothers Challenging 'Feminine' and 'Masculine' Concepts of Mothering." In O'Reilly and Abbey, 1999.

Downey, Douglas B., James W. Ainsworth-Darnell, and Mikaela J. Dufur. "Sex of Parent and Children's Well-Being in Single-Parent Households." *Journal of Marriage and the Family* 60, no. 4 (1998): 878–93.

Duncan, Erika. "The Hungry Jewish Mother." In Davidson and Broner, 1980.

Dworkin, Andrea. *Woman Hating.* New York: E. P. Dutton, 1974.

Easterbrooks, M. Ann, and Christine Graham. "Security of Attachment and Parenting: Homeless and Low-Income Housed Mothers and Infants." *American Journal of Orthopsychiatry* 69, no. 3 (1999): 337–46.

Eberly, Mary, Raymond Montemayor, and Daniel Flannery. "Variation in Adolescent Helpfulness toward Parents in a Family Context." *Journal of Early Adolescence* 13, no. 3 (1993): 228–44.

Ehrenreich, Barbara, and Deirdre English. *For Her Own Good: 150 Years of the Experts' Advice to Women.* Garden City, N.Y.: Anchor, 1979.

Eichenbaum, Luise, and Susie Orbach. *Between Women.* New York: Viking Press, 1988.

———. *Understanding Women: A Feminist Psychoanalytic Approach.* New York: Basic Books, 1983.

Eichler, Margrit. *Family Shifts.* Toronto: Oxford University Press, 1997.

Eisenberg, Ann R. "The Conflict Talk of Mothers and Children: Patterns Related to Culture, SES, and Gender of Child." *Merrill-Palmer Quarterly* 42, no. 3 (1996): 438–58.

Ellis, Albert, and Windy Dryden, eds. *The Practice of Rational-Emotive Therapy.* New York: Springer, 1987.

Engel, Barbara A. *Mothers and Daughters: Women of the Intelligentsia in Nineteenth-Century Russia.* New York: Cambridge University Press, 1983.

Epstein, Cynthia Fuchs, Carroll Seron, Bonnie Oglensky, and Robert Saute. *The Part-Time Paradox.* New York: Routledge, 1999.

Falk, Patricia. "Lesbian Mothers: Psychosocial Assumptions in Family Law." In

Psychological Perspectives on Lesbian and Gay Male Experiences. Between Men—Between Women: Lesbian and Gay Studies, edited by Linda Garnets and Douglas Kimmel. New York: Columbia University Press, 1993.

Faller, Kathleen Coulbourn. "Decision-Making in Cases of Intrafamilial Child Sexual Abuse." *American Journal of Orthopsychiatry* 58 (1988): 121–28.

Feldman, Maurice, Laurie Case, Maria Garrick, Wanda MacIntyre-Grande, et al. "Teaching Child-Care Skills to Mothers with Developmental Disabilities." *Journal of Applied Behavior Analysis* 25, no. 1 (1992): 205–15.

Fellman, Anita Clair. "'Don't Expect to Depend on Anybody': The Mother-Daughter Relationship of Laura Ingalls Wilder and Rose Wilder Lane." Paper presented to Institute of Section on Women and Psychology, Canadian Psychological Association, Vancouver, 1987.

Few, April L. "The (Un)making of Martyrs: Black Mothers, Daughters, and Intimate Violence." *Mothering and Motherhood* 1, no. 1 (1999): 68–75.

Fine, Michelle, and Adrienne Asch, eds. *Women with Disabilities: Essays in Psychology, Culture, and Politics.* Philadelphia: Temple University Press, 1988.

Fingerman, Karen. "Aging Mothers' and Their Adult Daughters' Perceptions of Conflict Behaviors." *Psychology and Aging* 10, no. 4 (1995): 639–49.

———. "Sources of Tension in the Aging Mother and Adult Daughter Relationship." *Psychology and Aging* 11, no. 4 (1996): 591–606.

———. "Tight Lips? Aging Mothers' and Adult Daughters' Responses to Interpersonal Tensions in Their Relationships." *Personal Relationships* 5, no. 2 (1998): 121–38.

Finkelhor, David. "Current Information on the Scope and Nature of Child Sexual Abuse." *The Future of Children* 4, no. 2 (1994): 31, 46–48.

Firman, Julie, and Dorothy Firman. *Mothers and Daughters: Healing the Relationship.* New York: Crossroad Publishing, 1989.

Fischer, Lucy Rose. *Linked Lives: Adult Daughters and Their Mothers.* New York: Harper and Row, 1987.

Fite, Karen, and Nikola Trumbo. "Betrayals among Women: Barriers to a Common Longing." *Lesbian Ethics* 1 (1984).

Fivush, Robin. "Exploring Sex Differences in the Emotional Content of Mother-Child Conversations about the Past." *Sex Roles* 20, nos. 11–12 (1989): 675–91.

———. "Gender and Emotion in Mother-Child Conversations about the Past." *Journal of Narrative and Life History* 1, no. 4 (1991): 325–41.

Flanagan, Patricia. "Teen Mothers: Countering the Myths of Dysfunction and Developmental Disruption." In Coll et al., 1998.

Flax, Jane. "The Conflict between Nurturance and Autonomy in Mother-Daughter Relationships and within Feminism." *Feminist Studies* 4 (1978): 171–89.

Flynn, Kristin, and Marian Fitzgibbon. "Body Image Ideals of Low-Income African American Mothers and Their Preadolescent Daughters." *Journal of Youth and Adolescence* 25, no. 5 (1996): 615–30.

Fodor, Renee. "The Impact of the Nazi Occupation of Poland on the Jewish Mother-Child Relationship." *YIVO Annual of Jewish Social Science* 11 (1956–57): 270–85.

Fraktman, Marilyn G. "Immigrant Mothers: What Makes Them High Risk?" In Coll et al., 1998.

Franco, Fabiana, Alan Fogel, Daniel Messinger, and Christopher Frazier. "Cultural Differences in Physical Contact between Hispanic and Anglo Mother-Infant

Dyads Living in the United States." *Early Development and Parenting* 5, no. 3 (1996): 119–27.

Fraser, Sylvia. *My Father's House: A Memoir of Incest and Healing.* Toronto: Doubleday Canada Limited, 1987.

Freeman, Lucy. "Family Theme Highlights Spirited Annual Meeting." *Ortho Newsletter,* Summer 1987, 1 and 17–39.

French, Marilyn. *Her Mother's Daughter.* New York: Ballantine, 1988.

Freud, Sigmund. "Femininity." In "New Introductory Lectures in Psychoanalysis" [1932], *The Standard Edition of the Complete Psychological Works of Sigmund Freud.* Vol. 22. Translated by James Strachey. London: Hogarth Press and the Institute of Psychoanalysis, 1964.

Freyd, Jennifer. *Betrayal Trauma: The Logic of Forgetting Childhood Abuse.* Cambridge, Mass.: Harvard University Press, 1996.

Friday, Nancy. *My Mother/My Self.* New York: Delacorte Press, 1977.

Friedan, Betty. *The Feminine Mystique.* New York: Dell, 1963.

Frost, Beth. "My Mother's Friend." *Radcliffe Quarterly,* December 1984, 26–28.

Fullmer, Elise, Sheldon Tobin, and Gregory Smith. "The Effects of Offspring Gender on Older Mothers Caring for Their Sons and Daughters with Mental Retardation." *Gerontologist* 37, no. 6 (1997): 795–803..

Fumia, Doreen. "Marginalized Motherhood and the Mother-Lesbian Subject." *Mothering and Motherhood* 1, no. 1 (1999): 86-95.

———. "By Any (M)other Name: Once-Married Lesbians." *Canadian Woman Studies/Les Cahiers de la femme* 18, no. 2 (fall/summer 1998): 41–45.

Galinsky, Ellen. *Ask the Children.* New York: William Morrow, 1999.

Gamble, Wendy, and Rochelle Dalla. "Parenting and Child Adjustment in Single- and Two-Parent, Euro- and Mexican-American Families." In McCubbin and Thompson, 1998.

———. "Young Children's Perceptions of Their Social Worlds in Single- and Two-Parent, Euro- and Mexican-American Families." *Journal of Social and Personal Relationships* 14, no. 3 (1997): 357–72.

Gardner, Howard. *Frames of Mind: The Theory of Multiple Intelligences.* New York: Basic Books, 1993.

Gavin, Leslie, and Wyndol Furman. "Adolescent Girls' Relationships with Mothers and Best Friends." *Child Development* 67, no. 2 (1996): 375–86.

Gee, Ellen M., and Meredith M. Kimball. *Women and Aging.* Toronto: Butterworths, 1987.

Genevie, Lois, and Eva Margolies. *Motherhood Report: How Women Feel about Being Mothers.* New York: McGraw-Hill, 1988.

Gerrard, Nikki. "A Critical Analysis of Guilt in Relation to Women with a Focus on Mothers and Daughters." Paper presented to Feminist Therapists' Association First Annual Meeting, Toronto, May 1987.

———. "Feminist Therapy and Oppression within Mental Health Systems: Contradictions, Struggles, Alliances, and Change." Paper presented to National Women's Studies Association Convention, Minneapolis, June 1988.

———. "Undoing Crazymaking: Feminist Therapy—A Stitch in Time Saves Nine." Popular Feminism Lecture Series, Paper No. 7, Centre for Women's Studies in Education, Ontario Institute for Studies in Education, Toronto, January 11, 1988.

———. "Women and the Psychological Development of Self: A Theoretical and Subjective Journey through Object Relations and Self-in-Relation Theories."

Paper presented to Institute of Section on Women and Psychology, Canadian Psychological Association, Montreal, June 1988.

Gilligan, Carol. *In a Different Voice: Psychological Theory and Women's Development.* Cambridge, Mass.: Harvard University Press, 1982.

Glickman, Rose. *Daughters of Feminists: Young Women with Feminist Mothers Talk about Their Lives.* New York: St. Martin's Press, 1993.

Goleman, Daniel. *Emotional Intelligence.* New York: Bantam, 1995.

Golomb, Anath, Pamela Ludolph, Drew Westen, M. Judith Block, et al. "Maternal Empathy, Family Chaos, and the Etiology of Borderline Personality Disorder." *Journal of the American Psychoanalytic Association* 42, no. 2 (1994): 525–48.

Golombok, Susan, Fiona Tasker, and Clare Murray. "Children Raised in Fatherless Families from Infancy: Family Relationships and the Socioemotional Development of Children of Lesbian and Single Heterosexual Mothers." *Journal of Child Psychology and Psychiatry and Allied Disciplines* 38, no. 7 (1997): 783–91.

Golombok, Susan, and Fiona Tasker. "Children in Lesbian and Gay Families: Theories and Evidence." *Annual Review of Sex Research* 5 (1994): 73–100.

Gombay, Brydon. "Mutual Empowerment: The Mother of a Daughter with Disabilities." *Canadian Woman Studies/Les Cahiers de la femme* 18, no. 2 (fall/summer 1998): 35–40.

Gonzales, Nancy A., Yumi Hiraga, and Ana Maria Cauce. "Observing Mother-Daughter Interaction in African-American and Asian-American Families." In *Resiliency in African-American Families,* edited by Hamilton I. McCubbin, Elizabeth A. Thompson, Anne I. Thompson, and Jo-A. Futrell. Thousand Oaks, Calif.: Sage, 1998.

Gordon, Linda. *Heroes of Their Own Lives: The Politics and History of Family Violence, Boston 1880–1960.* New York: Viking Press, 1988.

Gornick, Vivian. *Fierce Attachments.* New York: Farrar, Straus, and Giroux, 1987.

Gottfried, Adele Eskeles, Allen Gottfried, Kay Bathurst, and Colleen Killian. "Maternal and Dual-Earner Employment: Family Environment, Adaptations, and the Developmental Impingement Perspective." In Lamb, 1999.

Gottlieb, Alison. "Single Mothers of Children with Disabilities: The Role of Sense of Coherence in Managing Multiple Challenges." In McCubbin and Thompson, 1998.

Gottman, Julie. "Children of Gay and Lesbian Parents." *Marriage and Family Review* 14, nos. 3–4 (1989): 177–96.

Graber, Julia, and Jeanne Brooks-Gunn. "'Sometimes I Think That You Don't Like Me': How Mothers and Daughters Negotiate the Transition into Adolescence." In *Conflict and Cohesion in Families: Causes and Consequences,* edited by Martha Cox et al. The Advances in Family Research Series. Mahwah, N.J.: Lawrence Erlbaum Associates, 1999.

———. "Reproductive Transitions: The Experience of Mothers and Daughters." In Ryff et al., 1996.

Grant, Toni. *Being a Woman: Fulfilling Your Femininity and Finding Love.* New York: Random House, 1988.

Green, Fiona. "Living Feminism through Mothering." *Mothering and Motherhood* 1, no. 1 (1999): 99–104.

Greene, Beverly. "Sturdy Bridges: The Role of African-American Mothers in the Socialization of African-American Children." *Women and Therapy* 10, nos. 1–2 (1990): 205–25.

———. "What Has Gone Before: The Legacy of Racism and Sexism in the Lives of Black Mothers and Daughters." *Women and Therapy* 9, nos. 1–2 (1990): 207–30.

Greenglass, Esther. "A Social–Psychological View of Marriage for Women." *International Journal of Women's Studies* 8 (1985): 24–31.

Greenspan, Miriam. "'Exceptional' Mothering in a 'Normal' World." In Coll et al., 1998.

Griffin, Susan. "Forum: On Wanting to Be the Mother I Wanted." *Ms.*, January 1977: 98–105.

Griffith, Alison I., and Dorothy E Smith. "Constructing Cultural Knowledge: Mothering as Discourse." In *Women and Education,* edited by J. Gaskell and A. McLaren, 87–103. Calgary: Detselig Press, 1987.

———. "Coordinating the Uncoordinated: How Mothers Manage the School Day." *Perspectives in Social Problems* 2 (1990): 25–43..

Griffiths, Rosalyn A., Pierre J. Beumont, Daphne Beumont, Stephen W. Touyz, Hazel Williams, and Kitty Lowinger. "Anorexie à Deux: An Ominous Sign for Recovery." *European Eating Disorders Review* 3, no. 1 (1995): 2–14.

Grinnell, Gretchen. "Women, Depression and the Global Folie: A New Framework for Therapists." In Braude, 1987.

Gross, Zenith Henkin. *And You Thought It Was All Over! Mothers and Their Adult Children.* New York: St. Martin's Press, 1985.

Grotevant, Harold, and Julie Kohler. "Adoptive Families." In *Parenting and Child Development in 'Nontraditional' Families,* edited by Michael E. Lamb, 161–90. Mahwah, N.J.: Lawrence Erlbaum Associates, 1999.

Groze, Victor K., and James A. Rosenthal. "Single Parents and Their Adopted Children: A Psychosocial Analysis." *Families in Society* 72, no. 2 (1991): 67–77.

Gundlach, Julie Kette. *My Mother Before Me.* Secaucus, N.J.: Lyle Stuart, 1986.

Guy-Sheftall, Beverly. "Mothers and Daughters: A Black Perspective." *Spelman Messenger* 98 (1982): 4–5.

Hagan, John, John Simpson, and A. R. Gillis. "Feminist Scholarship, Relational and Instrumental Control, and a Power-Control Theory of Gender and Delinquency." *British Journal of Sociology* 39, no. 3 (1988): 301–36.

Hamilton, Sylvia. "African Nova Scotian Women: Mothering across the Generations." In Abbey and O'Reilly, 1998.

Hammer, Signe. *Daughters and Mothers: Mothers and Daughters.* New York: Signet, 1976.

Hampton, Mary Rucklos. "Adopted Women Give Birth: Connection between Women and Matrilineal Continuity." *Feminism and Psychology* 7, no. 1 (1997): 83–106.

Hancock, Emily. *The Girl Within.* New York: Fawcett, 1989.

Hanscombe, Gillian, and Jackie Forster. *Rocking the Cradle: Lesbian Mothers, a Challenge in Family Living.* Boston: Alyson, 1982.

Hare-Mustin, Rachel T., and Patricia C. Broderick. "The Myth of Motherhood: A Study of Attitudes toward Motherhood." *Psychology of Women Quarterly* 4 (1979): 114–28.

Harney, Patricia. "The Role of Incest in Developmental Theory and Treatment of Women Diagnosed with Borderline Personality Disorder." *Women and Therapy* 12, nos. 1–2 (1992): 39–57.

Hays, Sharon. *The Cultural Contradictions of Motherhood.* New Haven, Conn.: Yale University Press, 1996.

Heffner, Elaine. *Mothering: The Emotional Experience of Motherhood after Freud and Feminism.* Garden City, N.Y.: Doubleday, 1978.

Held, Virginia. "The Obligations of Mothers and Fathers." In Trebilcot, 1983.

Heller, Anita Fochs. *Health and Home: Women as Health Guardians.* Ottawa: Canadian Advisory Council on the Status of Women, 1986.

Hendrick, Susan. "'Carving Tomorrow from a Tombstone': Maternal Grief Following the Death of a Daughter." *Mothering and Motherhood* 1, no. 1 (1999): 33–44.

Henwood, K. L. "Adult Mother-Daughter Relationships: Subjectivity, Power, and Critical Psychology.," *Theory and Psychology* 5 (1994): 483–510.

Herman, Judith Lewis, and Helen Block Lewis. "Anger in the Mother-Daughter Relationship." In *The Psychology of Today's Woman: New Psychoanalytic Visions,* edited by Toni Bernay and Dorothy Cantor. Cambridge, Mass.: Harvard University Press, 1986, reprinted 1989.

Hirsch, Marianne. *The Mother/Daughter Plot: Narrative, Psychoanalysis, Feminism.* Bloomington: Indiana University Press, 1989.

———. "Mothers and Daughters." *Signs* 7 (Autumn 1981): 200–22.

Hite, Shere. "I Hope I'm Not Like My Mother." *Women and Therapy* 10, nos. 1–2 (1990): 13–30.

Hochschild, Arlie Russell. *The Second Shift.* New York: Avon, 1989.

———. *The Time Bind: When Work Becomes Home and Home Becomes Work.* New York: Metropolitan, 1997.

Holcomb, Betty. *Not Guilty! The Good News about Working Mothers.* New York: Scribner, 1998.

hooks, bell. *Bone Black: Memories of Girlhood.* New York: Henry Holt, 1996.

———. *Feminist Theory from Margin to Center.* Boston: South End Press, 1984.

Hooper, Carole Ann. "Child Sexual Abuse and the Regulation of Women: Variations on a Theme." In *Gender Violence: Interdisciplinary Perspectives,* edited by Laura L. O'Toole, Jessica R. Schiffman, et al., 336–51. New York: New York University Press, 1997.

Horney, Karen. *New Ways in Psychoanalysis.* New York: W. W. Norton, 1939.

Hossain, Ziarat, and Jaipaul L. Roopnarine. "Division of Household Labor and Child Care in Dual-Earner African-American Families with Infants." *Sex Roles* 29, nos. 9–10 (1993): 571–83.

Howe, Karen G. "Daughters Discover Their Mothers through Biographies and Genograms: Educational and Clinical Parallels." In Knowles and Cole, 1990.

———. "Telling Our Mother's Story." In *Representations: Social Constructions of Gender,* edited by Rhoda Unger, 45–60. New York: Baywood, 1989.

———. "Women and Work: Defining and Changing Students' Perceptions in a Women's Studies Course." Paper presented at Third Annual Women and Work Symposium, Women and Work Research and Resource Center, Graduate School of Social Work, University of Texas, Arlington, Tex., May 1–2, 1986.

Huh, Joonok. "Constantly Negotiating: Between My Mother and My Daughter." In O'Reilly and Abbey, 1999.

Humphries, Tom, Marcel Kinsbourne, and James Swanson. "Stimulant Effects on Cooperation and Social Interaction between Hyperactive Children and Their Mothers." *Journal of Child Psychology and Psychiatry* 19 (1978): 13–22.

Hunter, Nan D., and Nancy D. Polikoff. "Custody Rights of Lesbian Mothers: Legal Theory and Litigation Strategy." In *Homosexuality: Discrimination, Criminology, and the Law,* edited by Wayne R. Dynes and Stephen Donaldson, 225–67. *Studies in Homosexuality,* vol. 6. New York: Garland, 1992.

Hurley, Dan. "A Sound Mind in an Unsound Body." *Psychology Today,* August 1987, 34–43.

Hurston, Zora Neale. *Their Eyes Were Watching God.* Urbana: University of Illinois Press, 1987.

Hutchison, Elizabeth. "Child Welfare as a Woman's Issue." *Families in Society* 73, no. 2 (1992): 67–78.

Irigaray, Luce. "And the One Doesn't Stir without the Other." Translated by Helene Vivienne Wenzel. *Signs* 7 (1981): 60–67.

Johnson, Miriam M. *Strong Mothers, Weak Wives: The Search for Gender Equality.* Berkeley: University of California Press, 1988.

Jones, S. L., M. A. Moulton, P. Moulton, and S. Roach. "Self-Esteem Differences as a Function of Race and Weight Preoccupation." *Women's Health Issues* 9, no. 1 (1999): 50–55.

Jordan, Judith. "Empathy and Self Boundaries." In Jordan et al., 1991.

———. "The Meaning of Mutuality." In Jordan et al., 1991.

Jordan, Judith, Alexandra Kaplan, Jean Baker Miller, Irene Stiver, and Janet Surrey, eds. *Women's Growth in Connection: Writings from the Stone Center.* New York: Guilford, 1991.

Jordan, Judith, and Janet Surrey. "The Self-in-Relation: Empathy in the Mother-Daughter Relationship." In *The Psychology of Today's Woman: New Psychoanalytic Visions,* edited by Toni Bernay and Dorothy W. Cantor. Cambridge, Mass.: Harvard University Press, 1989.

Jordan, Judith V., Janet Surrey, and Alexandra Kaplan. "Women and Empathy." In Jordan et al., 1991.

Jordan, June. *On Call: Political Essays.* Boston: South End Press, 1985.

Joseph, Gloria I., and Jill Lewis. *Common Differences: Conflicts in Black and White Feminist Perspectives.* New York: Anchor Books, 1981.

Kagan, Jerome. *The Nature of the Child.* New York: Basic Books, 1984.

Kalergis, Mary Mottey. *Mother: A Collective Portrait.* New York: E. P. Dutton, 1987.

Kanakis, Deirdre, and Mark Thelen. "Parental Variables Associated with Bulimia Nervosa." *Addictive Behaviors* 20, no. 4 (1995): 491–500.

Kaplan, Alexandra. "Reflections on Gender and Psychotherapy." In Braude, 1987.

———. "The 'Self-in-Relation': Implications for Depression in Women." In Jordan, 1991.

Kaplan, Alexandra, Nancy Gleason, and Rona Klein. "Women's Self Development in Late Adolescence." In Jordan et al., 1991.

Kaplan, Elaine Bell. *Not Our Kind of Girl: Unraveling the Myths of Black Teenage Motherhood.* Berkeley: University of California Press, 1997.

Kaufman, Irving. "Father-Daughter Incest." In *Father and Child: Developmental and Clinical Perspectives,* edited by Stanley Cath and Alan Gurwitt, 491–507. New York: Basil Blackwell, 1988.

Kaufman, Michael, ed. *Beyond Patriarchy: Essays by Men on Pleasure, Power, and Change.* Toronto: Oxford University Press, 1987.

Kennedy, Florynce. *Color Me Flo: My Hard Life and Good Times.* Englewood Cliffs, N.J.: Prentice-Hall, 1976.

Kiley, Dan. *The Wendy Dilemma: When Women Stop Mothering Their Men.* New York: Arbor House, 1984.

King, Ti. "The Experiences of Midlife Daughters Who Are Caregivers for Their Mothers." *Health Care for Women International* 14, no. 5 (1993): 419–26.

Kinsbourne, Marcel, and Paula J. Caplan. *Children's Learning and Attention Problems.* Boston: Little, Brown, 1979.

Kirwin, Paul. "Affect Expression Training in Psychiatric Patients: The Verbalization of Feeling-Cause Relationships." Veterans Administration Hospital, Durham, N.C., 1970. Manuscript.

Kitzinger, Sheila. *Women as Mothers.* New York: Random House, 1979.

Knowles, Jane Price. "Introduction." In Knowles and Cole, 1990.

Knowles, Jane Price, and Ellen Cole, eds., *Woman-Defined Motherhood*. New York: Harrington Park Press, 1990.

Koblinsky, Sally, Kari Morgan, and Elaine Anderson. "African-American Homeless and Low-Income Housed Mothers: Comparison of Parenting Practices." *American Journal of Orthopsychiatry* 67, no. 1 (1997): 37–47.

Koch, Rebecca, Mary T. Lewis, and Wendy Quinones. "Homeless: Mothering at Rock Bottom." In Coll et al., 1998.

Kohn, Alfie. "Girl Talk, Guy Talk." *Psychology Today*, February 1988: 65–66.

Kome, Penney. *Somebody Has to Do It: Whose Work Is Housework?* Toronto: McClelland, 1982.

Koppelman, Susan, ed. *Between Mothers and Daughters: Stories across a Generation*. New York: Feminist Press, 1985.

Konstantareas, Mary, and Soula Homatidis. "Mothers of Autistic Children: Are They the 'Unacknowledged Victims'?" Paper presented to the Institute of the Section on Women and Psychology, Canadian Psychological Association Convention, Winnipeg, 1983.

Kramarae, Cheris, and Paula A. Treichler. *A Feminist Dictionary*. Boston: Pandora Press, 1985.

Krauss, Marty Wyngaarden, and Marsha Malick Seltzer. "Long-Term Caring: Family Experiences over the Life Course." In *Down Syndrome: Living and Learning in the Community,* edited by Lynn Nadel, Donna Rosenthal, et al., 91–98. New York: Wiley-Liss, 1995.

Kuebli, Janet, Susan Butler, and Robin Fivush. "Mother-Child Talk about Past Emotions: Relations of Maternal Language and Child Gender over Time." *Cognition and Emotion* 9, nos. 2–3 (1995): 265–83.

Kuebli, Janet, and Robin Fivush. "Gender Differences in Parent-Child Conversations about Past Emotions." *Sex Roles* 27, nos. 11–12 (1992): 683–98.

Ladd-Taylor, Molly, and Lauri Umansky, eds. *"Bad" Mothers: The Politics of Blame in Twentieth-Century America*. New York: New York University Press, 1998.

———. "Introduction." In Ladd-Taylor and Umansky, 1998.

Ladner, Joyce. *Tomorrow's Tomorrow: The Black Woman*. Garden City, N.Y.: Anchor Books, 1972.

Lamb, Michael E., ed. *The Father's Role: Applied Perspectives*. New York: John Wiley and Sons, 1986.

———, ed. *Parenting and Child Development in "Nontraditional" Families*. Mahwah, N.J.: Lawrence Erlbaum Associates, 1999.

Lamphere, Louise, Patricia Zavella, Felipe Gonzales, and Peter B. Evans. *Sunbelt Working Mothers: Reconciling Family and Factory*. Ithaca, N.Y.: Cornell University Press, 1993.

Landers, Ann. "It's Never Too Late for Forgiveness." *Toronto Star,* September 12, 1985, C5

———. "Too Few Phone Calls from Son Leave Mother Feeling Lonely." *Toronto Star,* May 22, 1986, D3

Landsberg, Michele. *Women and Children First: A Provocative Look at Modern Canadian Women at Work and at Home*. Toronto: Macmillan of Canada, 1982.

laSorsa Valerie, and Iris Fodor. "Adolescent Daughter/Midlife Mother Dyad: A New Look at Separation and Self-Definition." *Psychology of Women Quarterly* 14, no. 4 (1990): 593–606.

Laurence, Margaret. *The Diviners*. Toronto: Bantam-Seal Books, 1976.

Laws, Janice, and Joyce Strickland. "Black Mothers and Daughters: A Clarification of the Relationship as an Impetus for Black Power." *Black Books Bulletin* 6 (1980): 26–29, 33.

Lazarre, Jane. *Beyond the Whiteness of Whiteness: Memoir of a White Mother of a Black Son.* Durham, N.C.: Duke University Press, 1996.

———. *The Mother Knot.* New York: Dell, 1976.

Leaper, Campbell, Kristin Anderson, and Paul Sanders. "Moderators of Gender Effects on Parents' Talk to Their Children: A Meta-Analysis." *Developmental Psychology* 34, no. 1 (1998): 3–27.

Lee, Gary, Jeffrey Dwyer, and Raymond Coward. "Gender Differences in Parent Care: Demographic Factors and Same-Gender Preferences." *Journals of Gerontology* 48, no. 1 (1993): S9–S16.

Leifer, Myra. *The Psychological Effects of Motherhood: Study of First Pregnancy.* New York: Praeger, 1980.

LeMasters, E. "Parenthood as Crisis." *Marriage and Family Living* 19 (1957): 352–55.

Lerner, Gerda. *The Female Experience: An American Documentary.* Indianapolis: Bobbs-Merrill, 1977.

Lerner, Harriet Goldhor. *The Dance of Anger.* New York: Harper and Row, 1985. (Especially chapter on "Anger at Our Impossible Mothers," 67–87.)

———. *The Dance of Intimacy.* New York: Harper and Row, 1989.

Leve, Leslie, and Beverly Fagot. "Gender-Role Socialization and Discipline Processes in One- and Two-Parent Families." *Sex Roles* 36, nos. 1–2 (1997): 1–21.

Levene, Judi, and Mary Konstantareas. "Mothers of Disturbed Children." Presentation in panel at "Don't Blame Mother" conference, Toronto, May 22, 1987.

Levine, Helen. "The Power Politics of Motherhood." In *Perspectives on Women in the 1980s,* edited by Joan Turner and Lois Emery, 28–40. Winnipeg: University of Manitoba Press, 1983.

Lewis, Jane. "Introduction: Reconstructing Women's Experience of Home and Family." In *Labour and Love: Women's Experience of Home and Family, 1850–1940,* edited by Jane Lewis, 1–24. Oxford: Basil Blackwell, 1986.

Leyendecker, Birgit, and Michael E. Lamb. "Latino Families." In Lamb, 1999.

Lisi, Deborah. "Found Voices: Women, Disability, and Cultural Transformation." *Women and Therapy* 14, nos. 3–4 (1993): 195–209.

Liutkus, Joanne. Review of "To a Safer Place." *Healthsharing,* winter 1987, 33.

Loewenstein, S. "An Overview of the Concept of Narcissism." *Social Case-work* 58 (1977): 136–42.

Lorde, Audre. *From a Land Where Other People Live.* Detroit: Broadside, 1973.

———. *Sister Outsider.* Trumansburg, N.Y.: The Crossing Press, 1984.

———. *Zami: A New Spelling of My Name.* Trumansburg, N.Y.: The Crossing Press, 1982.

Low, Natalie. "Mother-Daughter Relationships: The Lasting Ties." *Radcliffe Quarterly,* December 1984, 1–4.

Lowell, M. C., and D. L. Fiorino. "Combatting Myths: A Conceptual Framework for Analyzing the Stress of Motherhood." In *Advances in Nursing Science* 1 (1978): 75–84.

Luxton, Meg. *More than a Labour of Love: Three Generations of Women's Work in the Home.* Toronto: The Women's Press, 1980.

Luxton, Meg, and Harriet Rosenberg. *Through the Kitchen Window: The Politics of Home and Family.* Toronto: Garamond, 1986.

Mahler, Margaret S. "On Childhood Psychoses and Schizophrenia: Autistic and Symbiotic Infantile Psychosis." In *The Psychoanalytic Study of the Child,* edited by R. Eissler et al. New York: International Universities Press, 1952.

———. *On Human Symbiosis and the Vicissitudes of Individuation.* New York: International Universities Press, 1968.

Mairs, Nancy. *Plaintext: Deciphering a Woman's Life.* New York: Harper and Row, 1987.

Marcow-Speiser, Vivien. "Coming Home: Midlife Rapprochement with the Mother." *American Journal of Dance Therapy* 15, no. 2 (1993): 77–87.

Margolis, Maxine. *Mothers and Such: Views of American Women and Why They Changed.* Berkeley: University of California Press, 1984.

Mary, Nancy. "Reactions of Black, Hispanic, and White Mothers to Having a Child with Handicaps." *Mental Retardation* 28, no. 1 (1990): 1–5.

Matsakis, Aphrodite. *Viet Nam Wife: The Other Forgotten Warrior.* Kensington, Md.: Woodbine Press, 1988.

Maynard, Fredelle Bruser. "A Mother and Two Daughters." *Lilith,* summer 1988, 29–31.

Maynard, Rona. "Let's Stop Blaming Mum." *Homemaker's Magazine,* May 1983, 8–26.

McBride, A. B. *The Growth and Development of Mothers.* New York: Harper and Row, 1973.

McBride, Brent, and Pernell Ferguson. "Parental Expectations for Young Children: Day Care versus Preschool." *Early Child Development and Care* 79 (1992): 47–53.

McCubbin, Hamilton, and Elizabeth Thompson, eds. *Resiliency in Native American and Immigrant Families.* Resiliency in Families Series, vol. 2. Thousand Oaks, Calif.: Sage, 1998.

McDonnell, Jane Taylor. "On Being the 'Bad' Mother of an Autistic Child." In Ladd-Taylor and Umansky, 1998.

McGinley, Phyllis. "Girl's-Eye View of Female Relatives." Poem in *Times Three.* New York: Viking Press, 1960.

McGoldrick, Monica, Nydia Garcia-Preto, Paulette Moore Hines, and Evelyn Lee. "Ethnicity and Women." In *Women in Families: A Framework for Family Therapy,* edited by Monica McGoldrick and Carol Anderson, 169–99. New York: W.W. Norton, 1989.

McKeever, Patricia. "Mothering Children Who Have Severe Chronic Illnesses." In *The Effect of Children on Parents,* edited by Anne-Marie Ambert, 170–90. New York: Haworth, 1992.

McLoyd, Vonnie. "Employment among African-American Mothers in Dual-Earner Families: Antecedents and Consequences for Family Life and Child Development." In *The Employed Mother and the Family Context,* edited by Judith Frankel, 180–226. Focus on Women Series, vol. 14. New York: Springer, 1993.

McLoyd, Vonnie C., Toby Epstein Jayaratne, Rosario Ceballo, and Julio Borquez. "Unemployment and Work Interruption among African American Single Mothers: Effects on Parenting and Adolescent Socioemotional Functioning." *Child Development* 65, no. 2 (1994): 562–89.

McMahon, Martha. *Engendering Motherhood: Identity and Self-Transformation.* New York: Guilford, 1995.

McMillan, Terry. *Mama.* New York: Washington Square Press, 1987.

Mens-Verhulst, Janneke van. "Reinventing the Mother-Daughter Relationship," *American Journal of Psychotherapy* 49, no. 4 (1995): 526–39.

Mercer, Ramona. *First-Time Motherhood.* New York: Springer, 1986.

Merkin, Daphne. *Enchantment.* New York: Fawcett Crest, 1984.

Miller, Barbara, and Robin Miller. "Mothering the Biracial Child: Bridging the Gaps between African-American and White Parenting Styles." In Knowles and Cole, 1990.

Miller, Casey, and Kate Swift. *Words and Women.* Garden City, N.Y.: Anchor Books, 1977.

Miller, Jean Baker. "Connections, Disconnections and Violations." Work in Progress Paper No. 33, Wellesley College, The Stone Center, Wellesley, Mass., 1988.

———. "The Construction of Anger in Women and Men." In Jordan et al., 1991.

———. "The Development of Women's Sense of Self." In Jordan et al., 1991.

———. *Toward a New Psychology of Women.* Boston: Beacon Press, 1976.

———. "What Do We Mean by Relationships?" Work in Progress Paper No. 22, Wellesley College, The Stone Center, Wellesley, Mass., 1986.

———. "Women and Power." In Braude, 1987.

———. "Women and Power: Some Psychological Dimensions." Work in Progress Paper No. 1, Wellesley College, The Stone Center, Wellesley, Mass., 1982.

Miller, Jean Baker, and Irene Stiver. *Healing Connections: How Women Form Relationships in Therapy and in Life.* Boston: Beacon, 1998.

Mills, Rosemary. "Paradoxical Relations between Perceived Power and Maternal Control." *Merrill-Palmer Quarterly* 44, no. 4 (1998): 523–37.

Minden, Ruth. "Glancing Backward, Looking Forward: Insights into Mothering." Paper, Ontario Institute for Studies in Education, 1986.

Miner, Valerie, and Helen Longino. *Competition: A Feminist Taboo?* New York: Feminist Press, 1987.

Moraga, Cherrie. *Loving in the War Years.* Boston: South End Press, 1983.

———. *Waiting in the Wings: Portrait of a Queer Motherhood.* Ithaca, N.Y.: Firebrand, 1997.

Morgan, Kathryn. "The Perils and Paradoxes of Feminist Pedagogy." *Resources for Feminist Research* 16 (1987): 49–51.

———. "Women and Moral Madness." In *Feminist Perspectives: Philosophical Method and Morals,* edited by S. Mullet, L. Code, and C. Overall, 146–67. Toronto: University of Toronto Press, 1988.

Morgan, Robin. *Dry Your Smile.* Garden City, N.Y.: Doubleday, 1987.

Morrison, Nancy. "Successful Single-Parent Families." *Journal of Divorce and Remarriage* 22, nos. 3–4 (1995): 205–19.

Morrison, Toni. *Beloved.* New York: New American Library, 1987.

———. "SEEMOTHERMOTHERISVERYNICE." In *Black-eyed Susans,* edited by Mary Helen Washington, 99. New York: Anchor Press, 1975.

———. *Sula.* New York: Knopf, 1974.

"Mothers Can't Win." Special issue. *New York Times Magazine,* April 5, 1998.

Nelson, Fiona. *Lesbian Motherhood: An Exploration of Canadian Lesbian Families.* Toronto: University of Toronto Press, 1996.

Newman, Barbara. "The Changing Nature of the Parent-Adolescent Relationship from Early to Late Adolescence." *Adolescence* 24 (1989): 915–24.

Nietzsche, Friedrich. *The Portable Nietzsche.* Edited and translated by Walter Kaufman. New York: Viking, 1954.

Niman, Harold. "The Price of Custody." Paper presented in "Domestic Law: A Colloquium on the Law and Practice of Custody," Annual Institute on Continuing Legal Education, Family Law for the Specialist, Toronto, 1987.

Norman, Marsha. *The Fortune Teller.* New York: Random House, 1987.

———. *'Night, Mother.* New York: Hill and Wang, 1983.

Obeidallah, Dawn, and Linda Burton. "Affective Ties between Mothers and Daughters in Adolescent Childbearing Families." In *Conflict and Cohesion in Families: Causes and Consequences,* edited by Martha Cox et al. The Advances in Family Research Series. Mahwah, N.J.: Lawrence Erlbaum Associates, 1999.

O'Brien, Mary. *The Politics of Reproduction.* Boston: Routledge and Kegan Paul, 1981.

———. "The Reproduction of Mothering." Paper presented at "Don't Blame Mother" conference, Toronto, May 21, 1987.

Ohye, Bonnie Y. "Safeguarding Wordless Voice in a World of Words." In Coll et al., 1998.

Olsen, Tillie. "I Stand Here Ironing." In *Between Mothers and Daughters: Stories across a Generation,* edited by Susan Koppelman, 177–87. New York: Feminist Press, 1985.

———. *Mother to Daughter, Daughter to Mother: A Daybook and Reader.* New York: Feminist Press at the City University of New York, 1984.

———. *Tell Me a Riddle.* New York: Dell, 1986.

Olsen, Tillie, et al. *Mothers and Daughters: That Special Quality, an Exploration in Photographs.* New York: Aperture, 1987.

Ontario Advisory Council on Women's Issues. "Sole Support M.O.M. (Mothers on the Move): Brief to the Ontario Government on Sole Support Mothers." November 1987.

O'Reilly, Andrea. "Across the Divide: Contemporary Anglo-American Feminist Theory on the Mother-Daughter Relationship." In Abbey and O'Reilly, 1998.

———. "'I Come From a Long Line of Uppity Irate Black Women': African American Feminist Thought on Motherhood, the Motherline and the Mother-Daughter Relationship." In O'Reilly and Abbey, 1999.

———, ed. *Mothers and Sons: Feminist Perspectives.* New York: Routledge, in press.

O'Reilly, Andrea, and Sharon Abbey, eds. *Mothers and Daughters: Connection, Empowerment, and Transformation.* Lanham, Md.: Rowman and Littlefield, 1999.

Osborn, Judith. "Mothers and Daughters in Ancient Near Eastern Literature." In Davidson and Broner, 1980.

Owen, David. "The Sultan of Stuff." *New Yorker,* July 19, 1999, 52–63.

Parker, G. "Re-Searching the Schizophrenogenic Mother." *Journal of Nervous and Mental Disorders* 170 (1982): 452–62.

Patterson, Charlotte. "Children of Lesbian and Gay Parents." *Advances in Clinical Child Psychology* 19 (1997): 235–82.

Patterson, Charlotte, and Raymond Chan. "Families Headed by Lesbian and Gay Parents." In Lamb, 1999.

Payne, Karen, ed. *Between Ourselves: Letters between Mothers and Daughters, 1750–1982.* Boston: Houghton Mifflin, 1983.

Pearce, Diana, and Hariette McAdoo. *Women and Children: Alone and in Poverty.* Washington, D.C.: National Advisory Council on Economic Opportunity, 1981.

Pearson, Jessica. "Mothers and Daughters: Measuring Occupational Inheritance." *Sociology and Social Research* 67 (January 1983): 204–17.

Peters, Joan K. *When Mothers Work: Loving Our Children without Sacrificing Ourselves.* Reading, Mass.: Addison Wesley, 1997.

Peters, John. "Gender Socialization of Adolescents in the Home: Research and Discussion." *Adolescence* 29 (1994): 913–34.

Petersen, Anne C. "Those Gangly Years." *Psychology Today,* September 1987: 28–34.

Phares, Vicky. *"Poppa" Psychology: The Role of Fathers in Children's Mental Well-Being.* Westport, Conn.: Praeger, 1999.

———. Perceptions of Mothers' and Fathers' Responsibility for Children's Behavior. *Sex Roles* 29, nos. 11–12 (1993):, 839–51.

Pike, Kathleen M., and Judith Rodin. "Mothers, Daughters, and Disordered Eating." *Journal of Abnormal Psychology* 100, no. 2 (1991): 198–204.

Pleck, Elizabeth. *Domestic Tyranny: The Making of American Social Policy against Family Violence from Colonial Times to the Present.* New York: Oxford University Press, 1987.

Pleck, Joseph. "Employment and Fatherhood: Issues and Innovative Policies." In *The Father's Role: Applied Perspectives,* edited by Michael E. Lamb, 385–412. New York: John Wiley and Sons, 1986.

———. "Paternal Involvement: Levels, Sources, and Consequences." In *The Role of the Father in Child Development,* edited by Michael Lamb, 66–103. New York: Wiley, 1997.

Pogrebin, Letty Cottin. *Among Friends.* New York: McGraw-Hill, 1987.

———. *Growing Up Free: Raising Your Kids in the 80s.* New York: McGraw-Hill, 1980.

Polakow, Valerie. *Lives on the Edge: Single Mothers and Their Children in the Other America.* Chicago: University of Chicago Press, 1993.

Polikoff, Nancy. "Gender and Child Custody Determination." *Women's Rights Law Reporter,* 1982, 183–202.

Pollack, Sandra, and Jeanne Vaughn, eds. *Politics of the Heart: A Lesbian Parenting Anthology.* Ithaca, N.Y.: Firebrand Books, 1987.

Pollitt, Katha. "'Fetal Rights': A New Assault on Feminism." In Ladd-Taylor and Umansky, 1998.

Powell, Gloria. "Growing up Black and Female." In *Becoming Female: Perspectives on Development,* edited by C. Kopp. New York: Plenum, 1979.

Press, Aida K. "Consider Naomi: In Defense of Mothers-in-Law." *Radcliffe Quarterly,* December 1984: 12–14.

Price, Jane. *Motherhood: What It Does to Your Mind.* London: Pandora Press, 1988.

Prozan, Charlotte Krause. "An Integration of Feminist and Psychoanalytic Theory." In Braude, 1987.

Quindlen, Anna. *Living Out Loud: Home Thoughts from the Front Lines of Life.* New York: Random House, 1988.

Rabasca, Lisa, "White House Conference an Important 'First Step,'" *American Psychological Association Monitor,* July/August 1999, 11

Rabinor, Judith Ruskay. "Mothers, Daughters, and Eating Disorders: Honoring the Mother-Daughter Relationship." In *Feminist Perspectives on Eating Disorders,* edited by Patricia Fallon, Melanie Katzman, et al., 272–86. New York: Guilford, 1994.

Rabuzzi, Kathryn Allen. *Motherself: A Myth Analysis of Motherhood.* Bloomington: Indiana University Press, 1988.

Rafkin, Louise, ed. *Different Daughters: A Book by Mothers of Lesbians.* Pittsburgh/San Francisco: Cleis Press, 1987.

———. *Different Mothers: Sons and Daughters of Lesbians Talk about Their Lives.* San Francisco: Cleis Press, 1990.

Ramey, Sharon Landesman, and Halldor-Kr. Juliusson. "Family Dynamics at Dinner: A Natural Context for Revealing Basic Family Processes." In *Families, Risk, and Competence,* edited by Michael Lewis and Candice Feiring, 31–52. Mahwah, N.J.: Lawrence Erlbaum Associates, 1998.

Randolph, Suzanne. "African American Children in Single Mother Families." In Dickerson, 1995.

Ransby, Barbara. "Another Black Woman Brutalized by the Courts," *In These Times,* July 11, 1999.

Ranson, Gillian. "Paid Work, Family Work, and the Discourse of the "Full-Time Mother." *Mothering and Motherhood* 1, no. 1 (1999): 57–66.

Raphael, Betty-Jane. "Mothers and Daughters." *Ladies' Home Journal,* September 1978.

Raymond, Janice. *A Passion for Friends: Toward a Philosophy of Female Affection.* Boston: Beacon Press, 1987.

Reddy, Maureen. *Crossing the Color Line: Race, Parenting, and Culture.* New Brunswick, N.J.: Rutgers University Press, 1996.

Reeves, Nancy. *Womankind: Beyond the Stereotype.* Chicago: Aldine and Atherton, 1971.

Reid, Pamela T. "Socialization of Black Female Children." In *Women: A Developmental Perspective,* edited by Phyllis W. Berman and Estelle R. Ramey. Bethesda, Md.: National Institutes of Health, 1983.

Reinelt, Claire, and Mindy Fried. "'I Am This Child's Mother': A Feminist Perspective on Mothering with a Disability." In *Perspectives on Disability: Text and Readings on Disability,* 2nd ed., edited by Mark Nagler et al., 195–202. Palo Alto, Calif.: Health Markets Research, 1993.

Renvoize, Jean. *Going Solo: Single Mothers by Choice.* London: Routledge and Kegan Paul, 1985.

Rich, Adrienne. "'Disloyal to Civilization': Feminism, Racism, and Gynephobia." *Chrysalis* 7 (1977): 9–27.

———. *Of Woman Born: Motherhood as Experience and Institution.* New York: W. W. Norton and Co., 1976.

———. *Snapshots of a Daughter-in-Law: Poems 1954–1962.* New York: W. W. Norton, 1967.

Riddington, Jillian. "Single Parenting in a Wheelchair: What Do You Do with a Sick Kid When You Can't Afford an Ambulance and You Can't Walk?" *Resources for Feminist Research/Documentation sur la recherche feministe* 14 (March 1985): 34–37.

Riley, Joan. *Waiting in the Twilight.* London: Women's Press, 1987.

Ritvo, Samuel. "Mothers, Daughters, and Eating Disorders." In *Fantasy, Myth, and Reality: Essays in Honor of Jacob A. Arlow, M.D.,* edited by Harold P. Blum, Yale Kramer et al. Madison, Conn.: International Universities Press, 1988.

Robb, Christina. "A Theory of Empathy: The Quiet Revolution in Psychiatry." *Boston Globe Magazine,* October 16, 1988, 10–56.

Robbins, Martha A. "Mourning the Myth of Motherhood: Reclaiming Our Mothers' Legacies." In Knowles and Cole, 1990.

Robinson, Lillian S. "Poverty, Purpose, Pride." (Review of *Dignity: Lower Income Women Tell of Their Lives and Struggles, Oral Histories Compiled by Fran Leeper Buss.* [Ann Arbor, Mich.: University of Michigan Press, 1985].) *Women's Review of Books* 3 (December 1985): 1 and 3–4.

Rodgers, Carolyn M. *IT IS DEEP, How I Got Ovah.* New York: Doubleday and Co., 1969.

Rodgers-Rose, La Frances, ed. *The Black Woman.* Beverly Hills, Calif.: Sage, 1980.

Rogers, Judi, and Molleen Matsumura. *Mother-to-Be: A Guide to Pregnancy and Birth for Women with Disabilities.* New York: Demos, 1991.

Rogerson, Carol. "Winning the Battle; Losing the War—The Plight of the Custodial Mother after Judgement." Paper presented in "Domestic Law: A Colloquium on the Law and Practice of Custody," Annual Institute on Continuing Legal Education, Family Law for the Specialist, Toronto, 1987.

Romano, Renee. "'Immoral Conduct': White Women, Racial Transgressions, and Custody Disputes." In Ladd-Taylor and Umansky, 1998.

Rosenfeld, Anne H. "Knowing When to Call the Doctor." *Psychology Today,* October 1987, 12.

Rosinsky, Natalie M. "Mothers and Daughters: Another Minority Group." In Davidson and Broner, 1980.

Rossi, Alice. "Transition to Parenthood." *Journal of Marriage and the Family* 30 (1968): 26–39.

Rossi, Alice, and Peter Rossi. *Of Human Bonding: Parent-Child Relationships across the Life Course.* New York: Aldine de Gruyter, 1990.

Rossiter, Amy B. "In Private: An Inquiry into the Construction of Women's Experience of Early Motherhood." Ph.D. diss., University of Toronto, 1986.

Rothman, Barbara Katz. *The Tentative Pregnancy: Prenatal Diagnosis and the Future of Motherhood.* New York: Viking Press, 1986.

Rotundo, E. Anthony. "Patriarchs and Participants: A Historical Perspective on Fatherhood." In Kaufman, 1987.

Rousso, Harilyn. "Daughters with Disabilities: Defective Women or Minority Women?" In Fine and Asch, 1988.

Rowbotham, Sheila. *Woman's Consciousness, Man's World.* Harmondsworth, England: Penguin, 1973.

Rubin, Nancy. *The Mother Mirror.* New York: G. P. Putnam's Sons, 1984.

Rucker, Naomi, and Karen Lombardi. "The Familial Menage-à-Trois: Mother-Daughter Sexuality and Father-Daughter Incest." *Journal of Contemporary Psychotherapy* 20, no. 2 (1990): 99–107.

Ruddick, Sara. "Maternal Thinking." *Feminist Studies* 6 (1980): 354–80.

Ruddick, Sara. "Maternal Thinking." In Trebilcot, 1983.

Rush, Florence. "The Myth of Sexual Delinquency." *Women: A Journal of Liberation* 3, no. 3 (1972): 38–39.

Rush, Florence. "The Sexual Abuse of Children: A Feminist Point of View." In *Rape: The First Sourcebook for Women,* edited by Noreen Connell and Cassandra Wilson, 64–75. New York: Signet, 1974.

———. "Woman in the Middle." In *Radical Feminism,* edited by Anne Koedt, Ellen Levine, and Anita Ropone. New York: Quadrangle Books, 1973.

Ruther, Nicole, and Charles Richman. "The Relationship between Mothers' Eating Restraint and Their Children's Attitudes and Behaviors." *Bulletin of the Psychonomic Society* 31, no. 3 (1993): 217–20.

Ryan, Mary P. *Womanhood in America: From Colonial Times to the Present.* New York: New Viewpoints, 1975.

Ryff, Carol, and Marsha Mailick Seltzer. *The Parental Experience in Midlife.* Chicago: University of Chicago Press, 1996.

SAGE: A Scholarly Journal on Black Women 1 (fall 1984). Special issue on Blacks' mother-daughter relationships.

Sanftner, Jennifer, Janis Crowther, Peggy Crawford, and Dana Watts. "Maternal Influences (or Lack Thereof) on Daughters' Eating Attitudes and Behaviors." *Eating Disorders: The Journal of Treatment and Prevention* 4, no. 2 (1996): 147–59.

Sanua, Victor D. "Sociocultural Factors in Families of Schizophrenics: A Review of the Literature." *Psychiatry: Journal for the Study of Interpersonal Processes* 24 (1961): 246–65.

Sarton, May. "The Muse as Medusa." In *Collected Poems*. Guilford, Conn.: Norton, 1974.

Scarr, Sandra. *Mother Care-Other Care*. New York: Basic Books, 1984.

Schneider, Susan Weidman. *Jewish and Female: A Guide and Sourcebook for Today's Jewish Woman*. New York: Simon and Schuster, 1985 (See especially the section called "Mothers and Daughters from a Feminist Perspective," 268–81.)

Schnitzer, Phoebe Kazdin. "He Needs His Father: The Clinical Discourse and Politics of Single Mothering." In Coll et al., 1998.

Secunda, Victoria. *When You and Your Mother Can't Be Friends*. New York: Delta, 1990.

Schonberg, Ila J. "The Distortion of the Role of Mother in Child Sexual Abuse." *Journal of Child Sexual Abuse* 1, no. 3 (1992): 47–61.

Schroeder, Karen, Linda Blood, and Diane Maluso. "An Intergenerational Analysis of Expectations for Women's Career and Family Roles." *Sex Roles* 26, nos. 7–8 (1992): 273–91.

Schweitzer, Ivy. "The Mammy and the Mummy: Cultural Imaginary and Interracial Coalition." In O'Reilly and Abbey, 1999.

Scott, Ann Crittenden. "The Value of Housework—for Love or Money." *Ms.*, July 1972: 56–59.

Sears, Priscilla F. "Cradling Your Mother." *Mothering and Motherhood* 1, no. 1 (1999): 149-58.

Seidman, Theodore R. and Marvin H. Albert. *Becoming a Mother*. Greenwich, Conn.: Fawcett Publications, 1956.

Seiffge-Krenke, Inge, and Frank Kollmar. "Discrepancies between Mothers' and Fathers' Perceptions of Sons' and Daughters' Problem Behaviour." *Journal of Child Psychology and Psychiatry and Allied Disciplines* 39, no. 5 (1998): 687–97.

Sen, Chandra, and Judith Daniluk. "Themes in the Relationships of Mothers and Their Incestuously Abused Daughters: A Feminist Analysis." *Feminism and Psychology* 5, no. 1 (1995): 47–60.

Sev'er, Aysan, and Marion Pirie. "Factors That Enhance or Curtail the Social Functioning of Female Single Parents: A Path Analysis." *Family and Conciliation Courts Review* 29, no. 3 (1991): 318–37.

Sexton, Anne. *The Book of Folly*. San Jose, Calif.: Gousha, 1972.

———. "The Double Image." In *To Bedlam and Part Way Back*. San Jose, Calif.: Gousha, 1960.

Shapiro, Susan. "Between Love and Ambition: A Daughter and Mother Find Each Other." *Cosmopolitan*, November 1986, 64.

Shen, Jerome T. Y. "Sexual Abuse of Adolescents." *Postgraduate Medicine* 71 (1982): 213–19.

Sherrard, Jain. *Mother-Warrior-Pilgrim*. Kansas City, Mo.: Andrews and McMel, 1980.

Shessel, Isabel. "On Being a Mother: Thoughts and Reflections." Paper, Ontario Institute for Studies in Education, 1986.

Shreve, Anita, and Julius Held. *Remaking Motherhood*. New York: Viking Press, 1987.

Shulman, Alix Kates. *A Good Enough Daughter*. New York: Schocken, 1999.

Sidel, Ruth. "Hearts of Iron." *READINGS: A Journal of Reviews and Commentary in Mental Health* 14, no. 9 (June 1999): 14–18.

Siegel, Rachel Josefowitz. "Antisemitism and Sexism in Stereotypes of Jewish Women." In *A Guide to Dynamics of Feminist Therapy,* edited by Doris Howard. New York: Harrington Park Press, 1986.

———. "Jewish Mothers: Beyond the Stereotype." In *Acts of Love: Jewish Mothers,* edited by Rachel Josefowitz Siegel, Ellen Cole, and Susan Steinberg-Oren (New York: Haworth, in press).

———. "My Legacy: Notes from an Alte Yiddene." *NASHIM: A Journal of Jewish Women's Studies and Gender Issues* (in press).

———. "Old Women as Mother Figures." In Knowles and Cole, 1990.

———. "Silencing the Voices of Older Women." In *Ageing in a Gendered World: Issues and Identity for Women,* edited by Julia Tavares. Santo Domingo and New York: INSTRAW/UN Publications, 1999.

———. "Women's 'Dependency' in a Male-Centered Value System: Gender-Based Values Regarding Dependency and Independence." *Women and Therapy* 7 (1988): 113–23.

Sigal, J. "Effects of Paternal Exposure to Prolonged Stress on the Mental Health of the Spouse and Children." *Canadian Psychiatric Association Journal* 21 (1976): 169–72.

Sigourney, Lydia Howard. *Letters to Mothers.* New York: Harper and Bros., 1845.

Silverstein, Louise, and Vicky Phares. "Expanding the Mother-Child Paradigm: An Examination of Dissertation Research, 1986–1994." *Psychology of Women Quarterly* 20 (1996): 39–53.

Silverstein, Louise. "Transforming the Debate about Childcare and Maternal Employment." *American Psychologist* 46 (1991): 1025–32.

Sluckin, Wladyslaw, Marin Herbert, and Alice Sluckin. *Maternal Bonding.* Oxford: Basil Blackwell, 1983.

Smith, Betsy, Janet L. Surrey, and Mary Watkins. "'Real' Mothers: Adoptive Mothers Resisting Marginalization and Re-creating Motherhood." In Coll et al., 1998.

Smith, Dorothy E., and Alison I. Griffith. "Mothering for Schooling." *Perspectives in Social Problems* 2 (1990): 3–24.

Smith, Liz. *The Mother Book: A Compendium of Trivia and Grandeur concerning Mothers, Motherhood and Maternity.* New York: Crown, 1984.

Smith-Rosenberg, Carroll. "The Female World of Love and Ritual: Relations between Women in Nineteenth-Century America." *Signs: Journal of Women in Culture and Society* 1 (1985): 1–29.

Snowden, Gail. "Mirror Images." *Radcliffe Quarterly,* December 1984, 29–30.

Solinger, Rickie. "Poisonous Choice." In Ladd-Taylor and Umansky, 1998.

Solomon, C. Ruth. "The Importance of Mother-Child Relations in Studying Stepfamilies." *Journal of Divorce and Remarriage* 24, nos. 1–2 (1995): 89–98.

Sommers, Evelyn K. *Voices from Within: Women Who Have Broken the Law.* Toronto: University of Toronto Press, 1995.

Sonkin, Daniel, ed. *Domestic Violence on Trial.* New York: Springer, 1987.

Sparks, Elizabeth. "Against All Odds: Resistance and Resilience in African American Welfare Mothers." In Coll et al., 1998.

Spender, Dale. *Man Made Language.* New York: Routledge, Chapman and Hall, 1985.

Stacey, Judith. "Gay and Lesbian Families: Queer Like Us." In *All Our Families: New Policies for a New Century,* edited by Mary Ann Mason and Arlene Skolnick, 117–43. New York: Oxford University, 1998.

Stack, Carol. *All Our Kin: Strategies for Survival in a Black Community.* New York: Harper and Row, 1974.

Starkman, E. "Hold the Blessing, Diaries." In *Women and Aging: An Anthology by Women,* edited by Jo Alexander, Debi Berrow, Lisa Domitrovich, Margarita Donnelly, and Cheryl McLean, 134–36. Corvallis, Ore.: Calyx, 1986.

Starrels, Marjorie. "Gender Differences in Parent-Child Relations." *Journal of Family Issues* 15, no. 1 (1994): 148–65.

Steele, Jennifer, and Julian Barling. "Influence of Maternal Gender-Role Beliefs and Role Satisfaction on Daughters' Vocational Interests." *Sex Roles* 34, nos. 9–10 (1996): 637–48.

Steinem, Gloria. "Ruth's Song: Because She Could Not Sing It Herself." In *Outrageous Acts and Everyday Rebellions,* 129–46. New York: Holt, Rinehart, and Winston, 1983.

Stiver, Irene. "Beyond the Oedipus Complex: Mothers and Daughters." In Jordan et al., 1991.

———. "The Meaning of Care: Reframing Treatment Models." In Jordan et al., 1991.

———. "The Meanings of 'Dependency' in Female-Male Relationships." In Jordan et al., 1991.

Straayer, Amy Christine. "High Heels." In *Between Mothers and Daughters: Stories across a Generation,* edited by Susan Koppelman, 279–84. New York: Feminist Press, 1985.

Strainchamps, Ethel. "Our Sexist Language." In *Women in Sexist Society,* edited by Vivian Gornick and Barbara K. Moran, 347–61. New York: Basic Books, 1971.

Streckert, William. *Their Mothers' Sons.* Philadelphia: Lippincott, 1956.

Strom, Kay, and Lisa Strom. *Mothers and Daughters Together.* Grand Rapids, Mich.: Baker Book House, 1988.

"Study of Family Interaction Leads to New Understanding of Abusive Parents." University of Toronto Research Highlights. Simcoe Hall, University of Toronto, Public and Community Relations, October 1987.

Strom, Robert, Diane Griswold, Shirley Strom, Pat Collinsworth, et al. "Perceptions of Parenting Success by Black Mothers and Their Preadolescent Children." *Journal of Negro Education* 59, no. 4 (1990):, 611–22.

Sugarman, Stephen. "Single-Parent Families." In *All Our Families: New Policies for a New Century,* edited by Mary Ann Mason and Arlene Skolnick, 13–38. New York: Oxford University Press, 1998.

Sunshine, Ilana. "Mother-Blaming by Mental Health Professionals: Update." Assisted by Maureen Gans. Paper, Toronto: 1987.

Surrey, Janet L. "Mother-Blaming and Clinical Theory." In Knowles and Cole, 1990.

———. "The Mother-Daughter Relationship: Themes in Psychotherapy." In *Daughtering and Mothering: Female Subjectivity Reanalysed,* edited by Janneke van Mens-Verhulst, Karlein Schreurs, et al., 114–24. London: Routledge, 1993.

———. "Relationship and Empowerment." In Jordan et al., 1991.

———. Personal communication, January 25, 1988.

———. "The 'Self-in-Relation': A Theory of Women's Development." In Jordan et al., 1991.

Tasker, Fiona, and Susan Golombok. "Adults Raised as Children in Lesbian Families." *American Journal of Orthopsychiatry* 65, no. 2 (1995): 203–15.

Taylor, Jill McLean. "Cultural Stories: Latina and Portugese Daughters and Mothers." In *Urban Girls: Resisting Stereotypes, Creating Identities,* edited by Bonnie J. Ross Leadbeater, Niobe Way, et al. New York: New York University Press, 1996.

Teichner, Gordon, Elinor Ames, and Patricia Kerig. "The Relation of Infant Crying and the Sex of the Infant to Parents' Perceptions of the Infant and Themselves." *Psychology: A Journal of Human Behavior* 34, nos. 3–4 (1997): 59–60.

Thomas, Helen. *Child Abuse, Neglect and Deprivation: A Handbook for Ontario Nurses.* Toronto: Registered Nurses Association of Ontario, 1983.

Thompson, Daniel. *Sociology of the Black Experience.* Westport, Conn.: Greenwood Press, 1974.

Thoreau, Henry David. *Walden and Civil Disobedience.* Combined edition. Harmondsworth, England: Penguin Books, 1985.

Thorne, Barrie. "Feminist Rethinking of the Family: An Overview." In *Re-thinking the Family: Some Feminist Questions,* edited by Barrie Thorne and Marilyn Yalom, 1–24. New York: Longman, 1982.

Thurer, Shari L. *The Myths of Motherhood: How Culture Reinvents the Good Mother.* Boston: Houghton Mifflin, 1994.

Trebilcot, Joyce, ed. *Mothering: Essays in Feminist Theory.* Totowa, N.J.: Rowman and Allanheld, 1983.

Turnage, Barbara. "The Global Self-Esteem of an African-American Female and Her Relationship with Her Mother." In O'Reilly and Abbey, 1999.

Umansky, Lauri. *Motherhood Reconceived: Feminism and the Legacies of the Sixties.* New York: New York University Press, 1996.

United States Department of Labor. *Occupational Outlook Handbook, 1998–99.* Washington, D.C.: U.S. Government Printing Office, 1999.

Valerio, Anita. "It's in My Blood, My Face—My Mother's Voice, the Way I Sweat." In *This Bridge Called My Back: Writings by Radical Women of Color,* edited by Cherrie Moraga and Gloria Anzaldua. New York: Kitchen Table, 1983.

VanVoorhis, Rebecca, and Linda McClain. "Accepting a Lesbian Mother." *Families in Society* 78, no. 6 (1997): 642–50.

Vincent, Clark. "An Open Letter to the 'Caught Generation.'" *Family Coordinator* 21 (April 1972): 148.

Wade-Gayles, Gloria. *No Crystal Stair: Visions of Race and Sex in Black Women's Fiction.* New York: Pilgrim Press, 1984.

———. "The Truths of Our Mothers' Lives: Mother-Daughter Relationships in Black Women's Fiction." *Sage: A Scholarly Journal on Black Women* 1 (fall 1984): 8–12.

Walker, Alexis, Clara Pratt, and Barbara Wood. "Perceived Frequency of Role Conflict and Relationship Quality for Caregiving Daughters." *Psychology of Women Quarterly* 17, no. 2 (1993): 207–21.

Walker, Alice. *In Search of Our Mothers' Gardens: Womanist Prose.* San Diego, Calif.: Harcourt Brace Jovanovich, 1983.

Walker, Alice. Quoted in "Author Alice Walker Discusses 'The Color Purple.'" *Wall Street Journal,* December 19, 1985, 26.

Walker, Lenore. Personal communication. August 29, 1999.

Wallerstein, Judith S. "Children of Divorce: A Society in Search of a Policy." In *All Our Families: New Policies for a New Century,* edited by Mary Ann Mason and Arlene Skolnick, 66–94. New York: Oxford University Press, 1998.

Wallerstein, Judith, and Shauna Corbin. "Daughters of Divorce: Report from a Ten-Year Follow-Up." *American Journal of Orthopsychiatry* 59, no. 4 (1989): 593–604.

Walters, Marianne, Betty Carter, Peggy Papp, and Olga Silverstein. *The Invisible Web: Gender Patterns in Family Relationships.* New York: Guilford, 1988.

Walton-Allen, Nicole. "Laypeople's Perceptions of Family Violence: An Examination of Stereotyped Learning." Master's thesis. Ontario Institute for Studies in Education, 1984.

Ward, Janie Victoria. "Raising Resisters: The Role of Truth-Telling in the Psychological Development of African American Girls." In *Urban Girls: Resisting Stereotypes, Creating Identities,* edited by Bonnie J. Ross Leadbeater, Niobe Way, et al. New York: New York University Press, 1996.

Washington, Valora. "The Black Mother in the United States: History, Theory, Research, and Issues." In *The Different Faces of Motherhood. Perspectives in Deveopmental Psychology,* edited by Beverly Birns and Dale Hay. New York: Plenum, 1988.

Wedenoja, Marilyn. "Mothers Are Not to Blame: Confronting Cultural Bias in the Area of Serious Mental Illness." In *Feminist Social Work Practice in Clinical Settings. Sage Sourcebooks for the Human Services,* edited by Mary Bricker-Jenkins and Nancy Hooyman. Newbury Park, Calif.: Sage, 1991.

Weingarten, Kathy. *The Mother's Voice: Strengthening Intimacy in Families.* New York: Harcourt Brace, 1994.

———. "Sidelined No More: Promoting Mothers of Adolescents as a Resource for Their Growth and Development." In Coll et al., 1998.

Weissman, Michaele. "At Home with Tira." *Ms.,* September 1987, 36–43.

Weitzman, Lenore. *The Divorce Revolution: The Unexpected Social and Economic Consequences for Women and Children in America.* New York: Free Press, 1985.

Westkott, Marcia. "Mothers and Daughters in the World of the Father." *Frontiers* 3 (1978): 16–21.

Wharton, Amy, and Deborah Thorne. "When Mothers Matter: The Effects of Social Class and Family Arrangements on African American and White Women's Perceived Relations with Their Mothers." *Gender and Society* 11, no. 5 (1997): 656–81.

Williams, Constance Willard. *Black Teenage Mothers: Pregnancy and Child Rearing from Their Perspective.* Lexington, Mass.: Lexington, 1991.

Williams, Kelly. *Single Mamahood: Advice and Wisdom for the African-American Single Mother.* Secaucus, N.J.: Carol Publishing, 1998.

Wilson, Melvin. "Child Development in the Context of the Black Extended Family." *American Psychologist* 44, no. 2 (1989): 380–85.

Wijnberg, Marion, and Susan Weinger. "When Dreams Wither and Resources Fail: The Social-Support Systems of Poor Single Mothers." *Families in Society* 79, no. 2 (1998): 212–19.

Wine, Jeri Dawn, Barbara Moses, and Marti Diane Smye. "Female Superiority in Sex Difference Competence Comparisons: A Review of the Literature." In *Sex Roles: Origins, Influences, and Implications for Women,* edited by Cannie Stark-Adamec. Montreal: Eden Press Women's Publications, 1980.

Wine, Jeri Dawn, Marti Diane Smye, and Barbara Moses. "Assertiveness: Sex Differences in Relationships between Self-Report and Behavioral Measures." In *Sex Roles: Origins, Influences, and Implications for Women,* edited by Cannie Stark-Adamec, 176–86. Montreal: Eden Press Women's Publications, 1980.

Wolfe, Susan T. "Jewish Lesbian Mother." In *Nice Jewish Girls: A Lesbian Anthology,* edited by Evelyn Torton Beck, 164–73. Trumansburg, N.Y.: The Crossing Press, 1982.

Wollstonecraft, Mary. *Vindication of the Rights of Woman.* 1792; Reprint, Harmondsworth, England: Penguin Books, 1982.

Wolofsky, Zella. "Reconciliation of the Mother-Daughter Relationship: A Personal Odyssey." Paper, Ontario Institute for Studies in Education, 1986.

Women's Health Issues, January/February, 1999, 50–55.

Woo, Merle. "Letter to Ma." In *This Bridge Called My Back: Writings by Radical Women of Color,* edited by Cherrie Moraga and Gloria Anzaldua. New York: Kitchen Table, 1983.

Woolsey, Lorette K., and Laura-Lynne McBain. "Issues of Power and Powerlessness in All-Woman Groups." *Women's Studies International Forum* 10 (1987): 579–88.

Worell, Judith. "Single Mothers: From Problems to Policies." *Women and Therapy* 7, no. 4 (1988): 3–14.

Wright, Carol, and Joseph Maxwell. "Social Support during Adjustment to Later-Life Divorce: How Adult Children Help Parents." *Journal of Divorce and Remarriage* 15, nos. 3–4 (1991): 21–48.

Wyche, Karen Fraser. "Let Me Suffer So My Kids Won't: African American Mothers Living with HIV/AIDS." In Coll et al., 1998.

Wylie, Philip. *Generation of Vipers.* New York: Rinehart and Co., 1946.

Yalom, Marilyn. *Maternity, Mortality and the Literature of Madness.* University Park, Pa.: Pennsylvania State University Press, 1985.

Yeats, William Butler. "A Prayer for My Daughter." In *Selected Poems and Plays of William Butler Yeats,* edited by M. L. Rosenthal. New York: Collier, 1962.

Yeoman, Elizabeth. "The Other within the Self: Black Daughter, White Mother and the Narrative Construction of Identity." In Abbey and O'Reilly, 1998.

Yezierska, Anzia. *Bread Givers.* New York: George Braziller, 1925.

Zamir, Aviva, and Cindy Cohen. *Mothers and Daughters: Interviews with Kibbutz Women.* Norwood, Pa.: Norwood Editions, 1986.

Zax, Barbara, and Stephen Poulter. "A Multigenerational Inquiry into the Relationship between Mothers and Daughters." In *The Handbook of Infant, Child, and Adolescent Psychotherapy,* vol. 2. *New Directions in Integrative Treatment,* edited by Bonnie Mark, James Incorvaia, et al. Northvale, N.J.: Jason Aronson, 1997.

Index

About the Author

Paula J. Caplan, Ph.D., is a clinical research psychologist and is an Affiliated Scholar at the Pembroke Center for Research and Teaching on Women at Brown University. Her work has been featured widely in both scholarly and popular publications. As an expert on mother-daughter relationships, she has appeared on many national television and radio programs, including *Oprah* and *The Today Show*. She is the author of *They Say You're Crazy: How the World's Most Powerful Psychiatrists Decide Who's Normal* and *The Myth of Women's Masochism*. She is pictured above with her mother, Theda Ann (Tac) Karchmer Caplan, and her daughter, Emily Julia Caplan.